THOREAU AS
ROMANTIC NATURALIST

His Shifting Stance toward Nature

THOREAU AS ROMANTIC NATURALIST

~ *His Shifting Stance toward Nature*

JAMES McINTOSH

Cornell University Press | ITHACA AND LONDON

International Standard Book Number 0-8014-0807-5
Library of Congress Catalog Card Number 73-8412

Printed in the United States of America by York Composition Co., Inc.

To my mother and father

Contents

Illustrations

Following page 32

Preface

This book is an attempt to read certain of Thoreau's writings by calling attention to his divided attitudes toward nature. Instead of smoothing over his inconsistencies, conflicts, and uncertainties, it makes the most of them. Yet it also underscores the steadiness of his commitment to the romantic idea of nature.

Thoreau is a romantic in that he is continually fascinated by the relation of the poetic mind to the external world. He is a "romantic naturalist" in that he regards man's communication with nature as spiritual, not as destructive of the human spirit. He is a late-coming heir to the reverence for nature of a Wordsworth or a Goethe. Thoreau absorbed a kind of antinaturalism from his mentor Emerson; but he resists the logic of Emerson's subordination of nature, even while he remains aware of this logic with a part of his mind.

Recent criticism of the English romantics, even of Wordsworth, has emphasized their preference for imagination over nature. This criticism provides us with a fundamental advance in the understanding of romanticism. I owe to it my tendency to treat nature as a world inevitably separate from the writer, with which he nevertheless interacts. But, against it, I posit a variety of romanticism in which nature is subtly affirmed, not subtly rejected. Thoreau is one of the more interesting figures in this naturalist tradition. The most important figure seems to me to be Goethe. I include a substantial section on his work, because he is an admirable and (by English-speaking readers) neglected writer, as well as a crucial one in a study of the romantic affirmation of nature.

The focus of the study is on essays and books that Thoreau published or clearly intended to publish during his lifetime; his journals, poems, and letters are treated as supporting evidence. The period after *Walden,* when Thoreau published little, receives here relatively little attention. Thus the Thoreau I describe is one who figures importantly in some of his most vital work; but there are other Thoreaus—in the spacious *Journal* of the 1850's, in the political essays, and also in the works I do examine, such as the *Week, The Maine Woods,* and *Walden.*

Though Thoreau's attitudes toward nature changed and matured to an extent, he is such a self-reflexive writer that he keeps rounding back to old positions and experimenting with what he seems to have outgrown and abandoned. Moreover, his methods of composition make a chronological analysis of his finished works difficult and inconclusive, except, perhaps, in the case of *Walden,* where we know a good deal about the sequence and internal order of his manuscripts. It may be as useful to consider Thoreau's work spatially, as large-scale mosaics of incidents and attitudes, as it is to consider them chronologically, as forms that evolved over a period of time. This book focuses not so much on the way Thoreau changes from work to work as on the way he shifts his attitudes within individual works. In these shifts one can discern an exciting interplay between contrasting perspectives, and one can also discover how Thoreau uses this interplay as a means to an end—the truthful representation of his mixed relation with nature.

In all the works I treat, though differences are obvious, Thoreau wants to be involved in nature; yet he feels that he is apart from it, either because he values the distinctiveness of his human state, or because he distrusts the nature he confronts, or both. And he fashions in the course of each work (though not necessarily at its climax or end) a more thoughtful attitude that is a synthesis of his wish for involvement and his sense of separation.

This third attitude is the result of a romantic learning process: his desire for involvement and his sense of separation work together in a dialectic. Thoreau does not always employ this dialectic intentionally. Instead, it is a semipermanent phenomenon of his mind that imbues his writing whether or not he chooses to call attention to it.

Thoreau evades generalization. He packs his thoughts close to one another and gives each thought such immediacy that it cannot be fitted neatly into an argument. This concentration demands unusual reading. It is one reason for examining his conflicting wishes alongside his ideas. One often needs to take moving pictures of his mind as it emerges from sentence to sentence within a given episode or essay.

As we read Thoreau closely, we discover that his work is shot through with what one might call a philosophical contrary-mindedness. He had a tendency to push ideas to extremes, and another tendency to take opposed positions on a given question if he felt the truth was not simple. These two tendencies often occur together. He pits one extreme statement against another in a rhetoric of "programmed inconsistency." This means that his writings on nature are full of consciously designed antithetical fragments for which he provides no obvious resolution. But though his fragments often pull against each other, and though Thoreau faces their awkward conjunctions honestly, the general thrust of his work is to make them subservient to a consistent larger purpose. He struggled not to get lost in fragments and to express, both subtly and simply, his own affirming vision of the life in nature and his relation to it.

The basic texts of Thoreau I use are *The Writings of Henry David Thoreau* (20 volumes; Boston: Houghton Mifflin, 1906); *Collected Poems of Henry Thoreau*, edited by Carl Bode (Baltimore: Johns Hopkins Press, 1964); *The Correspondence of Henry David Thoreau*, edited by Walter Harding and Carl Bode (New York: New York University Press, 1958); and *Consciousness in Concord*, edited by Perry Miller (Boston: Houghton

Mifflin, 1958). For *Walden* and *The Maine Woods* I use the CEAA Edition published by Princeton University Press: *Walden,* edited by J. Lyndon Shanley, 1971; *The Maine Woods,* edited by Joseph J. Moldenhauer, 1972.

Translations from German are my own.

I take pleasure in acknowledging the help and advice of teachers and friends. Above all, I am grateful to Charles Feidelson, Jr., who has been generous with his comments and criticisms at various stages of the writing. I also particularly thank Harold Bloom for his persistent and cheerful encouragement. I have a long-standing and happy debt to Alexander Gelley, who has often stimulated me to think through my methods and aims more precisely. I also owe thanks to Jean Alonso, Cleanth Brooks, Edward Casey, Warren and Judith Chernaik, Cyrus Hamlin, Geoffrey Hartman, Robert Lloyd, Margaret Means McIntosh, Jesper and Rosemund Rosenmeier, the late Eric Schroeder, Robert Weisbuch, Elizabeth Mary Wilkinson, and Thomas Woodson.

Finally I make grateful acknowledgment to the following publishers: Johns Hopkins University Press, for permission to quote six poems from *The Collected Poems of Henry Thoreau* (1965); Princeton University Press, for permission to quote a poem from *Walden,* in *The Writings of Henry Thoreau,* edited by J. Lyndon Shanley (copyright © 1971 by Princeton University Press; reprinted by permission of Princeton University Press); and Artemis Verlag, for permission to quote and translate seven poems of Goethe from *Gedenkausgabe der Werke, Briefe und Gespräche* (1949). I am especially grateful to the Henry W. and Albert A. Berg Collection, The New York Public Library, Astor, Lenox and Tilden Foundations, for permission to quote from the manuscript of Thoreau's 1846 Journal, which contains the unpublished first version of "Ktaadn."

J. M.

New Haven, Connecticut

Abbreviations

W   *The Writings of Henry David Thoreau*. Walden Edition. 20 vols. Boston: Houghton Mifflin, 1906.

J   *The Journal*. Edited by Bradford Torrey and Francis H. Allen. Vols. VII–XX of *The Writings of Henry David Thoreau*, Walden Edition. Boston: Houghton Mifflin, 1906. (Since the volumes of *The Journal* are also numbered I–XIV, I use this numbering.)

LJ   "Thoreau's Lost Journal." In *Consciousness in Concord*. Edited by Perry Miller. Boston: Houghton Mifflin, 1958.

THOREAU AS ROMANTIC NATURALIST

His Shifting Stance toward Nature

~ 1

Introduction

An informed reader may well ask, How can it be said that Thoreau *shifts his stance?* Was he not determined to stay put in Concord? Did he not establish his moral and poetic authority by speaking out firmly? And was he not an insistent spokesman for simplicity, and a constant lover of nature?

In time, a fuller answer to these questions will be apparent. A preliminary answer might run thus: The nature which Thoreau found around him was chaotic, various and ever changing, but was nevertheless also a single organic world, ever the same. In order to love it accurately, he learned to perceive its changes by adopting continually different stances toward it; he worked in his writing to express his shifting responses to a single, yet mutable reality. "I have travelled a good deal in Concord," he wrote in the third paragraph of *Walden*. This means in part that he reflectively explored a good deal in nature; and he developed a variety of modes of thought to do justice to the variety he found. If there is a moral lesson implicit in such tactics, it is a lesson in flexibility and faithfulness toward what one loves.

Unlike most recent critics of Thoreau, I have not looked, at least at first, for design and unity in his work, but for a kind of programmed inconsistency. It seems to me that one best approaches Thoreau's sensibility by noticing attentively his varied tangents and crotchets and by letting them establish their own patterns; eventually his designs, both intentional and half-conscious or "natural," emerge. His method of dealing with nature makes it difficult to generalize quickly or systematically about the structure of his work. Artistically fashioned fragments and segments may be found in profusion in Thoreau; it is one of my purposes to see the place of these in his larger finished and published essays. But these neater fragments exist alongside others less tidy and less tractable to criticism, and I try to get at them as well. Similarly, I avoid a discussion of Thoreau's "ideas" in the sense of his ideology, his message for the world. He has a vigorous message but, to borrow his words from another context, it is "a very untenable ground. . . . Its pleadings will not bear to be stereotyped" (*Walden,* p. 318). The categories of his thinking, like "nature," "the wild," "the good," and "the ideal," are not only words for adopted positions but are also shifting targets for imaginative hopes. Thoreau will think of these words in appropriately changing ways; they are not stable elements in his structures. Thus I study not so much his ideology as the way he feelingly maneuvers among his ideas.

Maneuvering is dull in itself; and we wish to follow the "crooked bent" of Thoreau's genius in order finally to understand him. (See *Walden,* p. 56.) We must ask what are the purposes of his maneuvering, what feelings impel him to shift his stance, and for what end does he go about and about his Truth. One of his central purposes is to keep in touch with the things of nature, with its temporal rhythms and its gifts to the senses, in order to apprehend more and more deeply the significance of nature as a whole. Nature writ large is Thoreau's chief article of faith and doubt, and writ small is the world he loved and expressed. (Some have argued that Thoreau was primarily an artist or a social thinker, not a writer concerned with nature, but we need not restrict his interest in nature to his skill in botany and surveying, or his talent for conversing with chipmunks.) Ultimately, nature with all its incoherency is one for Thoreau, one subject and one source for his being. Yet in the process of living with it, Thoreau maneuvers to accommodate his writing to its shifting appearances.

Obviously, he feels more than one way about nature. He is by turns braced and gentled by it; he loves and occasionally fears it. His relation with it is not so easy or automatic as we sometimes lazily think.

In his view of the promise and difficulty of nature, Thoreau resembles the great English and German romantic poets of nature from Goethe to Keats, especially Goethe and Wordsworth. We ask again as we read Thoreau, how valid is the romantic idea of Nature? Despite postromantic efforts to discredit and debunk this idea, we still powerfully inherit it and intermittently wish to hold to it. Victorian writers like J. S. Mill and Henry Adams argue that an attachment to Nature must be shed for the sake of sober truth, and they show a fierce pleasure in exposing romantic illusions. Adams, after standing by at the ghastly death of his sister, which he attributed to the impersonal savagery of nature, claimed to observe Mont Blanc without faith or affection: "For the first time in his life, Mont Blanc for a moment looked to him what it was—a chaos of anarchic and purposeless forces—and he needed days of repose to see it clothe itself again with the illusions of his senses, the white purity of its snows, the splendor of its light, and the infinity of its heavenly peace."[1] So much, Adams, would say, for romantic images of sublimity! Yet Adams himself, like most Victorians and moderns, continued to be moved, strengthened, baffled and provoked by the natural world as he lived in it, irrespective of his metaphysics. Reciprocally, the more thoughtful romantic naturalists, including Thoreau, found it by no means easy to live in nature; their complex engagement with its mystery is an eminent feature of their work.

A paramount reason for this complexity and difficulty for Thoreau is that as a self-conscious romantic he is always aware, with varying degrees of awareness depending on the occasion, that he cannot achieve identity or perfect sharing with nature, that indeed his spiritual concerns and his imagination tend to

[1] Henry Adams, *The Education of Henry Adams* (Boston: Houghton Mifflin, 1918), p. 289.

propel him away from nature toward higher—or more ephemeral—worlds. Like Goethe and Wordsworth he combines a powerful wish to love nature and even to merge with it, with a consciousness, sometimes explicit, sometimes concealed, of separation. Throughout this study the cutting edge of the argument is the idea that romantic self-consciousness necessarily separates the romantic observer from nature, however he may regret the separation. The understanding that "the poet's thought is one world, nature's is another," as Thoreau observed at the age of twenty-one,[2] forces him to make the best of the separation, or to pit himself against nature, or to lose the relation entirely. There is for Thoreau a shifting border between nature and mind, or soul, or spirit, or self, or imagination. (No single one of these words is continually operative for that "scene . . . of thoughts and affections" [*Walden*, p. 135] he knew as his detached self). Throughout his meditative life he is preoccupied with the questions, how close can I get to nature? if I get too close, shall I be hurt or undermined? how can I discover an appropriate distance from which to survey and use her? The uncertainties expressed in these shifting attitudes are the result of his consciousness of separation. A "natural man" like one of Thoreau's lumbermen or Indians would hardly be bothered by such reservations.

Thoreau is powerfully drawn both to the exaltation of self and to the unselfish enjoyment of nature. Other poets have been beset by analogous conflicts. In his *Wordsworth's Poetry*, Geoffrey Hartman imagines a Spirit-dialogue between Wordsworth and Blake, in which Blake snaps that Wordsworth is of "his [the mind's and imagination's] party without knowing it."[3] In such a controversy between parties, Thoreau is by preference a genuine mugwump, sitting resolutely on the fence between mind and

----

[2] *J*, I, 75—slightly modified. Thoreau actually wrote, in a paragraph on The Poet, "His thought is one world, hers another." For a discussion of this paragraph, see below, pp. 114–115.

[3] Geoffrey H. Hartman, *Wordsworth's Poetry, 1787–1814* (New Haven: Yale University Press, 1964), p. 233.

nature. When one contemplates in the Walden Edition of his
Works the accompanying photographs of New England scenes,
that of the Maine wilderness, for instance, they seem at once
appropriate reflections of the material in the text and singularly
incommensurate with it. (See Plate II of this book.) Thoreau
has invested the things he has seen with a mythical importance
and a mental grandeur that no literal reproduction of nature can
capture, but his descriptions are at the same time so accurate and
so detailed that the photographs cause in us a shock of half-
recognition.

My area of investigation, then, is Thoreau's romantic consciousness as it addresses itself to nature. This consciousness has
to be understood to include both his awareness of separation
and has desire to overcome it. Often Thoreau is trying to get
part way out of his own isolated mind and closer to nature, to
exist in a border area between that mind and nature. He often
conceives of the mental faculty of imagination not as separating
him from nature but as relating him to it. He imagined his bean
field and cabin as his own personal space between the town and
the forest, and he presented himself as a mediator between the
civilized and the wild. Similarly, he made it his business to think
his way back and forth between the civilizations of Europe and
Asia and the wilderness of America. In parallel maneuvers, he
was concerned to bring spirit and body, intellectual consciousness
and unconsciousness into harmonious relations. Though his attitude toward the body wavers, an early statement in his journal
perhaps expresses his most recurrent position: "The whole duty
of man may be expressed in one line,—Make to yourself a perfect body" (*J*, I, 147). With this duty in mind he carried out
sacramental rituals of bathing, baking, and house-building at Walden as demonstrations of the unity of the self. His prose itself
reflects his intention to express both spirit and body. It is a mixture of intellectual argument and indolent revery, along with
other elements. If a Thoreauvian pun may be forgiven, it is body-
English, as well as scripture of the spirit.

Like Thoreau himself I am concerned not exclusively with his intellect nor with his unconscious, but with an area in between. I would mark Thoreau's romantic consciousness with a shadowy outline on three sides. It is informed by impulses from the unconscious; it is conditioned by his intellectual inheritance from romanticism; and it reflects his contemporary awareness as a transcendentalist, a moral-minded New Englander, a student of Emerson. I picture Thoreau's consciousness of nature as a triangle-of-mind in which his thoughts and feelings intermingle, a triangle bound on three sides by these other more exclusively intellectual or emotional areas, and drawing constantly from them. My work is in part a description of Thoreau's "knowing-body" (*corps-connaissant*), to borrow an idea from the French phenomenologist Merleau-Ponty.[4] An attempt to understand Thoreau in this way seems to me justified in the terms of his own practice, for he was well aware that he projected himself as a "knowing-body" in his writing.

The basic conflicts in Thoreau, between the desire for a separated self and the desire for nature, between the aspiration for a higher law and the aspiration to live naturally in his own body, appear as formal elements, patterns of consciousness in his work. Indeed, he often attains form and coherence by a display of consciousness, rather than by a systematic argument or an arrangement of images or symbols. In this respect he is by no means alone in the egotistic nineteenth century. We are now often attracted by the conflicts, the maneuverings, and the strenuous reconciliations of nineteenth-century writers: by Coleridge's attempt to reconcile his romantic faith in the One Life with his Christianity in "The Rime of the Ancient Mariner"; by Wordsworth's eloquent sifting of attitudes and fantasies in the Intimations Ode; by Hawthorne's bemused, ambivalent, scattershot self-portrait in "The Customs House." As much as any of these writers, Thoreau makes literary use of his own conflicts and exploits

4 Maurice Merleau-Ponty, *The Phenomenology of Perception,* trans. Colin Smith (London: Routledge and Kegan Paul, 1962), p. 408.

his own inconsistencies. The patterns that we observe in his work are thus often patterns of consciousness: opposed attitudes vibrating against each other in the crucible of an essay, a poem, or a day's journal. Some of these patterns are intended; they are clear examples of Thoreau's conscious art. For example, in the chapter "Higher Laws" from *Walden* he is intentionally playing off his own opposed propensities toward "the wild" and "the good" against each other. Other patterns are generated less intentionally but are sometimes equally interesting. In such cases, his desires, as they are juxtaposed, reconciled, or left unreconciled, create their own patterns. For example, his account of his excursion up Mt. Wachusett is animated by two conflicting desires that are vivid in his mind as long as the episode lasts, but as he presents his narrative it seems that he is not aware of the conflict. In both these examples, whether the patterns we see are planned or unplanned, the play of conflict in Thoreau's attitude toward nature makes for intensity. Because they are full of intellectual and emotional excitement, his patterns solicit our attention, sometimes our affection, as readers. We are provoked and beguiled by them. They help us to make sense out of what we read as we take it in. Part of Thoreau's general aim is to work on us in this way. He is an artist who lets shapes happen within his writing.

Conflicts in Thoreau's consciousness create form and intensity in his work. One might conceivably explain these conflicts exclusively psychologically, but that would mean departing from our adopted triangle, and abandoning the effort to see his works as artistic endeavors in a historical context as well as expressions of his private self. The conflicts I discuss are seldom directly psychological, but are conflicts felt in an epistemological predicament: they result from his being a separated romantic observer trying to represent the truth and feel of nature, the facts as he sees them and his feelings about them. Though he is trying to sort out his attitudes as he writes, it would be a mistake to imagine that he wants his conflicts perfectly resolved. If nature is many-sided and his attitudes towards it diverse, he will seek to express that many-sided diversity. As he himself thought, his work in relation to nature is not dramatic (he does not cast out possibilities), but epic (he entertains them in a wavering and mixed and eternal dialectic). He achieves his amplitude of perspective by indulging in what one might call his contrary-mindedness: his specifically Thoreauvian tendency to contradict or qualify himself or write in paradoxes or pose a problem in several different ways. This contrary-mindedness often exasperates those who come upon him for the first time, in some instances justifiably. But it is a nettle that must be grasped, not merely an unnerving foible of Thoreau's character which his admirers should forgive because it comes with his high spirits and general gumption.

Let us look at a group of diverse, apparently contradictory statements about nature in *Walden*. Most of these are emphatically placed; all are sententious utterances that look like final answers to life questions; but each indicates a different direction chosen by Thoreau for a particular occasion. They illustrate not only his contrary-mindedness, but also his mixed feelings about a separated but beloved nature. Indeed, I take them from their contexts to show the divisions in Thoreau's mind in regard to nature. The first is from a climactic paragraph in "Solitude."

All Nature would be affected, and the sun's brightness fade, and the winds would sigh humanely, and the clouds rain tears, and the woods shed their leaves and put on mourning in midsummer, if any man should ever for a just cause grieve. Shall I not have intelligence with the earth? Am I not partly leaves and vegetable mould myself? [*Walden*, p. 138]

Thoreau seems to be saying that nature feels, sympathizes, is sentient, and that as the result of her kindness the relation between man and nature is one of intimate friendship. The second is from the last paragraph of "The Ponds," a chapter that also beautifully celebrates this intimacy.

Nature has no human inhabitant who appreciates her. The birds with their plumage and their notes are in harmony with the flowers, but what youth or maiden conspires with the wild luxuriant beauty of Nature? [*Walden,* pp. 199–200]

Here the capacity of youths and maidens and perhaps of the speaker himself to achieve intelligence with the earth is called into question. We are made to wonder whether man can be intimate with nature.

The third statement, from "The Pond in Winter," suggests that a comprehensive, analytic knowledge of nature is desirable and possible.

If we knew all the laws of Nature, we should need only one fact, or the description of one actual phenomenon, to infer all the particular results at that point. [*Walden,* p. 290]

But the fourth, from "Spring," suggests that the mystery of nature cannot be so codified.

At the same time that we are earnest to explore and learn all things, we require that all things be mysterious and unexplorable, that land and sea be infinitely wild, unsurveyed and unfathomed by us because unfathomable. [*Walden,* pp. 317–318]

The sentence following this in "Spring," in a passage that is generally a celebration of wildness and natural violence, is "We can never have enough of Nature." In "Higher Laws," on the other hand, Thoreau writes as if in opposition to the whole drift of argument and feeling in *Walden:* "Nature is hard to be overcome, but she must be overcome" (*Walden,* p. 221). By nature he means, in part, the human propensity for wildness.

Now if a reader were so disposed, he could fashion a consistency from these diverse statements, could see them as fragments of Thoreau's total point of view, could even point out that in each case Thoreau is secretly hedging and qualifying in order to advance his total meaning. But such an attempt at synthesis must be made circumspectly; otherwise it will be false to Thoreau's methods as a writer and false to his style of observation and reflection in nature. He intends, I think, that each of his sentences be read for itself as well as for its place in his total context, that it make its own sharp point. And he sees each moment in nature as valid in itself, not as wholly subject to a controlling ideology.

A reader hostile to Thoreau, on the other hand, might argue that he did not know what he meant by "nature," that he used the word to mean many different things, and that his inconsistency is really confusion. My position is the reverse of this: I think that he is trying to do justice to a single concept and a single reality that is itself full of contradiction and inconsistency. One purpose of Thoreau's programmed inconsistency is to make sense of nature as a whole, to comprehend the multiplicity of the entire natural world he lived in. The diverse meanings of "nature" shade into each other, even such a variety of meanings as appear in my illustrative statements. Taken together, they are to be regarded not as an array of concepts, to be separated from each other in the manner of Lovejoy, but as comprising a single beloved realm, a theatre of operation for Thoreau's psyche. Provisionally, I will define that realm: His "nature" is the nonhuman, external world of rocks, trees and plants, oceans and rivers, animals and insects. It is felt by him as interrelated, as one; and it is for him sometimes not only the aggregate of things but also the single, surging life force that animates and organizes these things. When he uses "nature" to refer to human beings, he means by it that part of man that is external to the human mind and not altered by it—thus nature may include a man's body, his unschooled impulses, his wildness, and his unconscious. Both the wildness of the landscape and his own sensual wildness, then, are nature. Both are outside of the more conscious self, part of a separate life that he would earnestly explore.

When Thoreau thinks of nature he does not jumble in confusion the disparate meanings of the word which he draws from the history of ideas. Rather, he takes the natural world as he conretely experiences it and calls that nature; for Thoreau, existence precedes essence, except that he is enough of a romantic holist and a ninetenth-century American to assume from the start that nature is one large realm to be identified with one large name. This implies, among other things, that when Thoreau experiences hostility in the natural world, he is still experiencing nature. Despite all his efforts to love and explore it, a residue of nature remains alien to him. "We live within her and are strangers to her."[5] It is natural to feel alienated in nature as well as to feel at home in it. Nature in its very being fosters in the romantic writer the desire to feel his connection with it; but it also fosters at times a different consciousness, a recognition of its difference from man.

Thoreau's changing feelings toward nature as he experiences it inform the dynamic texture of his writing. His attitude frequently shifts almost from sentence to sentence as the scene emerges before him. Indeed, his scenes are sometimes constituted and imagined from a series of changing perspectives. Nor does he shift his stance only by changing his abstract mind. Rather, he sometimes shifts with his whole knowing-body, changes the way he senses nature as well as the way he conceives it. Thus the texture of his descriptions and narratives is volatile and dramatic from moment to moment, even if his larger perspective remains epic and constant. The excitement of some of his work is created by this potential for flickering drama; yet we should recognize that this drama dissipates in a repeated experience of reassurance, that his volatile side is balanced by a contrary ability to rest in loving descriptions of the body of nature.

ii

Thoreau's intense attraction to nature sets him apart from Emerson, from whom he paradoxically derived the ideas that made possible an entrance into his own Thoreauvian nature. Emerson is Thoreau's chief human source of ideas and inspira-

[5] Christof Tobler, "Die Natur," in Johann Wolfgang Goethe, *Gendenkausgabe der Werke, Briefe and Gespräche*, ed. Ernst Beutler (Zurich: Artemis, 1949), XVI, 922.

tions during his formative years, between his graduation from Harvard and his move to the woods by Walden Pond. Indeed, so much of the abstract framework for Thoreau's thinking and feeling about nature comes from Emerson that it is proper to present that framework briefly here. Enmeshed in the tricky spiral structure of Emerson's *Nature,* a book that had an exhilarating and crucial influence on Thoreau,[6] is an argument that must have encouraged his intuitive belief in nature and inspired him to develop and clarify it. The familiar argument is this: The landscape, though an "inferior creation," is nonetheless an important teacher, set before us for our illumination, enjoyment, and spiritual instruction. As "man is a god in ruins," only dimly in touch with the divine sources within him, the natural world remains "the present expositor of the divine mind."[7] It behooves a man, now degenerate but still endowed with divine gifts, to learn to read the language of that exposition apparent everywhere around him. "The universe constantly and obediently answers to our conceptions" (*Walden,* p. 97), writes Thoreau, in the sense that the man who looks at natural phenomena finds models for human art, metaphors for human growth, assurances of human stability. For Emerson too, man's excursions into nature become a means of recovering his own "power," his charismatic capacity for the mastery of life. As he perceives and loves and organizes what he sees, he not only resurrects the divine within him but creates anew the world around him—before that creative point the world had no meaning for him, but now it exists in relation to his spirit as the leaves and branches of a tree relate to its central life.

For Thoreau, one idea that makes this pattern of renewal

[6] For proof of the immediate power of this influence, see the verbal borrowings from *Nature* in Thoreau's later college essays, especially in "Barbarism and Civilization," as cited by Sherman Paul in *The Shores of America* (Urbana: University of Illinois Press, 1958), p. 30.

[7] *The Complete Works of Ralph Waldo Emerson,* ed. E. W. Emerson, Centenary Edition (12 vols.; Boston: Houghton Mifflin, 1903), I, 71, 64, 65.

work in the actual experience of nature is Emerson's principle of correspondence. Emerson summarizes it in "Language": "Particular natural facts are symbols of particular spiritual facts. Nature is the symbol of spirit."[8] As a man studies the details of nature he discovers himself; he learns the natural and spiritual laws that operate in him and give him hope and being. Thoreau was as assiduous as Jonathan Edwards in seeking out these correspondences, these images and shadows of human things. As Ethel Seybold says, "He could not keep from speculating on them."[9] When he was excited by a new phenomenon he was ready to wonder what it symbolized. His exhaustive and obsessive effort in his journals to catalogue botanical facts as they appeared in the course of the seasons was based on the premise that he might thereby discover natural, seasonal rhythms in the human unconscious. In *Walden,* when he speaks of the purity of a pond or the peacefulness in the eye of a partridge, he is not just happening on casual metaphors but recording true symbols of his own inner possibilities.

A striking instance of correspondence occurs in a place one might not expect it, at the end of one of Thoreau's political essays, "Slavery in Massachusetts." He has fiercely condemned the courts and the governor in Boston for depriving the fugitive slave Anthony Burns of his liberty. "My thoughts are murder to the State," he says, "and involuntarily go plotting against her." But his passion is calmed because he can still read the exposition of divinity in nature.

But it chanced the other day that I scented a white water-lily, and a season I had waited for had arrived. It is the emblem of purity. It bursts up so pure and fair to the eye, and so sweet to the scent, as if to show us what purity and sweetness reside in, and can be extracted from, the slime and muck of earth. . . . If Nature can compound this fragrance still annually, I shall believe her still young

[8] Emerson, *Works,* I, 25.
[9] Ethel Seybold, *Thoreau: The Quest and the Classics* (New Haven: Yale University Press, 1951), p. 80.

and full of vigor, her integrity and genius unimpaired, and that there is virtue even in man, too, who is fitted to perceive and love it. . . . All odor is but one form of advertisement of a moral quality, and if fair actions had not been performed, the lily would not smell sweet. The foul slime stands for the sloth and vice of man, the decay of humanity; the fragrant flower that springs from it, for the purity and courage which are immortal. [*W*, IV, 407–408]

Thoreau, let us note, not only finds the white lily in his neighborhood; he also finds the foul slime. Natural facts can stand for human gloom, vice, incoherence, and disease, as well as for human health and virtue. And these less pleasant facts must be explored, for Thoreau's quest is comprehensive. "So much of nature as he is ignorant of, so much of his own mind does he not yet possess," as Emerson puts it in "The American Scholar."[10] When Thoreau sees the ugly or the sensual in nature, he regards and analyzes it as a symbol of ugliness or sensuality in himself, or in man generally.

Correspondence, then, might seem a perfect means for insuring one's relation to nature. All facts, even unpleasant ones, are made images to be discovered in the grand quest for the self. These facts, taken together, constitute "nature," the symbol of spirit. As Emerson said in his graveside eulogy of Thoreau, "Every fact lay in glory in his mind, a type of the order and beauty of the whole."[11]

Thus far I have been describing conventionally Thoreau's appropriation of Emersonian transcendentalism. But I do not think enough has been made of the strain Thoreau must have felt in adapting the injunctions in *Nature* to suit his own instincts and purposes. *Nature* contains a—perhaps wise—contradiction at its core that is deeply provocative of creative tension in Thoreau. On the one hand, as we have seen, Emerson urges his readers to study nature by living in it and learning to read God's uncorrupted revelation imprinted secretly on it. On the other

10 Emerson, *Works*, I, 86–87.
11 Emerson, *Works*, X, 471.

hand, Emerson keeps saying that nature is insignificant in itself, even untrustworthy. To introduce the first edition of *Nature* he used a motto from Plotinus that puts nature in its lowly place on the ladder of being: "Nature is but an image or imitation of wisdom, the last thing of the soul; Nature being a thing which doth only do, but not know."[12] After his famous narrative of ecstatic experiences on his walks ("I become a transparent eyeball; . . . I am part or parcel of God"), he warns the reader, "It is necessary to use these pleasures with great temperance."[13] In general, the intention of Emerson's book is not simply to urge a return to nature, but to show how to bring nature under the sway of man's spirit, so that the universe may at last be entirely spiritual.

True, Emerson has no more desire than Thoreau to be ensconced in a single philosophical box; he is justly famous for his cagey inconsistency. Thus in a crucial turn in *Nature* he refuses to attend to the implications of his antinaturalist arguments. After preaching the advantages of "idealism," he maneuvers to give due attention to the naturalist in himself. "But I own there is something ungrateful in expanding too curiously the particulars of the general proposition, that all culture tends to imbue us with idealism. I have no hostility to nature, but a child's love to it. I expand and live in the warm day like corn and melons."[14]

Nevertheless, Emerson asserts his kinship with nature only to deny it again. In "Prospects" he has his "certain poet" say, with oracular authority, "We distrust and deny inwardly our sympathy with nature. We own and disown our relation to it, by turns. . . . But who can set limits to the remedial force of spirit?"[15] Emerson eventually presents a more encompassing idealism according to which man uses nature to rise above it to the spiritual life. His motive, in *Nature* and elsewhere, is to see man as the happy master of his experience, including the experience of na-

[12] Emerson, *Works,* I, 403–404.
[13] Emerson, *Works,* I, 11, 12.
[14] Emerson, *Works,* I, 59.
[15] Emerson, *Works,* I, 70–71.

ture. Though he sometimes celebrates his own privately beloved landscape in his writings, this landscape remains a backdrop for the human quest. His Concord is a place for the Whole Man to find symbols, receive illuminations, and develop Himself; Thus It is subordinate to Him. In the last sentence of *Nature,* Emerson makes this subordination unmistakably clear. "The kingdom of man over nature, which cometh not with observation,—a dominion such as now is beyond his dream of God,—he shall enter without more wonder than the blind man feels who is gradually restored to perfect sight."[16]

Even the principle of correspondence, which opens the way for the poetic investigation of natural facts, can be conceived so as to slight nature as value. If one insists on its logic, nature as a self-creating realm disappears. If nature is the symbol of spirit, it can be argued that it exists only to be symbolized and means nothing of itself. So Emerson argues in "Spiritual Laws": "Not in nature but in man is all the beauty and worth he sees. The world is very empty, and is indebted to this gilded, exalted soul for all its pride. 'Earth fills her lap with splendors' *not* her own."[17] What happens in this effusion to "the order and beauty of the whole"? It exists only in the glorifying mind, not in the empty world. And if such logic is pushed still further, as it is in "Idealism," it leads to the position that nature is not a real "substance" but "an accident and an effect."[18] Emerson softens this harsh dictate of the philosophical understanding later in *Nature,* but he does not relinquish it.

As is his wont, Emerson seems in *Nature* to sail right past his key contradiction even as he acknowledges it. Thoreau, in contrast, gave forceful expression to both sides of the contradiction over and over throughout his career. If Emerson says "we own

[16] Emerson, *Works,* I, 77.

[17] Emerson, *Works,* II, 147. Wordsworth actually wrote, "Earth fills her lap with *pleasures* of her own" (my italics). Emerson is "correcting" the Intimations Ode to make it conform to his own idealism.

[18] Emerson, *Works,* I, 49.

I. Henry David Thoreau, 1856. From a daguerreotype by B. W. Maxham. Courtesy of the Concord Free Public Library, Concord, Massachusetts.

II. Spencer Mountains and vista through trees on the side of Longer Mountain, Greenville, Maine. By Herbert W. Gleason. Courtesy of Roland Wells Robbins. (This photograph appears with the caption "Maine Wilderness" in *The Writings of Henry David Thoreau* [Boston: Houghton Mifflin, 1906], III, 88.)

III. "Meditation by the Sea." Anonymous; American, about 1850–1860; oil on canvas, 13½ inches x 19½ inches. M. and M. Karolik Collection. Courtesy of the Museum of Fine Arts, Boston.

and disown our relation to nature by turns," Thoreau is ready to do just that. His disowning of it appears in occasional, recurrent antinaturalist reflections and even diatribes in his journal (though, as we shall see more extensively in later chapters, the character and being of nature itself gave him pause, not just what Emerson said about it). Thoreau himself is imbued with idealism. His reading of *Nature* inevitably made him acutely conscious of his separation from nature, conspicuously defined there as the Not Me.[19] And a certain idealism is necessarily at the center of his work, though he may sometimes ignore it. He conceives that his primary mission, as scholar and poet, is to imagine the renewal and redemption of the soul. He adopts this task above all others in the *Week* and *Walden,* and in pursuing it he is very much Emerson's disciple, as both are heirs of an idealizing Puritan evangelism. Renewal, Thoreau sometimes agrees, is a spiritual process, not a natural one. When driven to make this distinction he may explicitly prefer "spirit" or "thought" to nature.

Yet at the same time Thoreau has a quasi-pagan intuition, not perhaps so explicit but continually evident in his practice, that one renews oneself by going to the woods, forgetting the conscious self, and letting nature be. Under such circumstances nature has its own divinity, to which Thoreau often appeals. He is much more dependent on experience in the landscape than Emerson, and much more interested too in the wild nature in himself and other men. He wants, we remember, to get part way out of his mind and live in his natural body—which, in Emerson's definition, is merely a feature of the Not Me. In distinction from Emerson, he seeks to give full expression to nature's sensuous life and to make room for its mystery. (Emerson is as open to redemptive mystery outside of the conscious self as Thoreau; but for him the mystery is not located in nature.) Rather than building "a kingdom of man over nature," Thoreau seeks a partnership of equals with it. Or he thinks of nature as a fostering mother to a poetic child, more often than Emerson. All this

[19] Emerson, *Works,* I, 4.

means that the idea of nature as a single, living, existential being is much more prominent in Thoreau than in Emerson.

Most critics have followed Sherman Paul's formidable scholarly authority in assuming that Thoreau was an idealist in Emerson's mold. Paul properly says that in Emerson's early philosophy "the external world existed to be assimilated to the stuff of thought."[20] But most of the time Thoreau does not want to assimilate the world but to have "direct intercourse and sympathy" with it (*W*, V, 131); and he thinks of that intercourse as trustworthy. Nature is not a servant (Emerson's and Paul's metaphor), but a friend or sister or mother (Thoreau's metaphors). Thoreau seeks his knowledge not by mastering nature but in large part by involving himself in the experience of it. As Jonathan Bishop reminds us, he spent "a lifetime of afternoons" losing his fretful, daily self that he might, taught by nature, find himself more truly.[21] When Roderick Nash, following Paul, asserts that "much of Thoreau's writing was only superficially about the natural world,"[22] he makes a distinction that Thoreau usually avoids. For Thoreau the relation between fact and truth is mysterious, to be discovered by waiting and living, not to be analyzed into the categories of surface and depth. Even when a natural fact corresponds to a moral quality, it is not dismissed as superficial, as merely a "figurative tool."[23]

Correspondence itself, in so far as it takes Thoreau away from the actuality of nature, is not always a firm principle in his work. If a man focuses with exact attention on the specific intricacy of natural objects, he is by necessity distracted from human concerns. Because Thoreau makes us so distinctly aware of the objects he observes, his efforts to establish correspondence between nature and the soul sometimes seem hypothetical. Does the white

[20] Paul, *The Shores of America*, p. 7.

[21] Jonathan Bishop, "The Experience of the Sacred in Thoreau's *Week*," *Journal of English Literary History*, 33 (1966), 68.

[22] Roderick Nash, *Wilderness and the American Mind* (New Haven: Yale University Press, 1967), p. 89.

[23] *Ibid.*

water-lily's scent advertise a moral quality? Thoreau seems to entertain the thought as a speculative hope, not as a firm conviction. Moreover, he sometimes shows a clear awareness of the hypothetical character of his allegedly definite and true symbols in the way he develops them. After he measures the depth of Walden Pond by measuring its length and breadth, he attempts to apply his observations to "ethics."

What I have observed of the pond is no less true in ethics. It is the law of average. Such a rule of the two diameters not only guides us toward the sun in the system and the heart in man, but draws lines through the length and breadth of the aggregate of a man's particular daily behaviors and waves of life into his coves and inlets, and where they intersect will be the height or depth of his character. Perhaps we need only to know how his shores trend and his adjacent country or circumstances, to infer his depth and concealed bottom. [*Walden,* p. 291]

Thoreau is tossing out a thought to see what it is worth, though it may well be golden. Both the assertive opening ("It is the law") and the tentative working out of the thought ("Perhaps . . .") are typical. Thoreau's rhetoric when he uses the correspondences is often tinged with both bravado and skepticism. I do not mean that, because of the precariousness of the principle of correspondence, he is an ineffective or insincere symbolist. On the contrary, his evocations of value are usually convincing because they are supported by a factual texture. But he is a beleaguered symbolist, caught on the horns of the contradiction in *Nature,* doing his best to be faithful to both fact and value.

Thus Emerson, even while he offered Thoreau the very basis of his life's work, did not make things easy for him. Sturdy Yankee that he is, Thoreau is not openly bothered by Emerson's divided attitude toward nature. He does not dramatize the contradiction, but simply assumes it as a given that must be lived with. It lies embedded in his thought, ready to come out from time to time. He can take extreme positions, insisting oppositely that "we can never have enough of Nature" and that "Nature . . . must be overcome." But in general, because he loves "the wild not less than the good," Thoreau adopts a working compromise between the parties of spirit and nature in himself. According to this compromise, man needs nature to renew himself, to recover his natural healthy sense of the gift of life; but nature also needs and fosters man as her highest creation and her expressive representative. Man as the poet celebrates or "publishes" the truth of nature; he does not distrust or deny it. Nature is for him a powerful and mysterious independent realm, not a mere projection of himself. Yet it is inarticulate. It is of no use to him or to the human community until he perceives and describes it. This is a naturalistic version of Emersonian idealism; it may be found in *Nature,* but interwoven there with other strands of thought. Following Emerson, Thoreau lays great stress on inspired and creative human perception. A man must be up to what he sees if he is to travel effectively in Concord. He needs to educate his senses, that they may contribute to his regeneration. Perception for Thoreau, however, is not only visual and spiritual, but also sensuous and natural. He experiments with forms of perception in which he loses himself, desists from ordering or idealizing his observations, and thereby (he trusts) finds a more natural, unconscious way of being. This desire to naturalize himself exists alongside his desire for the spiritual, and he plays off the two against each other.

By a yoga of accommodation, then, the value of nature is secured for him. If he grants at logical moments that his intuition of nature as a real presence is an "illusion," that "strictly speaking . . . our ideal is the only real," he conveniently forgets such logic for the most part—it clarifies his thinking at the expense of his life, his "actual and joyful intercourse" with nature. (See *J,* XI, 281–282.) But we shall see this idealistic logical doubt surface from time to time, when the generosity of nature seems dubious to him. Part of Thoreau's courage as an artist and thinker lies in his willingness to juxtapose his doubts and his beliefs, as energetic members in a common dialectic.

To sum up: Emerson's theory led Thoreau to make a tremendous investment in the idea of nature. The principle of correspondence in particular enabled him to think about all the natural life that came into his ken, whether it was beautiful or ugly, wild or tame, exhilarating or boring. At the same time, the theory created difficulties, or at least tensions, for Thoreau. Out of its ambiguity towards nature he developed a double program, to live both an intensely natural and an intensely spiritual life; the two lives pull against each other in his work. The theory also made him acutely aware that he as a conscious seeker was separate from nature. And, finally, the theory covertly instilled in him the doubt that nature exists, a doubt that consorted uneasily in his mind with his acute appreciation of nature's presence.

iii

Thoreau learned from Emerson not only a set of ideals and a contradiction about nature in their midst. He also learned a way of writing that allowed him to live with the contradiction and to express the ideals with force and shrewdness. Emerson's change of stance toward nature in "Idealism" is an instance of his own programmed inconsistency, his delight in deftly turning an argument on its head for the sake of his larger subtleties. Thoreau's natural bent was to qualify and query, to say "yet . . . yet . . . "; but what might in other circumstances have been an idiosyncratic quirk in his style became an organizing method because he lived in Emerson's orbit. As he worked out patterns in his treatment of nature, he employed this strategy of "polarity," to use a Germanic-Coleridgean word also adopted by Emerson.[24]

Emerson uses polarity in his writing to demonstrate his sense of human complexity. However vibrant his faith in the Whole Man, he could not say everything about this Man at once, so he found strategies for emphasizing his occasional insights without relinquishing his basic desire for comprehensiveness. For instance,

[24] See Jonathan Bishop, *Emerson on the Soul* (Cambridge, Mass.: Harvard University Press, 1964), p. 80. See also Chapter 2, note 53, below.

he sees aspects of the Soul in pairs of opposites.. He will set one aspect off against its complementary opposite, will stress one and then the other, thereby giving a more inclusive illustration of both. In *Nature,* as we have seen, Emerson presents himself first as an idealist, then as a friend of nature, and finally (in "Spirit") as a judicious combination of the two. Charles Feidelson comments: "The whimsical veerings that led him at one time to plump for absolute spirit and at another to acknowledge the independence of nature were actually, as he said, 'somewhat better than whim at last,' for each extreme was tacitly conditioned by a third view in which both became partial."[25] Emerson also constructs individual essays by juxtaposing two points of view. "Experience," for example, stresses alternately the grinding power of the daily round and the uplifting power of illumination. Finally, he sometimes places essays in pairs within a series, thus achieving comprehensiveness: "Love" and "Friendship," "Prudence" and "Heroism."

Emerson's opposites are generally not specifically resolved, but left in a state of juxtaposition, so that the reader can draw his own "third view." Emerson wants to see each human trait he loves enthusiastically by itself; and to present practicality or the love of beauty or empirical scrupulousness in consistently just perspective would be to lose his encouraging and persuasive style. He would rather present his complementary opposites with equal fervor.

Polarity is also embedded in the texture of Thoreau's writing. Though he found it in Emerson, it is a conscious device and doctrine entirely congenial to his native contrary-mindedness. He is a man of strong, antithetical tendencies, all of which he would represent justly rather than disavow. Polarity is a useful means for leaving open such a conflict as that between his philosophical or puritanical asceticism and his romantic love of sensation. We have already seen him take diametrically opposed positions on

[25] Charles Feidelson, Jr., *Symbolism and American Literature* (Chicago: University of Chicago Press, 1959), p. 124.

nature, without trying to reconcile the differences. Some of his conscious oppositions are specifically Emersonian. The juxtaposition of chapter titles in *Walden* ("Solitude" and "Visitors," for example) recalls Emerson's juggling of abstractions in his own titles. Especially in the *Week*, Thoreau employs some of the same juxtapositions of values that one finds in Emerson—masculine and feminine, action and contemplation, East and West, Hindu and Yankee. As Emerson perhaps would not, Thoreau will sometimes introduce a polarity in a single, paradoxical phrase implying opposed points of view—"a wilderness domestic." (Emerson criticized this as a perverse mannerism when he read it in "A Winter Walk," but Thoreau not only elaborated on it in the *Week*, but also demonstrated its meaning in his life and work at Walden.)[26] Or Thoreau will insert an unresolved contradiction in statements that appear pages apart, thereby suggesting his mixed attitude indirectly:

We go on dating from Cold Fridays and Great Snows; but a little colder Friday, or greater snow, would put a period to man's existence on the globe. [*Walden*, p. 254]

The Great Snow! How cheerful it is to hear of! When the farmers could not get to the woods and swamps with their teams, and were obliged to cut down the shade trees before their houses, and when the crust was harder cut off the trees in the swamps ten feet from the ground, as it appeared the next spring. [*Walden*, p. 265]

Or sometimes he will express a complex moral idea in a single, polarized statement, as in a passage I have already alluded to from "Higher Laws": "I found in myself, and still find, an instinct toward a higher, or, as it is named, spiritual life, as do most men, and another toward a primitive rank and savage one, and I reverence them both. I love the wild not less than the good"

[26] See *The Correspondence of Henry David Thoreau*, ed. Walter Harding and Carl Bode (New York: New York University Press, 1958), p. 137, for Emerson's criticism; see *W*, I, 336, for Thoreau's use of the idea in the *Week*.

(*Walden,* p. 210). Finally, polarity is one of Thoreau's techniques of construction. At the end of "Economy," for example, he quotes what he calls "Complemental Verses" by Carew, whose opinion is that a heroic life can be achieved not by poverty and simplicity but by magnanimity and excess. Subtly and indirectly, Thoreau indicates that there is some complementary truth in an opposing way of managing one's personal life.

Thoreau's use of polarity is in general more aggressive-sounding than Emerson's because he uses it in connection with a device he calls "exaggeration" or "extra-vagance."[27] In "Walking" he begins, "I wish to say a word for Nature, for absolute freedom and wildness," and then explains, "I wish to make an extreme statement, if so I may make an emphatic one" (*W,* V, 205). In "Thomas Carlyle and His Works" the rationale for this strategy is set forth at length.

Exaggeration! was ever any virtue attributed to a man without exaggeration? was ever any vice, without infinite exaggeration? . . . He who cannot exaggerate is not qualified to utter truth. No truth, we think, was ever expressed but with this sort of emphasis, so that for the time there seemed to be no other. . . . By an immense exaggeration we appreciate our Greek poetry and philosophy, and Egyptian ruins; our Shakespeares and Miltons; our Liberty and Christianity. We give importance to this hour over all other hours. We do not live by justice, but by grace. [*W,* IV, 352–353]

A third statement of the idea, developed with considerable complexity, is in the "Conclusion" to *Walden.* I quote only a small part of it, for its subtle and wilful attempt to express the ineffable would be lost in my train of argument.

It is a ridiculous demand which England and America make, that you shall speak so that they can understand you. Neither men nor

[27] Even the idea for this device probably comes from Emerson—though Thoreau forcefully made it his own. For "exaggeration," see Emerson, *Works,* III, 184–185. For "extra-vagance," see *The Journals of Ralph Waldo Emerson,* ed. E. W. Emerson and E. W. Forbes (Boston: Houghton Mifflin, 1909–1914), IV, 482.

toad-stools grow so. . . . I fear chiefly lest my expression may not be *extra- vagant* enough, may not wander far enough beyond the narrow limits of my daily experience, so as to be adequate to the truth of which I have been convinced. *Extra vagance!* . . . I desire to speak somewhere *without* bounds; like a man in a waking moment, to men in their waking moments; for I am convinced that I cannot exaggerate enough even to lay the foundation of a true expression. [*Walden,* p. 324]

The psychological truth inhering in these meditations helps us to understand why Thoreau is a master of tendentious phrases and strong poetic fragments. He is right: Liberty and Christianity are not apprehended by the merely moderate man, but by the man who is able to focus his attention and imagination intensely on spiritual essences and values. We shall see how Thoreau uses exaggeration and extra-vagance in order to express the myriad intensities of his relation to nature; yet we shall also see that he is no simple fanatic or dogmatist in his allegiances. His conception of exaggeration contains in it the implication that he is capable of detachment from what attracts him.

Necessary to Thoreau's practice of exaggeration is his willingness to give himself up to the impression of the moment, on which he focuses only temporarily, and to allow each differing moment its own importance. The preference given to "this hour over all other hours," explicit in the essay on Carlyle and implicit in the other two quotations, is consonant with Thoreau's preference for living in the present, from moment to moment. If the truth of one moment contradicts the truth of he next—which frequently happens for him, he will exaggerate the expression of each, creating a polarity. He will not be bothered by the contradiction, but will exhibit it as a sign of his many-sidedness.

Thoreau's notion of extra-vagance is one feature of what amounts to a private theory of expression, which he developed over the years in his scattered comments on the process of writing. A central tenet of this theory is that a writer has a duty to the moment as it happens; it is his business to record the thoughts that occur to him in response to each moment, accurately, vigorously and expressively. By accumulating a store of such records, he will have honest materials with which to build his "true expression." Already in 1838 (and before, and after, in numerous similar passages),[28] Thoreau is thinking that he can best fulfill his calling as a writer by assembling transcriptions of his unforced, therefore true, responses.

COMPOSITION

March 7.   We should not endeavor coolly to analyze our thoughts, but, keeping the pen even and parallel with the current, make an accurate transcript of them. Impulse is, after all, the best linguist, and for his logic, if not conformable to Aristotle, it cannot fail to be most convincing. The nearer we approach to a complete but simple transcript of our thought the more tolerable will be the piece, for we can endure to consider ourselves in a state of passivity or in involuntary action, but rarely our efforts, and least of all our rare efforts. [*J*, I, 35]

But this emphasis on half-unconscious responsiveness is only one pole of Thoreau's theory. A central problem for him was how to become a "poet," a collector of beautiful moments and a bard of regeneration, without becoming what he sometimes called an "artist," an artificial writer, a poet encumbered with too much European form, too much inherited structure of any kind. Despite his disclaimers, Thoreau was an insistent artist of his own sort; his work is full of rare efforts. He is happy to collect and display "each smoother pebble and each shell more rare," as he wrote in "The Fisher's Son," his 1840 verse testament to his vocation. Thoreau was thus well aware that he was a careful writer; but at the same time the metaphor of the shell-collector is characteristic of him in its small-scale image of art and the artist. He generally describes the artistic process as one of selecting exquisite specimens or of refining rough materials into small, separable objects. He speaks of assembling "disjecta membra,"

28 *J*, I, 24; I, 206–207; II, 403; II, 457; III, 156–158; III, 231; III, 253.

"gleanings," and "kernels," or of hewing stone, of polishing a diamond, of winnowing a lecture, of whittling the staff of the Artist of Kouroo.[29] And he consciously allowed space between examples of his refined work for less refined materials. His alternate emphasis on craftsmanship and on spontaneity is nicely captured in a self-consciously contradictory passage in his journal for January 26, 1852, where he writes at first, "Whatever wit has been produced on the spur of the moment will bear to be reconsidered and reformed with phlegm," and then adds two paragraphs later, "Obey the spur of the moment. These accumulated it is that make the impulse and the impetus of the life of genius. . . . Let the spurs of countless moments goad us incessantly into life. I feel the spur of the moment thrust deep into my side" (*J,* III, 230–232).

The problem remained for Thoreau of finding an esthetic conception for works longer than single sentences or paragraphs. If his "compositions" were to be only accumulations of disparate transcripts, how could they appear as perspicuous wholes for his readers, even if each transcript were thoroughly reworked as a separate unit? Like his contemporaries, Hawthorne, Emerson and and Dickinson, Thoreau felt a Puritan's reticence in exercising his shaping spirit of Imagination openly and obviously on a large scale. Large artistic structures, like pyramids and temples, were likely to be violations of nature as well as monuments of human pride. How was he as a New England poet to devise structures that would be both natural and shapely?

Thoreau found no easy answers to this question, but his work everywhere bears the indications of his efforts to achieve a thorough yet natural craftsmanship. The labored deliberateness of his prose was observed and occasionally castigated by some of his first readers. If the young Thoreau was meticulously determined

---

[29] *J,* I, 24; I, 206; I, 275; I, 413; II, 418–419; *Walden,* pp. 326–327. Also compare Hawthorne's small-scale images for art and the artist in "Drowne's Wooden Image," "The Artist of the Beautiful," and even *The Scarlet Letter.*

to be passive and impulsive, he might have felt rudely noticed when Margaret Fuller returned him the manuscript of "The Service" with the comment, "I . . . seem to hear the grating of tools on the mosaic."[30] Miss Fuller had unsympathetically discerned the troubled echo of Thoreau's workshop, where he was forging his peculiar and difficult compromise between his art and his nature. His usual solution to the problem of structure was to allow his unforced responses to happen on paper, then arrange them in a careful mosaic. Short meditations or passages of immediately felt experience are selected from the journal and fitted together with studious care. Meanwhile, for each piece of writing he plans to publish, Thoreau keeps in mind a purpose or set of purposes that continually influences the process of selection and connection.

Yet Margaret Fuller's metaphor is by itself inadequate in that it makes Thoreau sound more arty than he is; it leaves out of account the crucial importance he attached both to spontaneity and to inspiration, to hearing "what was in the wind," to writing his "letters to heaven."[31] One reason for Thoreau's reticence as a New England poet is his deep-seated suspicion that he who turns his whole attention to art lacks love, distorts nature, and forgets heaven. Therefore, though Thoreau revised and reordered continually, it would be a mistake to conclude that his works are masterpieces of Byzantine ingenuity, highly finished artistic wholes controlled by the expert manipulation of structural and stylistic devices. Thoreau himself would not want so to encroach on nature as surely to control it, and thus become at last a mere artist. He would rather that his writing be free, natural, obedient to inspiration, and deviously true to his own crooked bent. Even *Walden* retains a healthy residue of the untransformed journal in its final composition. Descriptions of it as "intensely unified" are misleading and partial, even when made by Perry Miller, a commentator who has done more than anyone to illuminate

[30] Quoted in LJ, p. 137.
[31] *Walden*, p. 17; *J*, I, 207.

Thoreau's methods of composition.[32] Charles Anderson's distinguished effort to prove it a long prose poem may make questionable some of my assertions; indeed he has spurred me to re-
appraise my skepticism in regard to formalist readings of Thoreau; but I think that Anderson, like most good Thoreauvians, is
prone to extravagance. I am happiest when he imagines *Walden*
not as a "circle" or even as a "web," but as a "Ptolemaic system
of cycles and epicycles," or when he says that Thoreau sought
"an asymmetrical pattern that would satisfy the esthetic sense of
form and still remain true to the nature of experience."[33] Moreover, if Thoreau's works are the grand, diverse meditations I
think they are, they can be examined not only as achievements of
form but also as records of consciousness; indeed, I would argue
that in Thoreau's case consciousness is form, that the pleasing
structure of his work is often to be discovered in the persistent
operations of his mind and sensibility.

One reason for Thoreau's use of polarities is that he seems to
have felt that they provided a structure for his self-presentations
without the simple-mindedness of straightforward argument or
the factual distortion of fiction. By exhibiting his random responses in opposition to one another, he was being true to the
conflicts and inconsistencies in his own mind, and also giving
form to them. If he does not always use his polarities as features
of his conscious designs, they certainly find their way into the
underlying patterns which give coherence as well as dramatic and
intellectual tension to his writing. The works I discuss in subsequent chapters are alive with dialectical tensions of this sort: not
only the two major works, *Walden* and the *Week,* but the shorter
ventures into nature such as "A Walk to Wachusett," "The Shipwreck," "Ktaadn," and "Walking."

[32] Perry Miller, ed., *The American Transcendentalists* (New York:
Anchor, 1957), p. x. For Miller's discussion of Thoreau's methods of
composition, see his introduction in *Consciousness in Concord.*

[33] Charles R. Anderson, *The Magic Circle of Walden* (New York: Holt,
Rinehart and Winston, 1968), pp. 215, 18.

The device of polarity specifically helps Thoreau to write in depth about his chief epistemological concern, the separation he felt between mind and nature. If he presents one point of view toward nature in one paragraph and the opposite point of view in another, he may circumvent the demand of his readers that he say everything he has to say about the subject at once. Thoreau simply has too many diverse ideas and feelings about nature to fit them into a single sustained argument or description. His polarities then become part of a larger strategy of persistent self-qualification. By returning to nature over and over in separate compositions with a new perspective and a qualified attitude, he achieves a multiple perspective on a multifarious subject; he can thus reassess, correct and improve his account of his relation to nature. Thoreau never reaches final conclusions about nature, never attempts to define it, as Emerson rightly remarked in the Graveside address;[34] instead he presents us with a rich and varied collection of fragmentary attitudes. His relation to nature changes continually—his stance shifts. As he bends and turns he is always trying to discover or recover that perfect stance that will express a proper balance between himself and nature.

iv

The next chapter is intended to demonstrate how Thoreau's general approach to nature is romantic, how he may be compared with the great romantic poets whose wrestlings with nature preceded his by a generation or more. But Thoreau's romanticism has its own sensuous, anfractuous, and nervous character. Thoreau would clearly not shift his stance so habitually if he did not feel it a necessity of his temperament to do so. He is temperamentally of many successive dispositions, by turns a skeptic and an enthusiast, a humble poet and a bragging publicist, a hermit and an orator. I respond especially to two of his divergent qualities, both vividly present in his work. Indeed, the strangeness of their co-presence is part of what prompts me to write about him.

[34] Emerson, *Works,* X, 471.

The first quality is what I would call a residual pessimism. We are not accustomed to search in Thoreau for the power of New England bleakness; the prevalent unconscious image of him is of a spokesman for natural piety and heroic self-reliance. One should not slight his energy, or his firmness, or his wish to celebrate the gift of life. But this wish should be balanced by another, which Thoreau understood less well and articulated less often, the wish to "front the true source of evil" (*The Maine Woods*, p. 16). Curiously, it is deep in the wilderness that Thoreau expects to find this true source. His outbursts of misanthropy in *Walden* and elsewhere are familiar to us; not so familiar is his partially veiled willingness to distrust nature even as he searched for its secrets. His covert responsiveness to images of doom in both the human and the natural worlds struck me forcibly when I first read him. This seemed, and still seems, a comparatively unrecognized Thoreau. Perhaps now that the "Thoreau stamp" has been widely circulated, the public may view him differently. One may get a deeper impression of his darker side by looking at the tragic and determined face in the 1856 daguerreotype, which was Leonard Baskin's model for the stamp portrait.

The second quality is Thoreau's lyricism, especially in his descriptions of natural scenes. If Thoreau's pessimism implies his wariness in the face of nature, his lyricism suggests his openness to its gentler appearances. His descriptions show his ability and willingness to respond to what is beautiful in nature, either with overflowing sensuousness, or with strenuous exactness, or both. A memorable musical rendering of Thoreau's lyrical spirit is the last movement of Charles Ives' "Concord Sonata." The "program" for this movement, Ives suggested, was to "follow [Thoreau's] thought on an autumn day of Indian summer at Walden."[35] Ives' prose meditation in *Essays before a Sonata*, where this program is spun out at length, is one of the best of all eulogies of Thoreau. Of Thoreau's lyrical relation to nature Ives

[35] Charles Ives, *Essays before a Sonata and Other Writings*, ed. Howard Boatwright (New York: Norton, 1964), p. 67.

wrote: "Thoreau was a great musician. . . . He was divinely conscious of the enthusiasm of Nature, the emotion of her rhythms, and the harmony of her solitude. . . . [He knew that] he must let Nature flow through him . . . his search for freedom lies in his submission to her."[36] Part of Thoreau's personal vocation is to let those rhythms speak, that harmony emerge. Any account of his nature writings should provide a structure in which his lyricism can be felt again by the reader.

[36] Ives, pp. 51, 68.

~ 2

Thoreau and Romanticism

In one of his last essays Perry Miller places Thoreau in "the context of international romanticism."[1] Miller argues that Thoreau struggled throughout his career with the traditional romantic problems of "balance" and "combination" with the world outside him; and these problems, Miller remarks, are still a challenge to the mind and the artist.

We may say that the romantic movement breaks into being when the European man of feeling recognizes that he is alone with his imagination, with all the danger, fascination, and possibility for art, self-culture, and self-transfiguration that lonely recognition entails. A romantic is no longer related to the social and cosmic order by codified, inherited ties, but has to make his own peace or war with it, to decide on "an original relation to the universe." When Emerson in the opening address of *Nature* makes this appeal for a brave newness, he indicates how Americans of sensibility in his age found themselves in a romantic predicament. Emerson, Thoreau, Whitman, Melville, Hawthorne, and Poe all feel their connections with the European past frayed or severed; all are *isolatoes* who must construct imaginative lives for themselves. Thoreau chose to fashion his life in nature; as for many Americans, this was the legitimate and evident ground of

[1] Perry Miller, "Thoreau in the Context of International Romanticism," *New England Quarterly*, 34 (June, 1961), 147–159.

the imagination, on which castles-in-air might be built with solid foundations.

Thoreau's sense of nature as one, as alive, and as the aggregate of things is romantic, "Nature as a living whole" in René Wellek's formula, a living, growing, organic entity infused with spirit and in some way related to man.[2] Such a conception of nature is a very old one, not in itself original with the romantics; it is, perhaps, an abstraction arising from the human desire for an erotic relation with the land and from the human hope for an earthly paradise, whence its power and longevity as an idea. For example, in the Hellenistic world, when other gods receded or became incredible, men turned to "Nature as a living whole" in such cults as Orphism. In the Christian era this idea of nature surfaces on occasion, even if subversively and heretically. In the eighteenth and nineteenth centuries it appeals to romantic writers with renewed power.

But Thoreau and his European counterparts are romantics, not Orphists or Parsees or Buddhists, partly because they share a more or less open awareness of their separation from nature, however much they may desire to be at home in it. This awareness is of a piece with their awareness of themselves as isolated and self-conscious imaginative men, as unacknowledged prophets of a new society calling in a new language to the city from their personal exiles in the grove, the poetic commune, or the wilderness. As one great original feature of romantic structure is that it displays the self-conscious mind working out its own mental patterns, and as the spirit of the romantic age, in Emerson's words, is one of "protest and detachment,"[3] so the romantic nature poet finds his chief problem in his consciousness of isolation and separation.

The influence of European romantic writers on Thoreau and his American contemporaries is occasional, not central. Particular

[2] René Wellek, *Concepts of Criticism* (New Haven: Yale University Press, 1963), p. 160.

[3] Emerson, "New England Reformers," *Works,* III, 251.

poems, sayings, and ideas are occasionally echoed in Thoreau's writings, as we shall see; but he consciously avoids European influence and generally prefers not to exhibit his acquaintance with Wordsworth and Coleridge, Carlyle and Goethe. Nevertheless, he fights some of the same battles. Analogies between their work and his will throw into relief his own conflicts and preoccupations.

A major effort of romantics like Thoreau is to come to terms with the separation from nature. Goethe, Wordsworth, Thoreau, and others fight intimations that nature is estranged and alien to them.[4] Yet such intimations occur to the self-conscious romantic, and in his wish to be sincere and candid he allows them a place in his writing. One of Thoreau's most frequently used weapons in the struggle against estrangement is Emerson's idea of correspondence, according to which nature and mind are thought to have essentially identical structures, and nature is a grand collection of metaphors for human actions and relations. Yet, as we have seen, Emerson's program for putting nature to use may sometimes seem a metaphysical hat trick when applied to experience. We do not always feel our identity with nature spontaneously; in moments of doubt, correspondence becomes a conception imposed by the mind on nature.

Schelling, whose *Naturphilosophie* stands behind Emerson's, reveals in a programmatic espousal of nature not only that we need it, but also that we must choose to establish a relation with it.

So long as I am *identical* with nature, I understand what a living nature is as well as I understand my own life; I realize how this general life of nature reveals itself in the most various forms, in step-by-step developments, in gradual approaches to freedom. But as soon as I separate myself (and with me the whole ideal realm) from nature, nothing remains for me but a dead object and I cease to understand how a *life outside* me is possible. [Schelling's italics][5]

---

[4] Cf. E. Donald Hirsch, *Wordsworth and Schelling* (New Haven: Yale University Press, 1960), p. 18.

[5] F. W. J. Schelling, Introduction to *Ideen zu einer Philosophie der*

Behind this modern (1797) restatement of the importance of nature is the romantic fear that we may easily lose touch with the life outside ourselves. Schelling makes clear that a relation with nature is not automatic. The romantic has a choice, either to see nature as bearing an affinity to man or to see it without affinity. His realization of nature thus becomes an act of will and of awareness. The sudden and ever possible falling away of his creative relation with nature is represented in a passage from Emerson's 1839 journal, a rare direct expression of underlying doubt in his thinking.

> If, as Hedge thinks, I overlook great facts in stating the absolute laws of the soul; if, as he seems to represent it, the world is not a dualism, is not a bipolar unity, but is two, is Me and It, then is there the alien, the unknown, and all we have believed and chanted out of our deep instinctive hope is a petty dream.[6]

In the *Week,* Thoreau also makes it clear that his romantic faith is a conscious discovery.

> We do not commonly know, beyond a short distance, which way the hills range which take in our houses and farms in their sweep. As if our birth had first sundered things, and we had been thrust up through into nature like a wedge, and not till the wound heals and the scar disappears do we begin to discover where we are, and that nature is one and continuous everywhere. [*W*, I, 372]

Thoreau tried to act all his life as if he could maintain his sense of nature as one and continuous and as identical with man by schooling himself properly. But when he deals with nature moment by moment he does not always find his cherished affinity. There are times when nature becomes for him a dead object, or (we shall see) an object of terror. Even as he protests his faith this other alternative is always secretly possible for him. He is

---

Natur, in *Sämmtliche Werke,* ed. K. F. A. Schelling (Stuttgart: Cotta, 1855–1861), II, 47–48.

[6] Emerson, *Journals,* V, 206.

forever making Schelling's choice to believe, but the belief is unstable, the choice never permanently effective.

All the romantics concerned with nature vacillate at least occasionally in the ways they choose to relate to it—observe, for example, the vacillations within Coleridge's "Eolian Harp," or the changes in Wordsworth's *Prelude* from the 1805 to the 1850 version. Thus no romantic should be regarded exclusively as a believer or a disbeliever in the good of nature; yet each tends to believe one way or the other. Generally, Thoreau belongs with the naturalists, with those, like Goethe, Wordsworth, and the early Schelling, who give nature the dignity of an independent status, not with the antinaturalists, like Blake, Shelley, and Fichte, who regard nature at best as material to be transformed by the human mind and imaginaion, or at worst as a seductive and dangerous power in the self and the world which "must be overcome." These romantics either ignore the landscape or love it warily. The romantic naturalists, in contrast, feel that the desire for a total possession of nature by the separated mind leads to a selfish and dangerous distortion of the observed world and a reduction of this source of their being, a way of killing a god they need. Therefore they try to conceive the imagination as reconciled to nature, not as controlling it or wholly transforming it; and they seek an imaginative balance between mind and nature. If either is overemphasized at the expense of the other, the vital interchange which sustains the poet's life will be lost. In the work of all romantics of this tendency, the balance and interchange they desire is continually being threatened. Thoreau, we may expect, exaggerates at different times both nature and mind. On the one hand, he likes to experiment with self-forgetfulness, and thus with the dissolution of all cultural, civilized, mental patterns. He may choose to submerge himself in unconscious sympathy with the chaos of nature, giving as little mental shape as possible to the limitless all (the "living whole" in that sense). Or he may abandon reflection for the simply factual. In parts of his journal, especially after 1854, he accumulates vast records of natural phenomena, collections of named but unpoeticized facts, as if to preclude the mind's distortions.

On the other hand, Thoreau is intensely drawn at moments to "the mind's party," represented in his own reading by Emerson, or by the Coleridge of "Dejection."

> O Lady! we receive but what we give,
> And in our life alone does Nature live.[7]

I showed in the previous chapter how such idealism is built into the Emersonian framework of Thoreau's thought. And I indicated that Thoreau, imitating Emerson's "certain poet," grows on occasion vividly distrustful of nature. He makes demands on nature it cannot fulfill, and it becomes a dead object for him. For example, he writes, in a rare but memorable lament from the journal of 1854:

We soon get through with Nature. She excites an expectation which she cannot satisfy. The merest child which has rambled into a copsewood dreams of a wilderness so wild and strange and inexhaustible as Nature can never show him. The red-bird which I saw on my companion's string on election days I thought but the outmost sentinel of the wild, immortal camp,—of the wild and dazzling infantry of the wilderness,—that the deeper woods abounded with redder birds still; but, now that I have threaded all our woods and waded the swamps, I have never yet met with his compeer, still less with his wilder kindred. [*J*, VI, 293]

Yet it is characteristic of the ever polarizing Thoreau that this passage, which is a reworking of earlier ideas and not entirely a spontaneous overflow, is put together soon after the composition of the railroad cut episode in *Walden,* where he glories in creative nature proliferating and exfoliating in wet sand;[8] moreover, his dissatisfaction with nature does not deter him from im-

---

[7] *The Complete Poetical Works of Samuel Taylor Coleridge,* ed. E. H. Coleridge (Oxford: Clarendon Press, 1957), I, 365.

[8] J. Lyndon Shanley, *The Making of Walden* (Chicago: University of Chicago Press, 1957), p. 73. See also *J,* VI, 147–149.

mediately continuing his journal reports of seasonal circumstances in the swamps and woods.

The identity or intercourse between a romantic like Thoreau
and nature also tends to break down when he tries to get close to
the way nature grows, changes, and repairs itself. In so far as he
is a natural creature, he participates in the natural cycle of
growth, decay, death, and rebirth; but in so far as he is an intellectual creature he is wary of it and would get free of it. Within
the natural cycle is the continual alternation of creation and destruction; animals destroy each other in order to live. In romantic nature poetry there is a secret fear of this destructiveness.
Keats is a writer who tends, for example in his early sonnets and
in his last ode "To Autumn," to accept the English countryside
as his proper and familiar home, yet in the remarkable verse letter
to Reynolds from Teignmouth in March 1818 he reveals that he
has been troubled by a not-to-be-suppressed sense of nature's
savagery.

> I saw
> Too far into the sea, where every maw
> The greater on the less feeds evermore. . . .
> Still am I sick of it, and tho' today,
> I've gathered young spring-leaves, and flowers gay . . .
> Still do I that most fierce destruction see,--
> The Shark at savage prey,—the Hawk at pounce,—
> The gentle Robin, like a Pard or Ounce,
> Ravening a worm.[9]

This is not the self-consciously frantic Victorian Adams, but the
genial romantic Keats, caught up as he puts it in "moods of one's
mind."[10] Thoreau will find himself taking a similar view as he
looks out on the Atlantic from Cape Cod—and indeed it is a
view latent in romanticism. Northrop Frye writes, "The [roman-

[9] *The Letters of John Keats,* ed. M. Buxton Forman (London: Oxford
University Press, 1931), p. 126.
[10] *Ibid.*

tic] landscape is a veil dropped over the naked nature of scream-
ing rabbits and gasping stags, the nature red in tooth and claw
which haunted a later generation."[11] With sturdy determination,
Thoreau will try to see his correspondence with this wild and
naked nature. Yet on such occasions the reader may well feel the
strain in his prose.

Consistent with his fear of violence in the external world is the
romantic's occasional fear of the nature within himself. Man, in
so far as he is a body seeking to grow and survive, inevitably acts
aggressively in nature. And in so far as he is conscious of himself,
he is painfully or joyfully aware of his aggressiveness. The speaker
in Wordsworth's "Nutting," for example, feels first joy, then
pain: he thrusts his way joyfully into the forest, searching for
hazel nuts, but then feels guilty that he has broken a branch and
wounded the peace of nature. Thoreau repeats the pattern of
"Nutting" in some of his excursions, setting forth in high animal
spirits to confront the wilderness, but feeling as he proceeds that
his adventurousness is an intrusion and that his wildness must be
chastened.

Finally, there are times for some romantics when all correspondence breaks down, when nature is felt not as life or growth, but
as power or chaos. Shelley, who was especially conscious of power
in nature, allows to Mont Blanc a power for good, but as he describes it concretely it appears alien and terrific.

> The glaciers creep
> Like snakes that watch their prey, from their far fountains,
> Slow rolling on; there, many a precipice,
> Frost and the Sun in scorn of mortal power
> Have piled: dome, pyramid, and pinnacle,
> A city of death, distinct with many a tower
> And wall impregnable of beaming ice.
> Yet not a city, but a flood of ruin
> Is there, that from the boundaries of the sky

[11] Northrop Frye, ed., *Romanticism Reconsidered* (New York: Columbia University Press, 1963), p. 21.

Rolls its perpetual stream; vast pines are strewing
Its destined path, or in the mangled soil
Branchless and shattered stand. . . . The race
Of man flies far in dread;[12]

Shelley feels himself apart from the landscape he describes, even if he accepts it as the expression of an ultimately benign Necessity. In "Ktaadn," Thoreau will feel suddenly and violently cut off from nature as he watches the Katahdin rocks. At such times he tends to abandon the effort to include all nature in his vision and prefers to restrict his affection for nature to its kindlier aspects.

Yet for all these difficulties, Thoreau, following in the way of Goethe and Wordsworth, persists in the effort to revive and preserve the ancient belief in nature, and persists also in believing that a relation between a nineteenth-century *isolato* and nature is necessary and possible. Goethe, Wordsworth, and Thoreau go beyond most of the romantics in that the repeated experience of nature is for them a necessary way to enlightenment and truth. All the romantics participate in what Miller, following Coleridge, calls "combination,"[13] the effort to put the isolated self and the Not Me back together again, the combining of an active consciousness with everything that surrounds it and from which it stands apart—experience, the body, the world. The romantic believes that a man becomes creative when he can reassert his relation to the whole to which he belongs, when he can stimulate the intercourse between mind and world, soul and body, subject and object, value and fact, when he can see the minute particulars of existence under the light of the mind's eternity. But Goethe,

[12] *The Complete Works of Percy Bysshe Shelley,* ed. Roger Ingpen and Walter E. Peck, Julian Edition (London: Benn, 1927), I, 232.

[13] See Coleridge's well-known letter to William Sotheby for September 10, 1802, in which he writes: "We are all *One Life.* A poet's heart and intellect should be *combined,* intimately combined and unified with the great appearances of nature" (*Collected Letters of Samuel Taylor Coleridge,* ed. Earl Leslie Griggs [Oxford: Clarendon Press, 1956], II, 459).

Wordsworth, and Thoreau are all persistently intent on combination with a tangible and respected nature. Moreover, it is much the same nature that all three are attracted to, a world of generation which gives pleasure and peace to the man of restless mind because it is both ordered and alive; it is perpetually changing, eternally in flux. All three writers have sufficient belief in this Nature to bear with the inherent difficulties of the idea. And all three give lyrical and convincing testimony of the glory felt when the mind is reconciled to nature, when the individual is in lively touch with the great organic whole. The locus classicus of such hopes is a passage from Wordsworth's Prospectus to "The Recluse." As he writes, our moments of illumination and joy are moments of combination, when we realize

> How exquisitely the individual Mind . . .
> . . . to the external World
> Is fitted:—and how exquisitely, too . . .
> The external World is fitted to the Mind;

when we acknowledge

> . . . the creation (by no lower name
> Can it be called) which they with blended might
> Accomplish.[14]

Thus the works of Goethe and Wordsworth provide the most suggestive analogies to Thoreau's writing in the European romantic movement. As individual writers they are evidently different from each other and from Thoreau; their peculiar feelings for nature are as diverse as their minds; and these differences should not be forgotten. Nevertheless, as analogous examples their writings can help explain the vision Thoreau was trying for and the tortuous path he followed to reach it. Let us look at Wordsworth first, as the more familiar example for English-speaking readers.

[14] *The Poetical Works of William Wordsworth,* ed. Ernest de Selincourt and Helen Darbishire (Oxford: Clarendon Press, 1940–1949), V, 5.

ii

For nineteenth-century New Englanders, Wordsworth was *the* modern poet of nature. They might complain, as did both Emerson and Thoreau, of his "feeble poetic talents."[15] "More than any other poet his success has been not his own but that of the Idea or principle which he shared with his coevals and which he has rarely succeeded in adequately expressing."[16] But his genius seems nevertheless to have hovered by the mainstream of their thought. Wordsworth's influence is present in Thoreau's halting attempts to write a poetry of sincerity, in his more successful effort to create a sense of remembered place in *Walden,* and in his lifelong emphasis on childhood memory as a source of value. If Thoreau sometimes misquotes Wordsworth from memory, or consciously reinterprets him for his own purposes, or dismisses him in studied asides, this does not mean that he ignored him. On the contrary, he and Emerson wrestle with him as with an inevitable contemporary presence, an Englishman whose very power, currency, and appeal make it difficult for them to be authentically New-English themselves. One of the dramatic and choice moments in Emerson's journal occurs on the eve of his return from his first trip to Europe, when he indulges in reflections on his visits to Landor, Coleridge, Carlyle, and Wordsworth. He is glad that he has visited them because now he need not stand in awe of them. He decides that "not one of these is a mind of the very first class," and that they are "all deficient,—in insight into religious truth."[17] Now, having disburdened himself of their shadows, he can write *Nature.*

The "Idea" that possessed Wordsworth is in essence combination with nature through imagination and devotion. In the *Prelude* he tells how he overcame his early social and intellectual

[15] E[merson], "Thoughts on Modern Literature," *The Dial* (1844); rpt. *The Dial* (New York: Russell and Russell, 1961), I, 150.

[16] *Ibid.* See also *J,* I, 431.

[17] Emerson, *Journals,* III, 186.

confusions and freed himself from a compulsive interest in natural objects in themselves; he enters in the poetry of his great decade (1797–1807) on an impassioned and dedicated effort of mediation between the separated consciousness and the external world. He is an encourager of mankind, a preacher like Emerson, but he has not Emerson's need to qualify his ecstatic moments in nature. For they are central to the life he has found; he feels in them a luminous presence that irradiates his world,

> a sense sublime
> Of something far more deeply interfused,
> Whose dwelling is the light of setting suns,
> And the round ocean and the living air,
> And the blue sky, and in the mind of man:
> A motion and a spirit, that impels
> All thinking things, all objects of all thought,
> And rolls through all things.[18]

Implicit in these famous lines are two beliefs that inform both Wordsworth's and Thoreau's conception of nature. First, Wordsworth holds that there is a spiritual principle in nature and, moreover, that a properly enlightened and encouraged man is capable of apprehending this "wisdom and spirit of the universe."[19] Once in touch with this spirit, he feels that a special dimension of consciousness has opened for him, a "beyond," as Donald Hirsch calls it,[20] where all divisions between subject and object vanish. Wordsworth uses all his visionary expressiveness in "Tintern Abbey" to encourage his readers to share in his cosmic sympathy, his sense of the beyond. Second, it is important for Wordsworth that this spirit is also a "motion." His feeling for nature is for a world in motion, in flux, in circulation. Though he is a careful observer, he is not interested in displaying objects as

[18] Wordsworth, *Poetical Works*, II, 262.
[19] William Wordsworth, *The Prelude, or Growth of a Poet's Mind,* ed. Ernest de Selincourt, rev. Helen Darbishire (Oxford: Clarendon Press, 1926), p. 27, Book I, line 401.
[20] Hirsch, *Wordsworth and Schelling,* p. 16.

such, but tends rather to relate them to a whole with a life of its
own that has given him life. He feels that the whole is informed
by Presences moving among the waters and over the earth; his
images for this vital circulation are mists, dancing daffodils, inland seas stirring.

> Ye Presences of Nature in the sky
> And on the earth! . . . can I think
> A vulgar hope was yours when ye . . .
> Impressed upon all forms the characters
> Of danger or desire; and thus did make
> The surface of the universal earth
> With triumph and delight, with hope and fear,
> Work like a sea?[21]

Thoreau will share these images and hopes, but he is not so capable of a continually integrated vision. He is too contrary-minded
and subtly self-questioning to imitate Wordsworth's sustained
appeals. It is as if while he were listening for the sound of mighty
waters he were all the time fearful of stubbing his toe on a stone.
His nature is less general and visionary than Wordsworth's, more
earthy and obviously erotic. He is attracted not only to mists and
crags, as part of his romantic heritage, but also to weeds, swarming insects, small ponds, and individual trees.

Geoffrey Hartman sees Wordsworth as pursuing in passages
like the above lines from *The Prelude* and "Tintern Abbey" a
"dialectic of love with nature."[22] Many of his poems are suffused
by "a double generosity of Nature toward man and man toward
Nature."[23]

> There is a blessing in the air,
> Which seems a sense of joy to yield
> To the bare trees, and mountains bare,
> And grass in the green field. . . .

[21] Wordsworth, *Prelude,* I, 464–475.
[22] Geoffrey H. Hartman, *The Unmediated Vision* (New Haven: Yale
University Press, 1954), p. 9.
[23] *Ibid.,* p. 10.

> Love, now a universal birth,
> From heart to heart is stealing,
> From earth to man, from man to earth:
> —It is the hour of feeling.[24]

With this faith the Wordsworth of 1798 is able to saunter forth into the landscape and compose such hymns of encouragement as "To My Sister" and "Lines Written in Early Spring."

> The birds around me hopped and played,
> Their thoughts I cannot measure:—
> But the least motion which they made,
> It seemed a thrill of pleasure.
>
> The budding twigs spread out their fan,
> To catch the breezy air;
> And I must think, do all I can,
> That there was pleasure there.[25]

Thoreau may well be referring to this poem in his journal for July 9, 1851, when he writes of a Cambridge scene:

Coming out of town . . . when I saw that reach of Charles River just above the depot, the fair, still water this cloudy evening suggesting the way to eternal peace and beauty, whence it flows, the placid, lake-like fresh water, so unlike the salt brine, affected me not a little. I was reminded of the way in which Wordsworth so coldly speaks of some natural visions or scenes "giving him pleasure." [*J*, II, 295]

Thoreau's observation of the river is an instance of his own expressive nostalgia for landscapes losing themselves in time. But he has instructively missed Wordsworth's mood and point. The strength of "Lines Written in Early Spring" is shown in the way Wordsworth can repeat "pleasure" so self-delightingly, we might almost say mindlessly. He is not cold, but calm, slow, manly, confident, and easy—a way of feeling Thoreau was not easily given to experience.

[24] Wordsworth, *Poetical Works*, IV, 59, 60.
[25] Wordsworth, *Poetical Works*, IV, 58.

.The poem of Wordsworth's that seems to have affected Thoreau most strongly was "Ode on Intimations of Immortality from Recollections of Early Childhood." Surely, he responded sympathetically to Wordsworth's images of motion and circulation in the poem—the bounding lambs, the children that sport along the shore, the cataracts that blow their trumpets from the steep—and also to the vision of a landscape illuminated in a beyond, where "meadow, grove and stream" are "Apparelled in celestial light." But the significant element in the Ode for him, according to his own repeated testimony, was the evocation of a lost youth. Under Wordsworth's influence, he too yearns for ennobling memories of nature from his own past, images of faith on which to draw at need. He also feels a loss of visionary knowledge possessed before the advent of reflective consciousness. Some of the most moving passages in the journal are conscious efforts to use inspired memory. I would point out, however, in one such passage, his un-Wordsworthian insistence that these memories are of the body and the private self, of a time when his own body and soul were in perfect harmony. Thoreau may begin by echoing Wordsworth, but he moves to a transfiguration of memory peculiarly his own. His remembered paradise is a natural space inhabited by the senses, not a glorious, distant palace.

Methinks my present experience is nothing; my past experience is all in all. . . . As far back as I can remember I have unconsciously referred to the experiences of a previous state of existence. "For life is a forgetting," etc. Formerly, methought, nature developed as I developed, and grew up with me. My life was ecstasy. In youth, before I lost any of my senses, I can remember that I was all alive, and inhabited my body with inexpressible satisfaction; both its weariness and its refreshment were sweet to me. This earth was the most glorious musical instrument, and I was audience to its strains. . . . For years I marched as to a music in comparison with which the military music of the streets is noise and discord. I was daily intoxicated, and yet no man could call me intemperate. With all your science can you tell how it is, and whence it is, that light comes into the soul? [*J*, II, 306–307]

In *Walden* too Thoreau regrets, with the deliberate exaggeration of a pondered conviction, that he has never been as wise as the day he was born. And, reverently or curiously, he summons up memories of earlier experiences by the pond, as if to bind his days together in the single life of the nature he has known there. He would testify, in Coleridge's phrase, that "we are all *One Life.*"[26] Or rather, in his New England isolation, he might object to the "we." To his more prickly way of thinking, each conscious individual and his experience combine in one exemplary life: the satisfactions of his body and the inspirations of his soul, his memories of the past and his perceptions of the present, the vibrating earth and himself as a human audience.

If Wordsworth and Thoreau are inspired by the desire for combination with nature, they also must face the romantic dilemma of how to live with the estranging otherness of nature. Indeed, recent critics of Wordsworth, such as Hartman, David Ferry, Paul de Man, and Harold Bloom, have been preoccupied with his ambivalence toward nature; and they have made it clear that Wordsworth's naturalist faith is in part a beautiful and self-beguiling defense against other elements in his sensibility. Both Thoreau and Wordsworth use their love of nature to appease their inner violence. Wordsworth is less apt to put his violence on display, but it is part of the hidden power behind his poetry. The basic relation he envisions between his younger self and nature in *The Prelude* is one of conflict: the wild, unruly boy is uneasily in touch with an enigmatic, terrific-benign teacher. The conflict is lovingly resolved, yet it stays in our memory. Much of the poetry of 1793–1798, before his retreat to home and Grasmere, is enlivened by troubled protagonists who are out of harmony with the nature they move through: Peter Bell, the Sailor in "Guilt and Sorrow," Oswald in "The Borderers," the speaker in "Nutting," and the younger Wordsworth in "Tintern Abbey." Similarly, Wordsworth's early fascination with wild nature is associated with fear and self-loss, incommensurable emotions that are

[26] *Collected Letters of Coleridge,* II, 459.

tamed by being made to participate in the poet's education. Because he is honest to his memories he is apt to see nature even as he writes of its benevolence as the scene of terror and death, of graves, gibbets, looming mountains, and vast floods.

Furthermore, Wordsworth has a strong idealist bent that tends to disturb his balance with nature. In some ways, his tendency to relinquish the external world for a more exalted world within is an element of his conscious plan. One argument of *The Prelude* is that the love of nature may lead us beyond it to a sense of the human mind's pre-eminent grandeur. *The Prelude* ends with an Emersonian turn, no doubt recognized by Emerson himself when he wrote after reading it in 1850 that Wordsworth "almost alone in his generation has treated the Mind well."[27] Wordsworth writes of himself and Coleridge:

> Prophets of Nature, we to them will speak
> A lasting inspiration, . . . what we have loved,
> Others will love, and we will teach them how;
> Instruct them how the mind of man becomes
> A thousand times more beautiful than the earth
> On which he dwells, above this frame of things
> (Which, 'mid all revolution in the hopes
> And fears of men, doth still remain unchanged)
> In beauty exalted, as it is itself
> Of quality and fabric more divine.[28]

But the idealist in Wordsworth does not always consort so easily with the Prophet of Nature. His desire for a dialectic of love conflicts with another desire, that Hartman calls "apocalyptic," "to cast out nature and achieve an unmediated contact with the principle of things."[29] In the Intimations Ode we are left with an impression that the poet's apocalyptic nostalgia for a preconscious glory has hardly been appeased, even though the poem eventually becomes a major statement of Wordsworth's myth of poetic

[27] Emerson, *Journals*, IX, 53.
[28] Wordsworth, *Prelude*, XIV, 444–454.
[29] Hartman, *Wordsworth's Poetry*, p. x.

growth in nature. Some of his poems that would seem, to the uninstructed, simple narratives of experience in nature are really half-disguised visionary apostrophes: he will begin by observing a natural object, but this becomes an occasion for his ascending to the haunt of the mind. In "To the Cuckoo" he recovers "visionary hours" while ostensibly listening to bird songs.

> Thrice welcome, darling of the Spring!
> Even yet thou art to me
> No bird, but an invisible thing,
> A voice, a mystery.[30]

Thus he uses nature not to achieve a loving relation with it, but to go beyond it. In the Simplon Pass episode from *The Prelude* he experiences with greater precision a moment of apocalyptic vision that denies nature, and he is lost in "greatness":

> in such strength
> Of usurpation, when the light of sense
> Goes out, but with a flash that has revealed
> The invisible world, doth greatness make abode,
> There harbours; whether we be young or old,
> Our destiny, our being's heart and home,
> Is with infinitude, and only there.[31]

Thoreau's account of his life with nature also has its "apocalyptic" moments. He refers admiringly to several poems of Wordsworth's that contain submerged apocalyptic impulses: the Intimations Ode, "Stepping Westward," and "Peter Bell." The speaker of "Stepping Westward" (Thoreau naturally fixed on the title) sees a "wildish" and then a "heavenly" destiny in travelling through a western "region bright" "without place or bound."[32] And whether or not Thoreau read these poems as we read them, we may surely infer that he saw reflected in them his own love of the wildish and the heavenly. Thoreau's own desire for apoca-

[30] Wordsworth, *Poetical Works*, II, 207.
[31] Wordsworth, *Prelude*, VI, 599–605.
[32] Wordsworth, *Poetical Works*, III, 76.

lypse, for contact with the principle of things, propels him in two directions. On the one hand, especially in the *Week*, he is impatiently driven to "get through with Nature." On the other hand, he is ready at certain bold moments to envision an apocalypse *in* nature, to the extent that such a paradox can be managed in words. Like Wordsworth and other romantics who come from a tradition of radical Protestant feeling, he harbors deep within a hope for a millennium, an apocalypse that transforms society and ends history; and when he pictures such a total renewal he sees it distinctly on the actual soil of New England. Thus the light of a November sunset is beautifully made to figure forth the light of paradise restored at the end of "Walking":

We had a remarkable sunset one day last November. I was walking in a meadow, the source of a small brook, when the sun at last, just before setting, after a cold, gray day, reached a clear stratum in the horizon, and the softest, brightest morning sunlight fell on the dry grass and on the stems of the trees in the opposite horizon and on the leaves of the shrub oaks on the hillside, while our shadows stretched long over the meadow eastward, as if we were the only motes in its beams. It was such a light as we could not have imagined a moment before, and the air also was so warm and serene that nothing was wanting to make a paradise of that meadow. . . .

. . . We walked in so pure and bright a light, gilding the withered grass and leaves, so softly and serenely bright, I thought I had never bathed in such a golden flood, without a ripple or a murmur to it. The west side of every wood and rising ground gleamed like the boundary of Elysium, and the sun on our backs seemed like a gentle herdsman driving us home at evening.

So we saunter toward the Holy Land, till one day the sun shall shine more brightly than ever he has done, shall perchance shine into our minds and hearts, and light up our whole lives with a great awakening light, as warm and serene and golden as a bankside in autumn. [*W*, V, 246–248]

Thoreau is clearly aware of the danger, implicit in all Protestant visionary poetry, that the objective landscape and the earth on which man dwells will be forgotten at the bright glad day, under the great awakening light.

Wordsworth is thus a significant prototype for Thoreau because he helped to make a belief in nature possible for all New Englanders of Emerson's and Thoreau's generations, and because his faith in a loving relation with nature is closely analogous to a faith Thoreau found early and pursued like an evanescent ghost always afterwards. Wordsworth's affection for the external world sustains him because he has known it early, unconsciously, and long. It has been not only the scene but even the instrument of his conversion. The poet of the 1805 *Prelude* can speak with the confidence of a new faith, an evangelist of the New Word of Nature to an audience scarcely conscious of it. He can even afford to expose his inner paradoxes while at the same time putting them behind him. Thoreau, at his late date, cannot share this serene confidence. His "Nature" seems more threatened than Wordsworth's; he treats it as an idea to be experimented with; he constantly shifts his ground, while Wordsworth stands his.

On the other hand, Thoreau is more interested in knowing precisely and stubbornly what happens in the external world, "getting close to nature" in this sense. If Wordsworth has an instinctive sense of fact in his descriptions, he still does not go out and measure ponds or date the arrival of birds. Thoreau's stubbornness may be a reason that, for all his shiftiness, he stays longer with nature. Indeed his shifts help him to stay with it. Wordsworth is no self-conscious polarizer; his capacity for a poetry of relation with nature is more quickly spent, since that relation is expressed with more direct passion and defended with fewer strategies. It is true that a certain erosion of Thoreau's faith took place when he became aware of the difficulties of his position; yet he would not allow the distresses he felt so to humanize him as to separate him finally from the dialectic with nature. Instead, even after he lost the fervor that inspired his grandly hopeful images of combination in the *Week* and *Walden,* he stuck more or less to his own low-keyed and skeptical romantic naturalism to the end. He is, perhaps of all romantics writing in English, most tenacious in his adherence to the idea of nature.

iii

He is, however, exceeded, at least in the longevity of his commitment, by Goethe. Much of the work of this prolific and many-sided genius clearly has no relevance to Thoreau. Their social circumstances and their political prejudices were very different; and Goethe would have found a fanatic partisan of John Brown as uncongenial as Thoreau found a worldly state councillor at the court of Weimar. Moreover, Thoreau, as he himself admits in his essay on Goethe in the *Week*, knew only some of his writings. The Goethe Thoreau read was by and large the standard New England Olympian of *Wilhelm Meister's Apprenticeship, Poetry and Truth,* and the *Conversations with Eckermann*—wise old worldly Goethe, not the unpredictable youth of the pre-Weimar days, who might have appealed to Thoreau more. Thoreau explored the less familiar writings of Goethe at the time he first lived with Emerson, when he read *Tasso* and the *Italian Journey* in the original; but he soon gave up the effort to pursue things German as unfruitful for him. Nevertheless, there are reasons for a comparison. First, Goethe's influence on Thoreau is not negligible. If Wordsworth encouraged Thoreau in his mystical reveries in nature, prompted him to wonder "whence it is that light comes into the soul," Goethe provided a model of a poet-scientist and writer who would have the patience to see the particulars of nature accurately and lovingly—Thoreau especially admired his truthful descriptions in the *Italian Journey*.[33] Second, at least the younger Goethe and Thoreau resemble each other peculiarly in the ways they feel about nature. Third, the romantic idea of nature is at the heart of Goethe's achievement. Indeed, he should be recognized as romantic nature's most eminent, persistent, and

[33] See the essay on Goethe in the *Week, W,* I, 347–352.

convincing advocate. He may be said to stand at the other end of the romantic spectrum from Blake in his insistence on the independence and benevolence of nature.

Both Goethe's scientific activity, to which he attached great importance, and his poetry are expressions of his romantic naturalism. He shares with Thoreau an obsession with relating poetry to demonstrable fact. He has an almost religious sense of the value of fact and of the dignity of observation. At the same time Goethe would see facts in combination; he argues that isolated details by themselves are worse than useless. His quarrel with most scientists is that they are insufficiently sensuous and subjective. According to his own romantic science, the observer's subjective spirit properly comes into play as he combines what he sees and reflects on it. On another front, he opposed first the Orthodox Christian, later the Fichtean Idealist assumption that man was specially set apart from nature. Instead, man was "nature's highest creation," with the joyful privilege of "rethinking her highest thought,"[34] that of gradual evolution. Thus in his science Goethe stressed human affinities to animals, plants, and even rocks. One of his accepted achievements was the discovery of a bone in the human skull thought to exist only in animals, which was for him one more indication that men were creatures of nature, not exalted above it in a special creation. Goethe very much distrusted what he would call the arrogant anthropomorphism of man, who relegates nature to an inferior status or makes it over in his own image. Thoreau generally shares this opinion of human pretentiousness; and his own scientific studies are carried out in a Goethean spirit of careful observation that is meant to lead to well-grounded combination with the human spirit.

Both Goethe's science and his poetry originate in part in his passionate pleasure in landscape. Like Thoreau and Wordsworth, he starts with a vital sense of the nature around him as a source

---

[34] Goethe, "Metamorphose der Tiere," *Gedenkausgabe,* I, 521. All references to Goethe's works are to the *Gedenkausgabe* unless otherwise noted.

for his strength, and this early love sustains him for years through doubts and vicissitudes. He too feels nature as circulation, "a whole of moving, secret forces," according to Friedrich Gundolf.[35] He asks in an early poem, "Where is that original Nature which makes me, as I write, feel heaven and life stream forth into my fingertips?"[36] Barker Fairley comments, "This inchoate notion of organic forces thrusting into the life of the mind can be felt everywhere in his early writings and . . . was the germ from which his later wisdom grew."[37] He never quite loses this original sense. Wary of metaphysics and religion and of the human propensity to think only in anthropomorphic terms, he finds nature too good a refuge to be sacrificed for mind or men.

Yet in the course of his life Goethe did withdraw from nature, only to return to it later with renewed appreciation and conviction. In his early *Sturm und Drang* period he is immensely caught up in *Natur*—the word figures significantly in the poems, essays, dramas and fiction of that period. But when he went to Weimar in 1775 he seemed to drop his faith in nature, at least in the romantic sense of a beloved, friendly world that surrounds and nourishes us. The contact had been too ardent and too adolescent. It was only after he took up scientific studies—geology, botany, osteology and others—that he was able to return to his early faith, if never quite to his early ardor.

From the time of that return (fully accomplished, perhaps, during the Italian journey of 1786–1788) till his death Goethe continued to adhere to the idea of nature. His adherence was grounded in two concepts, important for our understanding of Thoreau, of nature as *growth* and nature as *structure*. By nature as growth I mean the organic body of nature, that lives, creates itself, dies, and comes to birth eternally. This is the volatile nature that Goethe had known early and wished always to be able to

[35] Friedrich Gundolf, *Goethe* (Berlin: Bondi, 1925), p. 65.

[36] Goethe, "Kenner und Künstler," I, 390.

[37] Barker Fairley, *A Study of Goethe* (Oxford: Clarendon Press, 1947), p. 130.

love. His idea of growth is analogous to the Greek idea of *phusis,* as described by Collingwood out of Aristotle, a nature imbued with creativity and given wholeness and energy by a single life force or animating spirit.[38] By nature as structure I mean what Collingwood describes as one Greek use of *kosmos:* the aggregate of things and their relations, the external world in all its thingness, "nature" as used in Thoreau's title "A Natural History of Massachusetts."[39] My chief reason, indeed, for introducing these two Greek words is that Thoreau also conceived nature as a similar Hellenic-romantic combination of *kosmos* and *phusis.*[40]

In one important respect, Goethe means by nature something other than what Thoreau means. He has no qualms in thinking of sexual love as nature. His affirmation of *eros* is by no means simple-minded; he is throughout his life concerned with its mysteries and dangers. But in Goethe's early work, where he is otherwise most like Thoreau, he pictures landscapes over and over as heightened by the presence of a lovable young girl or mother. In his poem "Der Wanderer" (1772),[41] for example, a youth making his way among classical sites in Italy comes upon a young wife who is suckling her child near the site of an ancient temple. The scenery is classical-Thoreauvian: the ruins are covered with ivy and moss and surrounded by blackberries, high grass, thistles, and a clear stream. But one Goethean point of the poem is that the wanderer reveres and loves both the people and the landscape as nature. The woman, her child (who is called a "full seed" coming to bloom), the stones, and the weeds—all are offshoots of

[38] R. G. Collingwood, *The Idea of Nature* (1945; rpt. New York: Oxford Galaxy, 1960), pp. 43–48 and 80–82.

[39] Collingwood, pp. 44–45.

[40] Thoreau sometimes uses the Greek κόσμος to mean the ordered beauty of the world (*J,* IV, 284–285), or order in itself (*J,* VIII, 88), or organized form (*J,* IX, 246–247). Thus his use of κόσμος has a trace of the idea of growth in it, indeed sometimes suggests a combination of growth and structure. In *Walden* he calls a mosquito "cosmical" because it expresses the everlasting vigor of the world. For the sake of clarity, I will use *kosmos* throughout to mean order in the sense of structure.

[41] Goethe, I, 378–384.

reichhinstreuende Natur, a nature that scatters its seeds richly about itself. It is clear, moreover, that the wanderer's affection for the landscape, as well as for the woman and the child, is informed by sexual feeling.

Thoreau's feelings for nature are also at times evidently erotic, even if to say that they are always so would be reductive. Sexual feelings run like submerged streams through his experience of growing nature.[42] His jagged changes in attitude are in part expressions of his inability to accept the sexual in nature, other persons, and himself. Thus he is fascinated but troubled by natural, primitive men. He is likely either to love his body or to hate it. He relishes the fertile swamps and bogs of Concord extravagantly, but is, one day in 1853, appalled to find phallic fungi growing there. He is always dimly aware of the traditional association of nature with sex, *phusis* with eros, but prefers not to focus on it. When this association creeps into his writing he generally excises it before publication. He is unlike Goethe in his wilful asceticism, his courageous and compulsive quest for the pure in the midst of the natural. "Oh, keep my senses pure!" he cries in a moment of happiness (*J,* II, 392); whereas Goethe urges more comfortably in a poem summarizing his beliefs at the end of his life:

> Den Sinnen hast du dann zu trauen,
> Kein Falsches lassen sie dich schauen,
> Wenn dein Verstand dich wach erhält.
> Mit frischem Blick bemerke freudig
> Und wandle, sicher wie geschmeidig,
> Durch Auen reichbegabter Welt.[43]

> (The senses then you have [been given] to trust;
> Nothing false do they let you behold,

[42] See Raymond Dante Gozzi, "Tropes and Figures: A Psychological Study of David Henry Thoreau," Ph.D. dissertation, New York University, 1957.

[43] Goethe, "Vermächtnis," I, 515.

> When your understanding keeps you awake.
> With fresh glance notice joyfully
> And wander, both assured and flexible,
> Through meadows of a richly gifted world.)

Though Goethe held persistently to nature, he had also to realize at times the precariousness of this belief. His later faith was elaborately shored up with his own science; he collected and investigated constantly, like Thoreau, and went to great pains to fill in the details of the structure he had posited for nature. I would, however, call attention to examples of his doubt, moments when he becomes acutely conscious of the implications of his separation from nature. There is an element of doubt in the core of his faith. He held that nature was an *offenbares Geheimnis,* an open, revealing secret; nature is full of revelations for us if we will simply look at it. At the end of the splendid poem, "Harzreise im Winter," Goethe looks thus at the Brocken mountain.

> Du stehst mit unerforschtem Busen
> Geheimnisvoll offenbar
> Über der erstaunten Welt
> Und schaust aus Wolken
> Auf ihre Reiche und Herrlichkeit,
> Die du aus den Adern deiner Brüder
> Neben dir wässerst.[44]

> (You stand with unexplored heart
> Revealed yet full of secretness
> Above the astonished world,
> And look from clouds
> Down on its kingdoms and its glory
> Which you water from the veins
> Of your brothers beside you.)

The speaker waits in awe before a mystery. Yet to call a mountain "full of secretness," however grand and kindly it shows it-

---

[44] Goethe, I, 311–312.

self in its gift of waters to the valleys of men, is to suggest the observer's distance from it. And at other times, though rarely, that
secret does not seem inviting, but estranging to Goethe.

In *Briefe aus der Schweiz* (1779), a letter diary of Goethe's
second voyage to the Alps, he experiences nature generally as
different and distant. The usual tone of the letters is detached,
even mildly grim. Goethe does not advertise his oneness with nature, but is content to make precise, cool observations of clouds
and rocks, as a way of living with what is strange to him. At
moments he feels himself threatened, like Thoreau on Katahdin.
As he climbs toward the Furka, the scene for him is "barren,"
"waste," "a huge, monotonous, snow-covered mountain-waste-
land." "I am convinced that one who let his imagination possess
him even partially on this path would die of fright, even though
there is no apparent danger."[45] Four years before Goethe on his
first Swiss voyage had taken a wild delight in the sublimity of this
landscape. But now the mountain's "open secret" is too powerful
to be easily borne.[46]

Goethe's sense of nature as in some way divided from man is
also implicit in his later theoretical writings. Rarely does he let
the division worry him; like his friend Schelling he is eager to
overcome it. Yet in a letter to Jacobi in 1801 he writes of German philosophy:

When it lays particular emphasis on separation, I cannot abide it
and can surely say that is has done me harm, in that it distracted
me from my natural way of feeling and thinking; when on the other
hand it brings together, or much more when it heightens the original
sensation that makes us feel *as if we were one with nature* [my
italics], heightens, secures and transforms this sensation into a deep,
peaceful beholding, . . . then philosophy is welcome to me and you
can count on my sympathy with your work.[47]

[45] Goethe, XII, 56.
[46] For Goethe's estrangement from nature in *Briefe aus der Schweiz,* see
Emil Staiger, *Goethe* (Zurich: Atlantis, 1956–1959), I, 336–341.
[47] Goethe, XIX, 414. Staiger also italicizes "als seien wir mit der Natur

The words I have italicized indicate the highly provisional quality
of Goethe's romantic naturalism, at least at this time. The feeling
that we are one with nature is regarded for the moment as a
useful fiction. It gives us an intimation of a "divine life,"[48] but is
vulnerable to doubt, and needs all the questionable support that
modern philosophy can give it.

Nevertheless, Goethe's attraction to nature was such that his
feeling of oneness was continually restored to him. Doubt would
vanish, as for Thoreau, with the inflow of natural life. Both
Thoreau and Goethe felt that their involvement with nature was
a kind of health, and all distraction from it a kind of sickness.
Very Goethean is the opening of "The Pond in Winter," in which
Thoreau forgets his nocturnal questionings in the radiance of a
winter morning. Goethe, like Thoreau, feels that imagination and
speculation must not be fragmented away from the objective
world, with which they belong in unceasing relation.

Despite Goethe's distrust of merely intellectual speculation, he
would not deny his conscious separation from nature, but would
see the independent mind as reflected in the grand, mysterious
structure of nature and also existing apart from it. "In nature is
everything that is in the mind [*im Subjekt*]—and something else
besides. In the mind is everything that is in nature—and something else besides."[49] Goethe regarded it as fundamental to recognize and properly use this subtle balance between world and self.
He felt as much as any romantic the desirability of keeping the
mind and the self related to the world. In the context of a short
philosophical essay he makes an extreme and emphatic statement
of the need for combination. He is writing of the difficulty of relating religious feeling to nature.

---

eins" when he quotes this passage, for he regards such an admission of
uncertainty as significant for this period of Goethe's development (Staiger,
Goethe, II, 367).

[48] Goethe, XIX, 414.

[49] Johann Wolfgang Goethe, *Briefe,* ed. Bodo Morawe (Hamburg:
Wegner, 1965), III, 304. The passage is discussed by Fairley, p. 263.

The real difficulty is that there seems to be a certain set gap between Idea and Experience, which all our powers strive in vain to bridge and cross. Nevertheless, it remains our eternal effort to overcome this hiatus, with Reason, Understanding, Imagination, Belief, Feeling, Madness, and, when nothing else avails, with Silliness [*Albernheit*].[50]

Thoreau might have appreciated the humorous variety of mental and emotional strategies Goethe would bring to bear on the romantic divisions that intrigued and disturbed them both. To convey his feeling for nature in *Walden* he is by turns imaginative, reasonable, down-to-earth, humbly affectionate, obstreperously arrogant, wild, dead-pan, and oracular.

The above whimsical fragment suggests that Goethe too is intent on getting at the truth of experience by a flexible response to man's ever-altering circumstances. Like Thoreau, he shifts his stance. He believes in stressing the exaggerated truth of the moment: "Man, whenever he speaks outside of poetry, is bound for the moment to become one-sided. There is no communication, no theory, without separation."[51] Yet as separation takes us from the wholeness of experience, Goethe also moves to recover that wholeness by espousing contradiction as a principle. A key maxim for the whole of his work is "Every outspoken statement excites its opposite" ("Jedes ausgesprochene Wort erregt den Gegensinn").[52] Thus he anticipates Emerson's strategy of polarity in his reflections on the workings of the mind. *Polarität* is a key term in his science and psychology. Indeed, polarity as a fundamental strategy of the literature of the American Renaissance may in part be derived from German origins, descending through Carlyle and Coleridge to Emerson, Thoreau, and other writers.[53]

[50] Goethe, XVI, 872.
[51] Goethe, X, 563.
[52] Goethe, IX, 499.
[53] See Oskar Walzel, *German Romanticism*, trans. Alma E. Lussky (1932; rpt. New York: Capricorn Books, 1966), pp. 22–23, 53; Albert La Valley, *Carlyle and the Idea of the Modern* (New Haven: Yale Uni-

iv

Goethe's early work has special relevance to Thoreau, for it illustrates the difficulties and opportunities of involvement with *phusis,* with the natural cycle, with nature as alive, responsive, threatening, and suffering. It is this sense of nature that Goethe and Thoreau especially share, more consciously and more intensely than other romantics. Goethe first seems to have become a poet of nature when he had his head romantically turned in Strassburg in 1771, by Herder, Friederike Brion, and the Alsatian countryside. He closes this phase of his career with his departure for Weimar in 1775. The responses to nature that he exhibits in his writings during this period are analogous to the young Thoreau's responses to his own local surroundings during his first years as a writer, before his settling in at Walden Pond in 1845. Thus the account of the young Goethe I present here is intended to foreshadow my account of the young Thoreau in the next chapter. Moreover, since the desires and strains in Thoreau's consciousness in respect to nature persist to a large degree throughout his life, the order I find in Goethe's various and sometimes discordant early writings will also serve as a phenomenological model for much of Thoreau's later work.

The early Goethe communicates his sense of nature through a series of personae, each of which is a vehicle for feelings of the moment but none of which reflects his whole attitude. Basically, Goethe is already committed to nature and regards his involvement as healthy. An atmosphere of healthy cheeriness in the face of dangerous possibilities informs the hermit's prologue to "Satyros" (1773). This hermit is a peculiarly Thoreauvian figure in

---

versity Press, 1968), ch. ii; and Richard Harter Fogle, *The Idea of Coleridge's Criticism* (Berkeley: University of California Press, 1962), chs. i and ii. Thoreau studied Coleridge's *Theory of Life* in the 1840s, which according to Fogle is Coleridge's central statement of the importance of polarity. See *Thoreau's Literary Notebook, 1840–48,* ed. Kenneth W. Cameron (Hartford: Transcendental Books, 1964), pp. 359–363.

Goethe, though he has the young Goethe's particular casual tone and carefree zest for the novelty of nature. He has retired like Thoreau in cheerful isolation from the city and the world. He describes his way of life and then meditates on his environment in spring.

Sick of the boring idiocy of the towns, I've withdrawn here to God's Town, where I admit life has its ups and downs, but in spite of them I don't go under.

I saw in the springtime countless buds and blossoms in the mountains and valleys. How everything drives and pushes its way up! No place remains without its seed. . . . The sunshine lures out for us storks and swallows from their strange world, the butterfly from its house, the flies from their crannies, the caterpillars and grubs, breeding in the earth. The whole swells with creative power, as if it had picked itself up from sleep. Birds and frogs and animals and bugs copulate in every moment—behind and in front, on their bellies and backs—so that on every leaf and blossom there is a marriage and confinement bed.

And I sing in my heart, and praise God with all the little worms. Yet all God's folk have to eat something; they consume God's gifts that are offered them. The worm eats a fresh seed-bud; the worm then feeds the lark; and since I am also here to eat, I pop down the lark for the well-being of my spirits.[54]

The hermit's joy in the swarming of creation is an example of a root feeling in both Thoreau and the early Goethe. The hermit delights in the living whole, the grand chaos of what he senses around him. He names natural things as if to articulate his intimacy with them: storks, swallows, moths, flies, caterpillars, insects, birds, and frogs. Yet there is an element of compulsiveness, of compulsively reaching out for what is strange, in his wish to accept all the manifestations of *phusis* and eros. Consider the association of ideas: Goethe's sense of the fullness and variety of the created world leads him to contemplate the creative *power* (*Erzeugungskraft*) in nature, which in turn suggests a world con-

[54] Goethe, IV, 198–199.

tinually and violently feeding on itself. The train of associations is creation, creative power, sex, eating, animal murder, and death.

At another time and in another mood, this rich aggregate of associations could become overpowering. Goethe sets forth such a mood in one of the letters from *The Sorrows of Young Werther* (1774). Werther is the persona in which Goethe chose to represent his own subjective vulnerability, including his vulnerability to nature. In a letter dated May 10, Werther too can delight like the hermit in "the swarming of the small world between grass-blades, the uncountable, unfathomable worms and insects."[55] But when his case gets more serious, he regards that delight as an illusion. His second thoughts about his rapture in spring come in a letter for August 18. Nature is no longer a decorated stage, but a place of mutual destruction.

The warm, full feeling of my heart for living nature, which swept over me with such joy, which made the world around into a paradise, becomes for me now an unbearable source of pain. . . . It is as if a curtain had been lifted from before my soul, and the stage-set of unending life were transformed before me into the abyss of an eternally open grave. Can you say *"This is,"* when everything dies? . . . Not a moment exists that hasn't consumed you and what is around you, not a moment when you are not yourself a destroyer and must be one. The most harmless of walks takes the life of a thousand poor worms; the step of a foot dismembers the labored structures of ants and stamps a little world into a wretched grave. . . . I feel sick at heart when I recognize the consuming power that lies hidden in the whole of nature, which has formed nothing that hasn't destroyed its neighbor and itself. . . . I can see nothing around me but an eternally self-gorging monster.[56]

We recall Keats's terror at the lifting of the veil of nature: "I saw too far." Thoreau will also feel threatened by the dynamism of the living whole even as he rejoices in it. But his usual response

[55] Goethe, IV, 384.
[56] Goethe, IV, 430–432.

to this "consuming power" is to protest his satisfaction with nature and to present himself as powerfully self-reliant and heroic
in its face. Goethe projects a similar stance in a short but extravagant review of Sulzer's *Die schönen Künste,* published in 1772
in a Frankfort journal.[57] Goethe's main point is that Sulzer has
sweetened the idea of nature in order to fit it painlessly into his
philosophy of art. Goethe, on the other hand, sees nature not as
neatly beautiful but as creative and violently destructive, the
scene of "raging storms, deluges, rains of fire, subterranean flame,
and death in all elements" as well as of "the gloriously rising sun
over full vineyards." Or, anticipating Werther, he writes: "What
we see of nature is power, the power consumes, nothing stable,
everything passing, thousands of seeds trampled and destroyed,
every moment a thousand born, great and significant, manifold
into the Limitless; lovely and ugly, good and bad, everything
with equal right existing alongside everything else."

If nature is so indiscriminately prolific and destructive, how
can man be at home with her and draw sustenance from her?
The answer given in the Sulzer review is not by any means the
early Goethe's only answer; he can also present himself as a naive
lover of nature, newly initiated and newly blessed, in poems like
"Satyros" or "Der Wanderer"; but it is an unusually self-conscious answer, one that shows him for the moment aware of the
problematic character of *phusis.* He suggests that the true man
does not withdraw from nature by beautifying it but stands up to
it and learns to live with it.

Nature hardens, thank the Lord, her true children against the pains
and evil [*Übel*] that she unceasingly prepares for them; so that we
call him the happiest man who is the strongest in setting himself
against that evil, pushing it aside and with scorn for it following
the path of his own will. For a great part of mankind this is too
arduous, even impossible.

In his own way the hermit in "Satyros" has adjusted himself

---

[57] Goethe, XIII, 26–32.

to nature's evils so as to enjoy her blessings. And his easy acceptance of nature is more often typical of Goethe and Thoreau
than the strained acceptance of the Sulzer review. Yet there is a
fierce side to Goethe's relation to nature, as represented in his
early "Titans," who are apt to strike a scornful pose: Prometheus, who thrives in nature in defiance of Zeus, or Faust (in the
early *Urfaust*), who mightily summons the Earth-Spirit only to
cringe before Him, or—for our purposes especially—Egmont.

Goethe later thought of Egmont specifically as a "daemonic"
hero, which means in this case that he is amoral, unpredictable,
radiating natural power and attractiveness. The daemonic man is
one who is in touch, whether he will or no, with the powerful
spirits (daemons) in nature, and who is able to sway others by
means of his own strange power. Recalling Egmont in *Poetry and
Truth*, Goethe tells how he imagined and created him in order to
come to terms with the daemonic in nature, man and himself.[58]
Thus Goethe felt at a certain distance from Egmont even as he
identified with him. Likewise, Thoreau feels enormously drawn
to his early soldiers, heroes, and natural men and at the same
time separated from them. Egmont, in his use of nature, does not
bother to restrain his aggressiveness. Meditating in prison, he
recalls how he used to fly the court for the wood and fields. But
as he thinks of the strength he got (like Antaeus) from his contact with earth, he pictures himself as a soldier who wastes and
deflowers the land. He is both a child and a ravager of nature.

Then I hurried away, as soon as it was possible, and to horse, with
a breathless rush. Then fresh, into the countryside, there where
we belong, where steaming from the earth every good deed of nature
and wafting through the heavens all the blessings of the stars pro-
tect and hover round us; where we, like earth-born giants, from the
touch of our mother rise up stronger into the heights; where we

[58] See Goethe, X, 839–842. Goethe kept returning to the idea of the
"daemonic" in his later years, and the word is subtly and variously used
in his writing. He applies it especially to historical personalities, such as
Napoleon or Karl August, Goethe's own Duke of Weimar.

feel humanity and human desire through all our veins; where the wish to push forward, to conquer, to seize, to use one's fist, to possess, to dominate burns through the soul of the young hunter; where the soldier claims with quick march his inborn right to the whole world and with his dreadful freedom strides destroying like a hail storm through meadow, field and wood, and knows no boundaries drawn by man.[59]

We notice a train of associations, similar to that in "Satyros" and *Werther,* of the teeming earth with power, eros, and destructiveness. In this case the destructiveness is clearly man's: Egmont destroys nature as he enjoys it. He has imbibed nature's consuming power into himself. Nature becomes, as in "Nutting," passive and vulnerable.

Egmont is thus a natural man destroying nature. Yet in this internecine combat, nature can in its turn appear terrifying and destructive to the aspiring man who would draw from its strength ––the Earth-Spirit so appears to Faust. Goethe himself must have found this aspect of his early relation with nature both fascinating and appalling, an exhausting struggle with daemonic powers that he preferred to relinquish in his poetry after his arrival in Weimar.

Fortunately, even the pre-Weimar Goethe had another way of living with nature than this mutually aggressive one, a way we shall find paralleled in Thoreau. Looking back in 1817 on his early work, Goethe commented that, in so far as it was concerned with nature, it seemed too brooding, anxious and ephemeral, not sufficiently grounded in a sense of natural structure. Yet "Here and there one may find a harmony arising from passionate delight in objects of the landscape, and from an earnest desire [*Drange*] to recognize the tremendous secret that reveals itself in continual creation and destruction."[60] Of Goethe's interest in natural creation and destruction we have already had an ade-

---

[59] Goethe, VI, 84.
[60] Goethe, XVII, 64.

quate sampling. His delight in particular natural objects is expressed characteristically in a short poem, "Auf dem See" (On
the Lake), written in June 1775 while visiting Lake Zurich during his first trip to Switzerland.

Und frische Nahrung, neues Blut
Saug ich aus freier Welt;
Wie ist Natur so hold und gut,
Die mich am Busen hält!
Die Welle wieget unsern Kahn
Im Rudertakt hinauf,
Und Berge, wolkig himmelan,
Begegnen unserm Lauf.

Aug, mein Aug, was sinkst du nieder?
Goldne Träume, kommt ihr wieder?
Weg, du Traum! so gold du bist;
Hier auch Lieb und Leben ist.

Auf der Welle blinken
Tausend schwebende Sterne,
Weiche Nebel trinken
Rings die türmende Ferne;
Morgenwind umflügelt
Die beschattete Bucht,
Und im See bespiegelt
Sich die reifende Frucht.[61]

(And fresh nourishment, new blood
I suck in from this open world;
How Nature is noble and good
Who holds me to her bosom!
The wave balances our boat,
Rocking it in time with the oars,
And mountains, rising cloudily toward heaven,
Meet our path.

[61] Goethe, I, 57.

Eyes, my eyes, why do you sink down and close?
Golden dreams, will you come again?
Away you dream, golden though you are!
Here also is life and love.

On the waves flicker
A thousand swaying stars,
Tender mists drink in
The towering distance around.
Morning wind flies about
The shadowed bay,
And in the lake is mirrored
The ripening fruit.)

The poem is a mosaic of three fragmentary meditations. The
first stanza is another expression of Goethe's need for nature, for
a motherly source of strength that restores and nourishes him.
Indeed, in the first, notebook version of the poem Goethe makes
the motherliness of nature outrageously clear. It begins: "Ich
saug' an meiner Nabelschnur / Nun Nahrung aus der Welt."[62]
(I am sucking on my umbilical cord / Nourishment from the
world.) But the voice and the message in this first version are
akin to those of the hermit in "Satyros," who also expresses a
whimsical and blissful acceptance of the sensuality of nature. In
neither version is the speaker dangerously involved. Goethe's feeling for *phusis,* for the life force in nature, causes him this time
not to feel oppressed or overwhelmed by it, or arrogant with its
strength, but to enjoy it as he sees it diffused in natural objects.
The last two stanzas display a characteristically Goethean progression of feeling. As Goethe moves from the thought of nature's
power to describe the particular landscape he cherishes, he turns
away from "dreams"—not only from the dream of his fiancée
Lili Schönemann, whom he had left in Frankfurt, but also from
all purely subjective fantasies—to relish a natural scene simply
as it is. The meeting of viewer and scene, man and nature, de-

[62] Goethe, I, 56.

scribed in the last stanza is a typically Goethean version of romantic combination. He cherished such moments of meeting, in
which the poet's private concerns were suspended in seeing, *An-
schauen,* "deep, peaceful beholding," in which, as it were, both
he and what he saw partook of a self-transcending interchange of
feelings. Here the objects themselves seem to share in this dance-
like ritual of love: the morning sun, reflected in "a thousand
swaying stars," glitters on the water. The sun thus meets the
waves, the mists the distances, the wind the shadowed bay, and
the ripening fruit the lake. The poet does not claim to understand
what he sees, but simply presents it as a transcendent moment. In
the stillness he is unconsciously caught up and entranced by the
gradual and silent growth of the world.

At such a moment Goethe neither isolates himself in his private
spirituality nor regards what he sees as a dead object, but meets
it as living and partakes of its life. He speaks to nature as to
another person, separate but beloved, whose very differences he
specifically cherishes—it is as if, in Martin Buber's terms, Goethe
said the primary word "I-Thou" to nature.[63] Perhaps one cannot
properly conduct such a dialogue with nature, for nature is not
human. To Blake, who was made ill by reading the Prospectus to
"The Recluse," the ultimate naturalist absurdity would be to
construe nature as a Thou, and thus to reduce the divine humanity to the natural level. But to the young Goethe nature is
this beloved opposite, this vehicle of religious hope. It is a secret

---

[63] Buber greatly respected Goethe's "dialogue" with nature. He writes:
"How lovely and how legitimate the sound of the full *I* of Goethe! It is
the *I* of pure intercourse with nature; nature gives herself to it and speaks
unceasingly with it, revealing her mysteries to it but not betraying her
mystery. It believes in her, and says to the rose, 'Then thou art it'—
then it takes its stand with it in a single reality. So the spirit of the real
remains with it when it turns back to itself, the gaze of the sun abides with
the blessed eye that considers its own radiance, and the friendship of the
elements accompanies the man into the stillness of dying and becoming"
(Martin Buber, *I and Thou,* trans. R. G. Smith [New York: Scribner's,
1958], p. 66). At least in this appreciation, Buber is himself a romantic
naturalist.

and strange presence that he nevertheless can relate to, both when he observes its organic life in detail and when he addresses it directly in the second person, "Natur! du ewig keimende."[64] Like Wordsworth, he carries on a dialectic of love, but with a partner more specific, more evidently alive and growing—yet paradoxically more ephemeral, for as Goethe's poems are the occasions of momentary moods, he is granted the power of seeing nature so freely and sympathetically only at moments.

Thoreau's relation to nature in some lyrical and characteristic descriptions is much like Goethe's in the last part of "Auf dem See." The idea of nature as a Thou appealed to him, both in his philosophical reflections and in his moments of observation. He writes in his early journal—at a time when he is responding to Goethe's influence and trying to modify Emerson's—that the poet is "that one especially who speaks civilly to Nature as a second person. . . . Though more than any he stands in the midst of Nature, yet more than any he can stand aloof from her" (*J*, I, 289). The I-Thou stance toward nature that Goethe and Thoreau are able at moments to discover allows them to hold in suspension the dangerous, daemonic elements in the relation. They would face "the tremendous secret of creation and destruction" by looking at it lovingly. Their stance at such times gives them a living and fragile tie to a nature that is both *kosmos* and *phusis*, both a varied structure of objects and a mystery of growth. They recognize that objects themselves can remain dead or can open into communal life. In their terms, a natural fact is an open secret, a lovable mystery, a fact that may flower into a truth.

These selections from Goethe's early work have been assembled in an order that illustrates the inner drama of his mind during one period of his life. They are not ordered chronologically (though indeed they move generally from earlier writings to later ones), for I have assumed that Goethe felt these varied impulses in his relation to nature throughout the period. They do

[64] Goethe, "Der Wanderer," I, 382.

show the necessity he felt, consciously or unconsciously, to extri-
cate himself from a destructive involvement in nature-as-growth.
Thoreau also felt intensely both the desire for such an involvement and its dangers. Thus he by turns enters nature and extri-
cates himself from it; and we can discover in his work too a
pattern of involvement in nature, detachment from it, and accommodation to it. Again, the pattern is not one that occurs
necessarily in consecutive time. Rather, his different attitudes inter-
act and intermingle in the mosaic of his constructed wholes, or
within the limits of particular periods. Nevertheless, this interaction
is itself a form of organization apparent in his work, a general
orientation of mind that has its own unity and effect.

v

The telos of much of Goethe's and Wordsworth's writing is to
show how a human sensibility is fitted to the external world, how
men create by being in touch with this world. At the same time,
we have seen both writers want other moods from the experience
of nature than a mood of joyful peace. They both enjoy being
dangerously excited by nature. In particular, they want "contact
with the principle of things," though each senses that principle
differently. Wordsworth uses nature to imagine the wildish and
the heavenly, to communicate with the mind's abyss, to remember a previous state of existence. Goethe's imaginative excite-
ments are more earth-bound. His Faust encounters not an "awful
Power"[65] rising from the abyss of the mind, but the power of the
Earth-spirit. Goethe himself identifies his chief source of wonder
and terror as "the daemonic," which might define as an unpredictable principle of power *within* nature.

Similarly, one of Thoreau's primary aims is to achieve an
affectionate balance with nature. We shall see him seeking this
balance in nearly every one of his works we discuss in detail. But
the young Thoreau especially does not want to be stranded for

[65] Wordsworth, *Prelude,* VI, 594.

too long in a state of peaceful equilibrium. He also desires to be excited by supernatural principles, however threatening they may be. Like Wordsworth he yearns for revelations of origins and ends, and he presses nature into the service of this yearning. Like Goethe he wants the natural magnified, as well as nature in intimate detail. He knew Goethe's meditation on "the daemonic" in *Poetry and Truth;* he occasionally uses the word in Goethe's sense; and it is probable that some of his reflections on power in nature are colored by Goethe's conception.[66] But Thoreau's own word for the intensely, unredeemably natural, for the volatile principle in nature and the natural man, is *wild*. When he gives his attention to wildness he generally associates it with the Indians and the wilderness, with *phusis* in its American manifestations, not with Germans, Greeks, or redefined demons. While Goethe shies away from the daemonic, the young Thoreau fancies himself part of the wild. He brags of his own wildness in a lively self-description in a letter of 1841 to Mrs. Lucy Brown.

I grow savager and savager every day, as if fed on raw meat, and my tameness is only the repose of untamableness. I dream of looking abroad summer and winter, with free gaze, from some mountain side, while my eyes revolve in an Egyptian slime of health,—I to be nature looking into nature with such easy sympathy as the blue-eyed grass in the meadow looks in the face of the sky. [*Correspondence,* p. 45]

Though "wildness" is an obvious attribute of unexplored, American nature, Thoreau uses the word ambiguously. First, by correspondence, it refers to what is most intense and vital in the soul as well as in nature. Thus he treats wildness as a desirable quality in literature, present in the *Iliad* and *Hamlet*. Or some-

[66] See Chapter 5, note 13, below, for clear evidence of this influence in a passage from a Thoreau manuscript. Emerson translated the meditation on the daemonic in *Poetry and Truth* for his 1839 lecture "Demonology," and it was well known in transcendentalist circles. In the *Week,* Thoreau criticizes Goethe for being too much an artist, not enough "an inspired or demonic man" (*W,* I, 350).

times he makes it a spiritual principle, and associates it with images of ecstasy and desire for the beyond; he applies it to the red bird he never found in his threading through the woods, and to the song of the thrush that beckons toward "a fertile unknown" (*J*, V, 293). We may already guess, from the fact that he never found that bird, that these are *images,* not simply natural objects, that they represent a human, imaginative desire that cannot always be satisfied by local and ordinary nature. Thus even when Thoreau seeks the wild, he may be transported in his mind beyond the experience of nature.

"Wildness" has this ambiguity because Thoreau's whole project in regard to nature is ambiguous: he is using nature both to get deeply into it and to get beyond it. He both wishes to be a savage whose eyes revolve in a slime of health and aspires toward "a wilderness so wild and strange and inexhaustible as Nature can never show him." And these two wishes are both referred to as "dreams," fundamental desires of his imagination. Thus his desire for the wild is laden with the same epistemological conflict that besets his relation to nature generally. True, as Thoreau grows older as a writer he learns to blur the sharpness of the conflict. When he is nudged by transporting intensities, his penchant is gently to naturalize what he has envisioned and to harmonize the inspirations of spirit and nature. Nevertheless, his conception of wildness keeps its sting and resonance because of the tension latent in it. "Walking," Thoreau's most concentrated and dialectically subtle treatment of the wild, moves from resonant bragging to a final peacefulness. Thoreau has realized in it once again his chief romantic naturalist aim, to discover the fullness of the human spirit by means of a generous interchange with nature.

This aim appears in Thoreau's youthful writings too. But in them he is less tempered and temperate, and our pleasure as we examine them will come in part from their heady variety.

⮂ 3

Early Reflections
and Excursions

The Thoreau of the journals and essays written after his graduation from Harvard (1837) and before the experiment at Walden Pond (1845) is a fledgling romantic in his approach to nature. Fresh from his adolescent encounters with Wordsworth and Coleridge, he is himself still reading the European romantics and their forbears, even if he insists from the start on keeping them at arm's length. And he is vividly experiencing the direct influence of Emerson—living for two years at his house, keeping company with his children, absorbing his library. He is not yet individualistically estranged from him—nor has Emerson himself yet grown respectably detached from the romanticism of *Nature*.

The journal that covers these years—at least in the truncated form it has come down to us—is more laconic, more gnomic, more self-consciously philosophical than the expansive journal of the 1850's. There are fewer narratives of walks and listings of local details and seasonal events; instead the early journal bristles with sententiae, with experimental, tentatively radical attitudes, with seeds of thought that may later flower or burst into paragraphs and extra-vagances. Later—in *Walden* and especially in the fine nostalgic late essays such as "Wild Apples," "Fruits and Seeds," and "Autumnal Tints"—he will pare his ideas to essentials, indulge his imagination more prudently, and speak out his views more simply. But the complex immature Thoreau offers a special and rarely faced challenge to his reader.

Thoreau is already working his journals into brief essays for the transcendentalist *Dial* and other magazines during these years. The masks which he shows in public, however, only partly reveal the experimental and churning self behind them. In his essays he is more patently Emerson's student; in his journals he is working out his own romanticism. True, in the journals also he is eager to try out Emerson's principle of correspondence as a method of speculating on the meaning of natural phenomena; but correspondence can become for him an intellectual screen, behind which he meditates on the psyche and the world in adventurous and defiant ways. I will not insist on this distinction between a public and a private Thoreau too definitely—it sometimes disappears both in the early and the later work, and in any case Thoreau tended to keep his most personal concerns out of everything he wrote—but we should understand that the tone Thoreau adopts for publication, that of a promising local American scholar, is representative of an early mask, and that a more tentative and volatile writer and artist waits behind it.

The early journals and essays, then, already exhibit Thoreau's many-sidedness and contrary-mindedness. No consistent doctrine of nature emerges from them. What does emerge is a wish to keep returning to nature, and a persistent concern with the problem of romantic combination. As we shall observe in detail, Thoreau exhibits many different moods as he approaches nature. He is by turns presumptuous and humble, manic and placid; he revels in nature's sensuousness; he is caught up in the day's dreaminess; he scrutinizes the details of the landscape in a clear light. But through all these separate experiences and experiments runs a desire for an appropriate balance and a usable faith. With a shifting stance but a constant motive he wrestles with his epistemological and literary task, how to realize and express his sensuous and spiritual delight in nature.

Though the early Thoreau never follows one approach or assumes one role in relation to nature for very long, his disparate thoughts tend to group themselves into particular modes of dealing with nature. I will call them the mode of involvement (a wilful sharing of the wild life of nature); the mode of detachment (an aware contemplation of a separate nature); and the mode of comprehensive understanding (an attempt to know and feel nature as a whole). In each mode Thoreau runs into difficulty: the contact with nature may prove too intense; the proper balance between man and nature may be lost; the very existence of a relation may seem suspect. None of the modes does Thoreau find permanently satisfying. In his longer works they often appear in juxtaposition or in conflict with each other. But by isolating them and showing their relations, I hope to present a composite and true portrait of his mind—a mind energetically seeking at this stage to come to grips with itself and its experience.

These modes have a dialectical relation with each other. Any spectator might be moved to lose himself in nature, then feel his difference and think of withdrawing, and later (in tranquility) wish to secure his experience of unpremeditated joy and excitement with a strategy of cautious and contemplative empathy. This is Thoreau's basic pattern, as it is Goethe's in his early writings. Yet, though Thoreau usually operates within this romantic framework, the course he follows in his particular expressions of thinking and feeling is not so linear, logical, and neat. The conflicts in his relation to nature, as they appear, do not resolve themselves so neatly in "comprehensive understanding," and sometimes what is most interesting about his mind is the incompatibility of its tendencies.

Involvement

A fundamental desire of Thoreau's mind, as of Goethe's, is the wish to be in touch with growing things. This sensitivity to the living, changing activity of the earth deeply informs his appreciation of nature and provides the impulse for his involvement.

Men tire me when I am not constantly greeted and refreshed as by the flux of sparkling streams. Surely joy is the condition of life. Think of the young fry that leap in ponds, the myriads of insects ushered into being on a summer evening, the incessant note of the hyla with which the woods ring in the spring, the nonchalance of the butterfly carrying accident and change painted in a thousand hues upon its wings, or the brook minnow stoutly stemming the current, the lustre of whose scales, worn bright by attrition, is reflected upon the bank! ["Natural History of Massachusetts," *W,* V, 106]

If we compare this passage with Wordsworth's "Lines Written in Early Spring"—where the scene is also crowded with multitudes of living things, where as we have seen there is also "motion" and "pleasure"—we may isolate its more typically Thoreauvian features. Wordsworth's poem derives its strength from the earnestness of the poet's faith. He stands at the center of the scene drinking in the vague cross-currents. In "Surely joy is the condition of life," the natural details tend to crowd out the observer. The landscape is more belligerently alive: the colors are brighter, the sounds louder, the outlines sharper and less ethereal. We have not only motion, but a "flux of sparkling streams." The animal life is vigorous and aggressive, with fish leaping, the minnow buffeting the stream, and the tree-frog insisting on his note. The emphasis is all on the joyful, earthly here-and-now. Thoreau relishes "accident and change"; he delights in insects being born and banks being worn away, in the multitude, even the chaos, of detail.

Thoreau is then responsive to growth, movement, chaos in the American scene around him. He has a strong tactual sense of the richness of things germinating in the earth's crust.

Fat roots of pine lying in rich veins as of gold or silver . . . make you realize that you live in the youth of the world, and you begin to know the wealth of the planet. . . . Bring axe, pickaxe, and shovel, and tap the earth here where there is most sap. The marrowy store gleams like some vigorous sinew, and you feel a new suppleness in your own limbs. [*J*, I, 76]

As in many later passages, Thoreau gets strength from the earth. He feels bound to it while he digs at it. It too is alive, sinewy, flowing with sap.

In an entry for the summer of 1840, this feeling of being in contact with the flowing earth becomes a wish to be immersed in it.

Would it not be a luxury to stand up to one's chin in some re-tired swamp for a whole summer's day, scenting the sweet-fern and bilberry blows, and lulled by the minstrelsy of gnats and mosquitoes?
. . Surely, one may as profitably be soaked in the juices of a marsh for one day, as pick his way dry-shod over sand . . .
So is not shade as good as sunshine, night as day? Why be eagles and thrushes always, and owls and whip-poor-wills never? [*J*, I, 141–142]

In such a fantasy Thoreau chooses, first, to be as close with his senses to nature as possible and, second, to enter into the unorga-nized organic chaos we saw him enjoying earlier. Moreover, to be close to nature he must dissociate himself from conventional hu-man prejudices. He here prefers not only the company of natural things to human, but a wild, American, disordered style in nature to its more elegant and formal style, also night to day, uncon-scious murkiness to conscious clarity. He wilfully accepts aspects of nature that the civilized reader normally rejects: swamps, soakings, gnats and mosquitoes. He seeks the chaotic, the phys-ically disagreeable, the dark and the wild in nature.

I place these three passages next to each other because I re-gard them as belonging to a single complex, or progression of feelings that belongs to this mode in Thoreau. The passages do not follow a temporal sequence; but I am not thinking of such a progression as occurring temporally, rather as one possible to the early Thoreau at any time, given the conditions of his mind.

We may detect the same progression, from delight in movement to delight in wildness, in Thoreau's early reflections on music. These two entries appear consecutively in the journal for April 23 and 24, 1841:

When I hear music, I flutter, and am the scene of life, as a fleet of merchantmen when the wind rises. [April 23]

Music is the sound of the circulation in nature's veins. It is the flux which melts nature. Men dance to it, glasses ring and vibrate, and the fields seem to undulate. The healthy ear always hears it, nearer or more remote. [April 24—*J*, I, 251]

Let us take the two entries as one. What do they then say to us about music and nature, and about the man who experiences them? First, Thoreau is asserting that his enjoyment of music is an enjoyment of nature. Music is the audible expression of nature, "the sound of the circulation in nature's veins." We are reminded of "Surely joy is the condition of life," where the vital principle in nature, as often in Goethe and Wordsworth, is *circulation:* the flow of sap, the flux of sparkling streams. The two entries above may be condensed to "When I hear music, I am in nature." Second, this circulation is felt, more explicitly than we have seen before, as the flowing between nature and man. To be involved in nature means to be involved in the flowing and thus to flutter and dance oneself, and be the scene of organic life. Thoreau is using the principle of correspondence: The fat roots of pine and the swamp bilberries are symbols that represent inner needs. Yet as is nearly always the case in Thoreau, the natural details are more than mere symbols. Thoreau is so interested in them as things that their symbolic meaning is half forgotten in the process of perception. They call attention to themselves as real and independent facts. When Thoreau seeks involvement, he is getting in touch with his own "unconscious"; but this means that he turns his attention to the chaotic facts of his experience, which includes the stubbornly separate natural facts he has known. In "Surely joy is the condition of life," for example, we feel the overbearing presence of nature at the same time that we discern a writer trying to make his correspondence to nature felt.

If music is to stand for circulation in nature, it cannot signify only Beethoven and "The Battle of Prague." For Thoreau, these artifacts are but a fraction of nature's musical output. His idea of music includes the unpretentious, the accidental, and also the raucous sounds he bears: his neighbor's pump at night, the offerings of the Italian organ grinder, the barking of dogs, and the humdrum of insects. Much as Thoreau enjoys man-made harmonies and melodies, music is for him, of course, primarily an expression of nature, "sphere music," the sounding of the earth on a universal aeolian harp.

We may expect, and we find, that Thoreau will on occasion associate music with wildness and turbulence.

When I hear a sudden burst from a horn, I am startled, as if one had provoked such wildness as he could not rule nor tame. [*J*, I, 163]

How can a man sit down and quietly pare his nails, while the earth goes gyrating ahead amid such a din of sphere music, whirling him along about her axis some twenty-four thousand miles between sun and sun, but mainly in a circle some two millions of miles actual progress? And then such a hurly-burly on the surface wind always blowing—now a zephyr, now a hurricane—tides never idle, ever fluctuating—no rest for Niagara, but perpetual ran-tan on those limestone rocks. [*J*, I, 35]

In the second entry, the sound of circulation has become "hurly-burly," Niagara's perpetual ran-tan. The movement Thoreau wishes to be involved in is so rapid as to be remote from the daily round, from "paring one's nails." Indeed, part of his purpose in entertaining such a fantasy is to escape from mundane duties to a more intense life. His desire for wildness here verges on the apocalyptic. He imagines a scene of star-wide turbulent activity, and a responsive self-consciousness ready to run wild round the universe. At such moments ordinary human intercourse and ordinary observation of nature no longer seem valid. The poet wants to be involved in something more extreme—an encounter with a local *Erdgeist,* perhaps, or a confrontation with death or eternity.

Thoreau sometimes presents his moments of apocalyptic desire in images of a millennium, for example in this vision of a millennial community in which speech has become music: "At length music will be the universal language, and men greet each other in the fields in such accents as a Beethoven now utters but rarely and indistinctly" (LJ, p. 140). Or, like Wordsworth on occasion, he imagines a transformation of nature in the form of a universal flood or engulfing ocean.[1] In a curious passage for February 1841, he intimates how drawn he is to the idea of death by drowning.

Shipwreck is less distressing because the breakers do not trifle with us. We are resigned as long as we recognize the sober and solemn mystery of nature. The dripping mariner finds consolation and sympathy in the infinite sublimity of the storm. It is a moral force as well as he. With courage he can lay down his life on the strand, for it never turned a deaf ear to him, nor has he ever exhausted its sympathy. [*J,* I, 217]

Thoreau attributes a "moral force" to the storm because he seeks to understand his correspondence with it. But as we read the passage, his studied pursuit of correspondence comes to seem subordinate to his "sympathy" with natural violence and his enjoyment of self-dissolution. His imagined mariner merges with the sea and welcomes his own destruction at the hands of infinite sublimity.

In the spring of 1840, Thoreau entertains his fantasy of engulfing in conjunction with the event of the Concord River's overflowing.

Feb. 22.   The river is unusually high, owing to the melting of the snow. Men go in boats over their gardens and potato-fields, and all the children of the village are on tiptoe to see whose fence will be

[1] See Hartman, *The Unmediated Vision,* pp. 29–31.

carried away next. Great numbers of muskrats, which have been driven out of their holes by the water, are killed by the sportsmen.

They are to us instead of the beaver. The wind from over the meadows is laden with a strong scent of musk, and by its racy freshness advertises of an unexplored wildness. Those backwoods are not far off. I am affected by the sight of their cabins of mud and grass, raised four or five feet, along the river, as when I read of the Pyramids, or the barrows of Asia.

People step brisker in the street for this unusual movement of the waters. You seem to hear the roar of a waterfall and the din of factories where the river breaks over the road. [*J*, I, 121–122]

Thoreau and his townsfolk are aroused to briskness by the circulation of the waters. They are not only more alive; they are also wilder. They are drawn to the scent of musk, the undercurrent of wildness in nature. The muskrats themselves are driven forth from their homes in the meadows and take part in the general movement. Yet all this stimulation also brings out another aspect of wildness in man, his enjoyment of destruction. Thoreau observes: the children are on tiptoe to see fences carried away; the scent of musk brings out the hunter's instinct.

Thoreau's own wish to destroy appears in his poem, "The Freshet," recorded two days later. Most of the poem, a playful description of Concord in flood-time, with the dubious point that the local fen is then "Far lovelier than the Bay of Naples," is reprinted in "Natural History of Massachusetts." Omitted from the published version, however, is this awkwardly unplayful stanza.

> O that the moon were in conjunction
> To the dry land's extremest unction,
> Till every dike and pier were flooded,
> And all the land with islands studded,
> For once to teach all human kind,
> Both those that plow and those that grind,
> There is no fixture in the land,
> But all unstable is as sand. [*J*, I, 122]

Thoreau's impulse is to use the river's rising as an occasion for his nascent apocalyptic imagination. His intuition of nature as circulation is embodied in the apocalyptic image of a universal flood. Yet we should remember that Thoreau is still a neophyte at such imaginings and is trying to work out his artistic vocation in a Massachusetts household hedged round by loquacious sisters, mothers, and aunts; he is constrained in his impulses as in his imagination. The vision of flood is irresolutely merged with a pleasant scene of "land with islands studded." The implied extreme wish, that men should be annihilated, becomes in overt expression the sentiment that they should be taught the mutability of life. We recognize, however, Thoreau's nonmoral intent when we recall how he delights in mutability, accident and change, instability.

For March 8 of the same spring (1840), we find Thoreau enjoying not only the change of seasons and the discomfiture of men who would control nature commercially, but also the raucous noise and untamable activity of ice cracking. "In the ponds the ice cracks with a busy and inspiriting din and down the larger streams is whirled, grating hoarsely and crashing its way along, which was so lately a firm field for the woodman's team and the fox" (*J*, I, 126). The pleasure in upheaval and destruction implicit in these descriptions is made explicit in a pithy entry for May 14.

> Every man is a warrior when he aspires. . . . The soldier is the practical idealist; he has no sympathy with matter, he revels in the annihilation of it. So do we all at times. When a freshet destroys the works of man, or a fire consumes them, or a Lisbon earthquake shakes them down, our sympathy with persons is swallowed up in a wider sympathy with the universe. A crash is apt to grate agreeably on our ears. [*J*, I, 135]

Here he alludes directly to the freshet and the grating ice and explains their meaning to himself. This meaning is that his "wider sympathy with the universe" justifies a sympathy with natural violence. This is all the easier because Thoreau's own inner violence corresponds to nature's. The Emersonian circle of perception boomerangs on the observer; Thoreau perceives that he enjoys the storm without and must acknowledge that it is related to a storm within.

We should notice in passing that Thoreau is by now imagining himself as a "practical idealist" who "revels in the annihilation of matter." That is, a curious thing has happened to his involvement with nature. When that involvement leads to an interest, not only in circulation but in wild tumult, Thoreau is apt to be so caught up in his mood of excitement as to leave ordinary nature behind him. To annihilate matter is to forsake it. The original, mutually affectionate relation felt in "Surely joy is the condition of life" has been abandoned for a relation of soldier to victim.

In "The Service," that abrasive and labored essay which Margaret Fuller rejected for *The Dial* in 1841, Thoreau presents a mythical conception of the spiritual hero as a warrior or recruit. We may understand his choice of this image not only as a result of his Puritan training in sturdiness and his early reading in militantly imaginative Puritan writers like Milton, but also as in part an expression of his own appetite for heroic violence. "Offer not only peace offerings but holocausts unto God," he quotes, somewhat out of context, from Sir Thomas Browne.[2] Just as he is pleased by storms that "do not trifle with us," he prizes aggressiveness in other writers and men. In the fine essay of 1847, "Thomas Carlyle and his Works," Carlyle receives Thoreau's most enthusiastic praise for his polemical energy and destructiveness.

With his brows knit, his mind made up, his will resolved and resistless, he advances, crashing his way through the host of weak, half-

---

[2] Sir Thomas Browne, "Letter to a Friend," quoted in Kenneth W. Cameron, ed., *The Transcendentalists and Minerva* (Hartford: Transcendental Books, 1958), p. 283. Thoreau's college reading notes have been collected in Cameron's volume.

formed, *dilettante* opinions, honest and dishonest ways of thinking
. . . and tramples them all into dust. See how he prevails; you
don't even hear the groans of the wounded and dying. [*W*, IV, 329]

What a cutting cimeter was that "Past and Present," going through
heaps of silken stuffs, and glibly through the necks of men, too,
without their knowing it, leaving no trace! [*W*, IV, 333]

When Thoreau draws from his journal for his early essays, he
tends to tone down or eliminate indications of his own aggressiveness. But the qualities of mind I have been documenting are also
evident in all his larger published writings. We shall see more of
his wish to involve himself intensely or violently in nature, and
of his sympathy with natural violence.

Why, on the other hand, the restraint and caution in Thoreau?
Why is he not wholly an artist of the wild—*Henry Thoreau,
Sauvage,* as one French title has it?[3] If he is more than this, what
place have these volatile and exciting feelings in the complex
mosaic of his self-representation? For like the early Goethe, the
early Thoreau turns several faces towards nature, and his wildness interacts with other elements in him. First, his appreciation
of nature's growth does not inevitably lead to a wish to destroy
it; rather he tends in the presence of *phusis* to oscillate between a
mood of cheerful aggressiveness and a mood of vulnerable, yearning receptivity. He may as easily adopt a passive and gentle persona as an active and fierce one in his involvement with the flux.
Many of his early poems express this gentleness—none, perhaps,
more appropriately in this context than "Nature."

> O nature I do not aspire
> To be the highest in thy quire,
> To be a meteor in the sky
> Or comet that may range on high,
> Only a zephyr that may blow
> Among the reeds by the river low.
> Give me thy most privy place

[3] Léon Balzagette, *Henry Thoreau, Sauvage* (Paris: Rieder, 1924).

Where to run my airy race.
In some withdrawn unpublic mead
Let me sigh upon a reed,
Or in the woods with leafy din
Whisper the still evening in. [*Collected Poems*, p. 216]

We notice that Thoreau's sensibility appears to be polarized: He tends to be either radically belligerent or radically self-effacing as he submerges in nature. Here he will turn into a wind, sigh upon a reed, and disappear in nature's recesses.

More self-consciously and programmatically, Thoreau is already at this stage playing off the wild against the good, the gentle, the civilized. In the passages I have cited, there is a recurrent double emphasis on opposite aspects of his values. The music of the spheres includes zephyrs as well as hurricanes; the swamp poet allows that we may be eagles and thrushes as well as owls and whippoorwills; the recruit brings God peace offerings as well as holocausts. Thoreau stresses the wild not only because he considers himself wild, but also because he wishes to give recognition to those elements in nature and the soul that are usually ignored. "We have not yet met with a sonnet, genial and affectionate, to prophane swearing, breaking on the still night air, perhaps, like the hoarse croaking of some bird. Noxious weeds and stagnant waters have their lovers, and the utterer of oaths must have honeyed lips" (*J*, I, 140). Yet such reflections are experimental. As I have intimated, the journal is a private repository for outlandish ideas and sometimes for forbidden feelings. Not only the wild, but also the immoderately gentle are kept from public scrutiny. "Nature," like a number of his more affecting poems, remained unpublished during his lifetime.

Thoreau has an instinctive sense that his inner wildness is a dangerous gift to be warily used. That he censors it out of his essays is an indication of his fear of it. Only later, as in "Walking," will he find ways of giving it pungent but careful public expression. He writes in his early journal that he identifies "at times" with the soldier who revels in annihilation. But there are other times when he would control his wish to annihilate. The hero then becomes not a wanton youth like Goethe's Egmont, but a demon of self-restraint.

The brave man does not mind the call of the trumpet nor hear the idle clashing of swords without, for the infinite din within. War is but a training, compared with the active service of his peace. Is he not at war? Does he not resist the ocean swell within him, and walk as gently as the summer's sea? [*J*, I, 247]

Thoreau's concept of adult, manly social relations is based on self-resistance and self-restraint—on regulated gentleness. One feels from the 1856 photograph and from various surprising documents and anecdotes that he was a powerfully and uncomfortably affectionate person. (For example, when he was in his last illness, he heard a boy singing in the street below where he lay in his sick bed, and he is said to have cried out, "Give him some money! give him some money!")[4] But in the *Week* he wrote, as if in defense against his nature, "The violence of love is as much to be dreaded as the violence of hate" (*W*, I, 290). The drama of his mind is in part a struggle between his impulse toward violence and his determination to restrain and organize himself.

Detachment—The Poet

To this point, we have been observing Thoreau as one who wants to feel nature with all his senses, even to shed his humanity and become a zephyr or a storm. His involvement has meant a wilful lack of control, a surrender to unconscious or natural forces. If he celebrates a human type, it is the soldier, who is himself caught up in violence. Yet we have also seen him draw back from the dangers of involvement. One way of protecting himself from these dangers, while at the same time preserving a closeness to nature, was to become what he called a "poet." Dur-

---

[4] See Walter Harding, *The Days of Henry Thoreau* (New York: Knopf, 1966), p. 463.

ing this same period he is trying in his journal to define his role as a poet, the role of a conspicuous human capable of detachment as well as involvement. By poet, Thoreau does not mean primarily a maker of verses (though he sometimes means that too), but a man of inspired genius and imagination, whose specific task is that of romantic combination. He transforms facts into symbols; he relates conscious and unconscious; he mediates between man and nature. By imagination, similarly, he means not so much the poet's shaping spirit as a more general power of his mind, an intense energy of his consciousness. Thoreau already recognizes that the self-conscious imaginative man cannot wholly lose himself in nature, and must be separate from it. This is the subject of "The Thaw."

> I saw the civil sun drying earth's tears—
> Her tears of joy that only faster flowed,
>
> Fain would I stretch me by the highway side,
> To thaw and trickle with the melting snow,
> That mingled soul and body with the tide,
> I too may through the pores of nature flow.
>
> But I alas nor trickle can nor fume,
> One jot to forward the great work of Time,
> 'Tis mine to hearken while these ply the loom
> So shall my silence with their music chime.
>   [*Collected Poems*, p. 107]

Nature is alive in the thaw, steaming from all her pores, and Thoreau wants to touch that life but cannot. The first two lines beautifully suggest Thoreau's concept of nature as circulation. Quite explicitly in the next four he wants to join that circulation and disappear as a man. But in the last four he recognizes that he cannot so dissolve in mist or water. His role is other: it is to stand aside and "hearken." He alone can appreciate, in a detached and sympathetic fashion, the work that he contemplates. This is the poet's role, that of a self-conscious appreciator.

How is one to think of the distinct, separated poet in relation to nature? The early Thoreau ponders this romantic question often and comes up with a spectrum of romantic answers. In "The Thaw" he gropes toward his deepest, most characteristic answer. The poet's role is to stand off from nature in an attitude of affection and reverence; in his reverence he both contributes to the harmony of nature and ennobles himself. One might call this Thoreau's preferred stance, the approach to which he would keep returning in his assured and peaceful moments. But at this stage especially, Thoreau experiments with other answers. He shifts in complicated ways from one romantic position to another. He searches in his reading to find formulations of the subtle relation for which he is striving.

At one end of the spectrum Thoreau repeats the message of Emerson's "Idealism": Nature exists as the result of man's thought.

> Packed in my mind lie all the clothes
>   Which outward nature wears,
> And in its fashion's hourly change
>   It all things else repairs. ["The Inward Morning,"
>   *Collected Poems,* p. 74]

Or, what amounts to the same Emersonian position, nature is raw material, an inferior world barren in itself that exists to be transformed by the poet. Such a sentiment Thoreau found in Sidney's "Apology for Poetry" and copied into his commonplace book for August 11, 1837, two months before he began his journal: "Nature never set forth the earth in so rich tapestry as divers poets have done; neither with so pleasant rivers, fruitful trees, sweet-smelling flowers, nor whatsoever else may make the too-much-loved earth more lovely; Her world is brazen, the poets only deliver a golden."[5] Yet if Thoreau responds to the power of Emerson's and Sidney's imaginative thought, he never adheres to such a mentalist concept of the poet for long. The sensation of

---

[5] Quoted in Cameron, *The Transcendentalists and Minerva,* p. 229.

being in touch with untransformed creative nature, as described in "Surely joy is the condition of life," is too necessary to his experience for him to deny it.

A more ambiguous relation to nature appears in a passage from Goethe's *Tasso,* which Thoreau translated and copied into his four-day-old journal on October 26, 1837. This is the first of a number of early entries to be labelled "The Poet." According to this fragment of Goethe, the poet is an exalted and favored being, above nature, yet also deeply in touch with it.

> His eye hardly rests upon the earth;
> His ear hears the one-clang of nature . . .
> His mind collects the widely dispersed,
> And his feeling animates the inanimate.
> Often he ennobles what appeared to us common,
> And the prized is as nothing to him.
> In his own magic circle wanders
> The wonderful man, and draws us
> With him to wander, and take part in it:
> He seems to draw near to us, and remains afar from us.
>
> [*J,* I, 4 5]

Tasso is hardly aware of the earth, yet he feels intuitively the harmony of the whole (*den Einklang der Natur*)—Thoreau's "the one-clang of nature" is not only an expressive but also a prophetic phrase for a writer who was to take pleasure in distantly booming drums and ringing telegraph wires. Dreamily, the poet stands aloof.

The figure of the exalted dreamer appeals to Thoreau. Later he will reappear as the "hermit" or the "mystic" of *Walden,* where Thoreau is seen to enjoy abstracted revery as intensely, perhaps as frequently, as he enjoys sensuous contact with nature. Though, in such moments, his reveries begin in nature, they transport him beyond it. In "The Cliffs and Springs," one of his best early poems, a moment of ecstasy in nature gives Thoreau a fleeting sense of some pure, paradisaical world that is apart from this world. At such a time he will be in a special sense "de-

tached"—withdrawn in his imagination, isolated and ecstatic.
I quote the whole poem. It seems to me in its hesitant and varied
lines to conform to the rhythm of the experience described; it is
simply faithful to a significant moment.

> When breathless noon hath paused on hill and vale,
> And now no more the woodman plies his axe,
> Nor mower whets his scythe,
> Somewhat it is, sole sojourner on earth,
> To hear the veery on her oaken perch
> Ringing her modest trill—
> Sole sound of all the din that makes a world,
> And I sole ear.
> Fondly to nestle me in that sweet melody,
> And own a kindred soul, speaking to me
> From out the depths of universal being.
> O'er birch and hazle, through the sultry air,
> Comes that faint sound this way,
> On Zephyr borne, straight to my ear.
> No longer time or place, nor faintest trace
> Of earth, the landscape's shimmer is my only space,
> Sole remnant of a world.
> Anon that throat has done, and familiar sounds
> Swell strangely on the breeze, the low of cattle,
> And the novel cries of sturdy swains
> That plod the neighboring vale—
> And I walk once more confounded a denizen of earth.
>   [*Collected Poems,* p. 92]

Thoreau does not try at such a delicate time to celebrate the
disagreeable in nature; there is nothing here of swamps and insects. The speaker wants to be alone with the veery, so alone that
the "faintest trace of earth" is excluded from his consciousness.
The desire of his imagination is for a timeless, placeless realm,
of which nature can only give him intimations. The experience is
mystical and ideal in that the speaker feels the rest of the world

blotted out while he communes ecstatically in solitude with the sole representative of eternity. When the veery's song stops, the speaker's feelings toward the restored natural setting are ambiguous. He is confused, "confounded," a "denizen" now of the earth, no longer attuned to a melody coming from the sky—the veery's province of imaginative freedom.

"The Cliffs and Springs" thus suggests a potential conflict between imagination and nature. Nature stimulates the man of imagination to want more from it than it can give. His logical choice is then to transcend nature and "become a living soul." Yet Thoreau does not entertain this choice for more than a brief moment. He senses that to exclude nature and to opt for mind is to bind the hand that feeds him. The poem has a characteristically Thoreauvian turn. Immediately after the speaker has asserted that he is free of earth, he acknowledges that he is surrounded by "the landscape's shimmer." He claims to have managed a mystical escape and then qualifies the claim in the same breath. His functions of sense, like Wordsworth's in "Tintern Abbey," are "almost suspended" but not quite. And as he returns to the world, he covers up his own tracks. "The low of cattle and the novel cries of sturdy swains" are not unpleasant—nature is good to come back to just as it was good to leave. Moreover, that familiar nature may even have been enhanced by the experience; it has become "novel" and "strange." Whenever Thoreau is drawn to such a mystical escape, we find a similar irresolution in the relation between imagination and nature.

Thoreau's pronouncements on poetry and the poet bear the traces of this conflict. They constitute an elaborate balancing act. He begins his essay on Goethe in the *Week* with "A true account of the actual is the rarest poetry" (*W*, I, 347) and closes it with "Poetry is the mysticism of mankind" (*W*, I, 350). Poetry is thus a record both of nature (the actual) and of heightened consciousness (mysticism). The poet is both apart from nature and involved in it. "Though more than any he stands in the midst of

Nature, yet more than any he can stand aloof from her" (*J*, I, 289). "The Fisher's Son" is a poem about poetry in which Thoreau adopts a persona who embodies this paradoxical stance. It is a didactic parable that describes Thoreau's attitude toward his vocation in concentrated form. The ideal represented by the fisher's son satisfies most of the opposing needs of Thoreau's romantic sensibility.

> I know the world where land and water meet,
> By yonder hill abutting on the main,
> One while I hear the waves incessant beat,
> Then turning round survey the land again.
>
> Within a humble cot that looks to sea
> Daily I breathe this curious warm life,
> Beneath a friendly haven's sheltering lea
> My noiseless day with myst'ry still is rife. . . .
>
> And yonder still stretches that silent main,
> With many glancing ships besprinkled o'er,
> And earnest still I gaze and gaze again
> Upon the self same waves and friendly shore
>
> Till like a watery humor on the eye
> It still appears whichever way I turn,
> Its silent waste and mute oerarching sky
> With close shut eyes I clearly still discern.
>
> And yet with lingering doubt I haste each morn
> To see if Ocean still my gaze will greet,
> And with each day once more to life am born,
> And tread the earth once more with tott'ring feet.
>
> ———————
>
> My years are like a stroll upon the beach,
> As near the ocean's edge as I can go;
> My tardy steps its waves sometimes o'erreach,
> Sometimes I stay to let them overflow.

Infinite work my hands find there to do,
Gathering the relics which the waves up cast;
Each tempest scours the deep for something new,
And every time the strangest is the last.

My sole employment 'tis and scrupulous care,
To place my gains beyond the reach of tides,
Each smoother pebble and each shell more rare
Which ocean kindly to my hand confides.

I have but few companions on the shore,
They scorn the strand who sail upon the sea,
Yet oft I think the ocean they've sailed oer
Is deeper known upon the strand to me.

My neighbors sometimes come with lumb'ring carts,
As if they wished my pleasant toil to share,
But straightway go again to distant marts
For only weeds and ballast are their care.

———————

'Tis by some strange coincidence if I
Make common cause with ocean when he storms
Who can so well support a separate sky,
And people it with multitude of forms.

Oft in the stillness of the night I hear
Some restless bird presage the coming din,
And distant murmurs faintly strike my ear
From some bold bluff projecting far within.

My stillest depths straightway do inly heave
More genially than rests the summer's calm,
The howling winds through my soul's cordage grieve,
Till every shelf and ledge gives the alarm.

Oft at some ruling star my tide has swelled,
The sea can scarcely brag more wrecks than I,

Ere other influence my waves has quelled
The staunchest bark that floats is high and dry.
[*Collected Poems,* pp. 121–123]

The fisher's son is a poet seeking an angle of vision, an appropriate stance from which to conduct his vocation in the presence of a separate nature. He is said to live by a "world where land and water meet." This "world," I take it, is the Not Me, nature as a whole, the poet's subject matter and environment. "Land" clearly refers to ordinary circumstances, ordinary nature, the plodding farms of Concord. "Water" is more obscure. I interpret it to refer to those regions of being that his neighbor farmers would not explore. The sea (or ocean) is symbolic of the distant, the divine, the sublime; it is the area from which he extracts his spiritual gains. Yet Thoreau, as usual eschewing pure symbolism out of respect for nature, also writes of it as a physical, palpable sea, a pleasant place for meditation and a wild place where storms breed. Thus the sea is also nature, a sublime feature of the landscape, a nature beyond the ordinary that most men never properly perceive.

The fisher's son, then, lives where he may be aware of both ordinary and sublime, extraordinary nature. It is significant that he lives neither within the land nor on the sea, but has chosen a border region between them. In neither will he be so involved that he ignores the other; his position toward both land and sea is that of friendly detachment. But he is chiefly interested in the sea, interested in what inspiration he can draw from nature as her poet. Permanently encamped on his appropriate narrow strip, he stands apart from the sea, yet gazes on it continually. He has Thoreau's tenaciousness; daily, scrupulously, incessantly he keeps at his task, to learn the meaning of Ocean. He is rewarded with everything a poet might want. He creates the poetry of the actual and lives in an atmosphere of the mystical. The ocean is the kindly source of pebbles and shells and strange relics, which he gathers on his adopted strand; and life in the ocean's vicinity is "rife with mystery"—with the possibility of mystical experience. He enjoys both the calm and the storm of the ocean. His poetry is drawn not only from the world of external nature but also from the world within, from his own "separate sky" with its "multitude of forms." Psychologically also his stance is advantageous. The fisher's son is isolated and superior. He is presumably wiser than both the lumbering land-dwellers who ignore the sea and those rash voyagers who sail unreflectively on it.

Yet how clearly this remains a stance, a means of holding varied and opposite wishes in balance. His strand *is* narrow, his position precarious, and his opportunities uncertain. Like the speaker in "The Thaw," he is doomed to be separate from the mystery of nature even as he seeks to know it. His knowledge, his intuition of the meaning of ocean, is evanescent; it must be renewed over and over. Thus, despite his affirmations, he is something of a homeless wanderer, a romantic consciousness bound only to itself, hardly the settled and voluble vagrant we know from *Walden*.

He is homeless in part because his relation to land and sea is provisional, because nature exists independently in "The Fisher's Son" and is not felt to be subordinate or insignificant. Though there is correspondence between the worlds without and within, though the speaker may have his own ocean of unconsciousness from which he can draw his own treasures, that other ocean on which he gazes is tremendous, unfathomable, incommensurable, and separated. He would step just close enough, but not too close, to its edge. He does not wish to be shipwrecked in the infinite sublimity of its storms. He does not create the sea, but observes it. His wrecks are one world; its are another.[6]

[6] For a different reading of part of this poem, see Joel Porte, *Emerson and Thoreau: Transcendentalists in Conflict* (Middletown, Conn.: Wesleyan University Press, 1965), pp. 101–102. Porte interprets it as a poem in which Thoreau consciously sets himself apart both from his neighbors and from the vaguer transcendentalists, including Emerson. Yet Emerson himself responded approvingly, at least to the first line, for he thought it good enough to use for his own purposes. He wrote in his journal in July,

Nature's independence is openly asserted in a journal entry for March 3, 1839. Yet as Thoreau works out his difficult thought in this appealing meditation, the position he comes to is a somewhat confusing compromise, which I will try to disentangle.

THE POET

He must be something more than natural,—even supernatural. Nature will not speak through but along with him. His voice will not proceed from her midst, but, breathing on her, will make her the expression of his thought. He then poetizes when he takes a fact out of nature into spirit. He speaks without reference to time or place. His thought is one world, hers another. He is another Nature,—Nature's brother. Kindly offices do they perform for one another. Each publishes the other's truth. [*J*, I, 74–75]

Thoreau is trying in the paragraph both to follow Emerson closely and to assert a difference from him. Thus it contains two tendencies of thought that do not quite mesh. On the one hand, this poet is a self-and-world-builder out of Emerson's *Nature*. He is "more than natural,—even supernatural" (he is a godlike being, above nature); he takes facts "out of nature into spirit" (he gives spiritual meaning to the Not Me); he "speaks without reference to time and place" (he resembles Emerson's Orphic Poet more than he resembles Thoreau). On the other hand, Thoreau indicates in other phrases that nature is separate from but equal to the poet. Her expression (her "speech" or "thought") is distinct

---

1841: "Yet we care for individuals, not for the waste universality. . . . Who would value any number of miles of Atlantic brine bounded by lines of latitude and longitude? Confine it by granite rocks, let it wash ashore where wise men dwell, and it is filled with expression; and the point of greatest interest is *where the land and water meet*" (Stephen E. Whicher, ed., *Selections from Ralph Waldo Emerson* [Boston: Houghton Mifflin, 1957], pp. 184–185—my italics). Emerson used these sentences from his journal later that summer in "The Method of Nature" (*Works*, I, 205). In this instance of influence Thoreau has clear chronological priority. He transcribed "The Fisher's Son" in *his* journal on January 10, 1840 (*J*, I, 110–113).

from his. Only thus separate can she perform "kindly offices" for him—otherwise he performs them for himself by realizing nature as his own creation. And Thoreau's normal tendency in practice is just this: to feel nature as another world, alive and real in itself, to which he may speak in the second person. In such a meditation Thoreau is working away from Emerson, perhaps with the help of Goethe and Wordsworth, toward his own sense of the brotherly potency of nature.

Sight and Insight

Thoreau thus makes several attempts to describe the poet's subtle relation to nature; but he gravitates in his practice toward the idea of the poet as "Nature's brother." In his many early statements on the act of seeing we can discern a similar variety of opinions, a spread of attitudes ranging from an almost exclusive emphasis on the man who sees to an equally exclusive emphasis on the things seen. Yet if we examine this spread to learn what it means as a whole, we sense that in his total effort he is trying to achieve a stance of detached sympathy—the stance he ultimately prefers—in the way he looks at nature. He will "hearken" while she "plies the loom."

If Thoreau is to be a poet of Emerson's school, sight will be crucial for him as the most spiritual of the senses. "The eye does the least drudgery of any of the senses. It oftenest escapes to a higher employment—The rest serve, and escort, and defend it" (LJ, p. 165). The eye is the sense most apt for detachment, even for "escape" from nature to the ideal realm of the living soul. With its proper use man expresses and creates himself. This is Emerson's stress in "Behavior" (from *The Conduct of Life*), where he describes man seeing at enthusiastic length.[7] And it is also Thoreau's in some formulations, which are clearly indebted to Emerson.

Much credit is due to a brave man's eye. It is the focus in which

[7] Emerson, *Works*, VI, 177–181.

all rays are collected. It sees from within, or from the centre, just as we scan the whole concave of the heavens at a glance, but can compass only one side of the pebble at our feet. [*J*, I, 171]

How much virtue there is in simply seeing! We may almost say that the hero has striven in vain for his preeminency, if the student oversees him. The woman who sits in the house and *sees* is a match for a stirring captain. . . . We are as much as we see. [*J*, I, 247–248]

But Thoreau is too interested in nature for its own sake to abide by this stress. He will feel nature as his opposite partner, not merely as an instrument for building up his soul. "We do not learn with the eyes; they introduce us, and we learn after by converse with things" (*J*, I, 142). "Converse" is one of Wordsworth's words for the generous interchange between man and nature.[8] "Converse with things," as well as echoing Wordsworth, points toward Thoreau's Goethean interest in simple, separate, natural facts. His "seeing" often tends to mean "seeing-what-is-really-there," without metaphor or ornament.

The poet does not need to see how meadows are something else than earth, grass, and water, but how they are thus much. He does not need discover that potato blows are as beautiful as violets, as the farmer thinks, but only how good potato blows are. [*J*, I, 114]

I like better the surliness with which the woodchopper speaks of his woods, handling them as indifferently as his axe, than the mealy-mouthed enthusiasm of the lover of nature. Better that the primrose by the river's brim be a yellow primrose and nothing more, than the victim of his bouquet or herbarium, to shine with the flickering dull light of his imagination, and not the golden gleam of a star. [*J*, I, 237–238]

The second of these pronouncements is a reflection on some lines from Wordsworth's "Peter Bell." But Thoreau is transmuting Wordsworth for his own purposes. Early in the poem Peter is

[8] See Carl Bode's comment in Thoreau, *Collected Poems*, p. 357.

but an unenlightened plowman without the moral wit to see beyond the primrose itself.

> In vain, through every changeful year,
> Did Nature lead him as before;
> A primrose by a river's brim
> A yellow primrose was to him,
> And it was nothing more.[9]

Unlike Wordsworth's narrator, Thoreau finds this attention to
the object a virtue, not a fault. Whereas Emerson in "Spiritual
Laws" can rewrite a line from the Intimations Ode to give it an
idealist coloring ("'Earth fills her lap with splendors' *not* her
own"),[10] Thoreau here wants to be rid of Wordsworth's Emersonian stress on moral sentiment and imagination, and reverses
this stress to help articulate his own desire for an independent
nature.

One early journal passage on perception, a precisely worked-
out theoretical fragment, suggests a justification for Thoreau's
catalogues of facts in the *Week* and in the journals of the late
1850s. We are not likely to find in these catalogues, however,
such a confluence of the wish for accuracy with the wish for sympathy, or such an explicit attempt to understand his knowledge
of the minnow in the context of his total knowledge.

Only their names and residence make one love fishes. I would know
even the number of their fin-rays, and how many scales compose the
lateral line. I am the wiser in respect to all knowledges, and the
better qualified for all fortunes, for knowing that there is a minnow
in the brook. Methinks I have need even of his sympathy, and to be
his fellow in a degree. ["Natural History of Massachusetts," *W*, V,
118]

"I have need of his sympathy" recalls us to "The Poet is Nature's
brother," where Thoreau envisions an equal balance between
man and nature. (In this period especially he is interested in both

[9] Wordsworth, *Poetical Works*, II, 341.
[10] See p. 32, above.

getting sympathy from nature and giving it to her, as evidence of their mutual equality.) This balance, however, tends to be upset even as Thoreau's mind expands on his thought. "I have need . . . to be his fellow" reminds us more of his wish to lose himself in nature, to declare his fellowship with the dog who bays at the moon.[11] The qualification "in some degree" suggests that Thoreau is aware that there is a danger in going too far into nature, one by which the poet of "The Thaw" would naturally be tempted.

There may be a related danger for him in counting fin-rays and scales. By attending exclusively to things-as-they-are the poet may become so involved in phenomena, so much "in a state of subjection to external objects" as Wordsworth put it,[12] as to lose the vital double emphasis on man *and* nature. Sight, as well as being the most spiritual of the senses, can also be the most passive, the least conducive to imagination. Thoreau is aware, along with Wordsworth and Keats, that sight can take over the soul, can distract a man from himself so that his poetic faculties are dissipated in compulsive observation. As if to restore the balance, Thoreau will at times pull back in his theoretical statements and refuse to employ sight at all: "It is only by a sort of voluntary blindness, and omitting to see, that we know ourselves, as when we see stars with the side of the eye. The nearest approach to discovering what we are is in dreams" (*J*, I, 253). This is an early example of extra-vagance: What is for Thoreau a partial truth is enunciated boldly and unequivocally; the claims of subjectivity must get a fair hearing. When he praises potato-blows, he argues as one-sidedly for the objective presentation of observed facts.

Occasionally, when Thoreau writes of the act of seeing, we catch him striving to blend fact and feeling in a way that does

---

[11] See *J*, I, 147; *W*, I, 40; LJ, p. 138. Thoreau enjoyed this image of combination, probably adopted from Shakespeare's *Julius Caesar*, IV. iii. 27–28.

[12] Preface to *Poems* (1815), in *Wordsworth's Literary Criticism*, ed. Nowell C. Smith (London: Milford, 1925), p. 150.

equal justice to the seer and to the seen: "The eye must be firmly anchored to this earth which beholds birches and pines waving in the breeze in a certain light, a serene rippling light" (*J*, I, 351). The poet here arrives at a carefully measured stance toward nature. His truth and hers are published in a way that marries them.

Comprehensive Understanding

While Thoreau developed more privately his penchant for wildness, his image of the heroic recruit, and his conception of the poet, in public he first appeared most often in another role, that of a transcendentalist writer on natural history. Spurred by Emerson in this role, Thoreau presented himself not just as an amateur botanist and ornithologist, but as a thoughtful observer of variety, unity, and correspondence in the *kosmos*. Emerson himself had inclinations to be a scientist or "naturalist" of this sort in the early 1830s;[13] when he found Thoreau endowed both with a "free and erect mind" and a knowledge of "boatcraft and fishcraft,"[14] he encouraged him to write two of the best of his early esays, "Natural History of Massachusetts" and "A Winter Walk." In these, Thoreau attempts to see man and nature as a living unity by observing the composite natural world around him—the Concord *kosmos*.

These essays are pages of illustration for Emerson's principles, public performances carried out in the transcendentalist cause of the 1840's; thus they are self-consciously soul-affirming and healthy-minded; they exhibit little of the wanton romantic desire or the circumspect doubt Thoreau might allow himself in his journals. They are also written appropriately in prose; Thoreau's accurate seeing follows the irregular rhythm of juxtaposed natural detail. In romantic verse the poetic, subjective mind pro-

---

[13] See Emerson's well-known account of a visit to the Jardin des Plantes in Paris during 1833, in *Journals*, III, 163.

[14] Emerson, *Journals*, IV, 395; *The Letters of Ralph Waldo Emerson*, ed. Ralph L. Rusk (New York: Columbia University Press, 1939), III, 47.

vides a measure that suits its own inner rhythm, but part of Thoreau's intention in the essays—as in much of his prose—is that the dreaming mind should move out of the way and allow nature its irregularities. After careful and humble observation, the unity of the *kosmos* would emerge, and man could feel that he was at home in a place enlivened by mysterious spirit and ordered by secret law.

One way the Thoreau of this mode apprehends unity is to look for indications of the total structure of nature in each thing he sees. An object ceases to be a spiritless fragment when it is made an organic part of a larger structure. Thoreau undoubtedly came upon prescriptions in Emerson and Coleridge for seeking the whole in the parts.[15] But let us see how he himself actively searches out the organic, for example in this description of a stump of wood from "A Winter Walk":

See how many traces from which we may learn the chopper's history! From this stump we may guess the sharpness of his axe, and from the slope of the stroke, on which side he stood, and whether he cut down the tree without going round it or changing hands; and, from the flexure of the splinters, we may know which way it fell. This one chip contains inscribed on it the whole history of the woodchopper and of the world. [*W*, V, 173]

The manifest exaggeration of the last sentence nevertheless suggests Thoreau's intention: to discern the whole history of a man and of the world inscribed on a single chip. A literal reading of the book of nature affords us a glimpse of that whole. Thoreau affirms the importance of a thing by making it the object of attention for an act of the mind, his penetrating seeing of particulars. Moreover, becouse his recognition of behavior and detail is so clear, his visualization of the scene is a persuasive instance of combination: the woodchopper is related to the stump, the world to this place, the observer to the living thing observed.

---

[15] See Sherman Paul, *Emerson's Angle of Vision* (Cambridge, Mass.: Harvard University Press, 1952), pp. 37ff.

Not only do the parts of the *kosmos* relate to the whole; they also relate to each other. For Thoreau, as for Emerson, nature is full of observable and significant likenesses. Thoreau seeks out these likenesses on his walks: "I am struck with the pleasing friendships and unanimities of nature, as when the lichen on the trees takes the form of their leaves" ("Natural History of Massachusetts," *W*, V, 124). The friendship of lichen and leaf is different in kind from the love in nature evoked, say, at the end of Coleridge's "Frost at Midnight," where the eave-drops hang "in silent icicles, / Quietly shining to the quiet moon." Coleridge would not pretend to assert that there is a structural or scientific relation between the icicles and the moon; they are both features of his landscape, and he provides the unity. But Thoreau makes just this claim in "A Natural History of Massachusetts." "Foliate structure is common to the coral and the plumage of birds, and to how large a part of animate and inanimate nature." "Vegetation is but a kind of crystallization." "The . . . independence of law on matter is observable in many . . . instances, as in the natural rhymes, when some animal form, color, or odor has its counterpart in some vegetable. As, indeed, all rhymes imply an eternal melody, independent of any particular sense" (*W*, V, 127).

Let us, however, understand the character of these claims. Thoreau's method is not rigorously scientific. It is rather a means of managing a stance by which he may relate to nature. He is not surveying a limited mass of observed facts to arrive at a modest generalization—this he was more likely to do late in his career, as in the carefully researched essay "The Succession of Forest Trees." Instead, he is using a few fashionable ideas, stemming from the German romantic science of the period, to provide a framework for his seeing and thinking. His purpose is not to weigh facts in his study but to use the evidence of his senses to jump as readily as he can to the conclusion that nature is a living whole. Thoreau read about the foliate structure of animal parts, for example of lungs and entrails, in Menzel's synopsis of Oken;[16] and he seems to have adopted the idea as a principle he would look for everywhere. "Vegetation is but a form of crystallization" might seem to come from Goethe, who recognized that all parts of a flowering plant are leaf-life in structure. (And indeed Thoreau and Emerson are drawn to the Goethean notion of *Urphänomene,* of fundamental structural elements in nature, evident to the observer, from which the particular forms of all natural things derive.) But in fact Goethe expressly repudiated such a connection between leaves and crystals as unfounded empirically.[17] Though he too used his science for the romantic purpose of buttressing his relation to nature with his factual knowledge, the older Goethe was more scrupulous than the younger Thoreau in discovering his friendships and unanimities. Thoreau's are in effect extra-vagances; he goes out of his way to find them. His strategy is so to shower our minds with images of the unity of nature that we will share his belief in the possibility of that unity out of sheer imaginative response.

An errand of extra-vagance in Thoreau tends to hide its opposite which, in this case, is a covert skepticism regarding everything he does not know empirically, a skepticism that tends to erode his faith not only in likenesses within nature, but more significantly in the human bond with nature. When he accepts the Emersonian imperative, "Go out and look at nature, and demonstrate its unity with man," he is not really content with whimsical evidence. Let us look closely at a paragraph from the "Natural History."

I am particularly attracted by the motions of the serpent tribe. They make our hands and feet, the wings of the bird, and the fins of the fish seem very superfluous, as if Nature had only indulged her fancy in making them. The black snake will dart into a bush when pursued, and circle round and round with an easy and grace-

[16] Quoted in Cameron, *The Transcendentalists and Minerva,* pp. 293–295.

[17] See Fairley, *A Study of Goethe,* p. 206.

ful motion, amid the thin and bare twigs, five or six feet from the ground, as a bird flits from bough to bough, or hang in festoons between the forks. Elasticity and flexibleness in the simpler forms of animal life are equivalent to a complex system of limbs in the higher; and we have only to be as wise and wily as the serpent, to perform as difficult feats without the vulgar assistance of hands and feet. [*W*, V, 123–124]

Snakes are linked not only to men, but also to fishes and birds, all belonging together as features of evolution. But this is a "fancy" for Thoreau, an interesting speculation. His language reveals the fanciful tentativeness of his ideas. The fins of the fish only "seem" superfluous. When the paragraph is stripped of conjecture and imaginative projection, what remains is "I am attracted by the motions of the serpent tribe" and the description of the black snake itself. The conjecture Thoreau would not dismiss; he is interested in anything that might certify the intuition, expressed in "Surely joy is the condition of life," that nature is one and man belongs with it. Yet the unity of nature remains a threatened hypothesis; we seldom find him arguing for it openly or straightforwardly—rather he will declaim it expansively, suggest it obliquely, or persuade us of it cleverly. Later Thoreau's skepticism will get the better of his fondness for fanciful experiment. His last published scientific writings, "Wild Apples" and "The Succession of Forest Trees," have a sobriety that Goethe would have respected. Also, even in these late essays he is pursuing his Goethean faith in the unity of nature. By endless records, by habitual gazing and accurate seeing, he may silence the "lingering doubt" of the fisher's son and reassert the truth of his original intuition.

Phusis

What Thoreau cares about, early and late, is not so much his speculations on formal relations between observed phenomena as his intuition of an "eternal melody," which he may or may not parse into natural rhymes. He hardly thinks of the structure of nature without thinking of the force that makes it live. He sees the woodman's chip not only as a piece of wood that is structurally a part of the forest, but also as the end result of an animating process in which the work of nature is conceived as one growth with one history. As he contemplates the idea of nature as a living whole, he is most drawn to the creative, changing activity within nature. His early speculations and later labors concerning *kosmos* are means of indicating the truth of Phusis, the Mother of Joy, who sustains him. It is this nature with which he would be involved, in all his various roles. The chief metaphor with which he clothes his sense of the oneness of growing things is that of nature as a great, single organism that never dies. Nature is inhabited by a spirit, a "slumbering subterranean fire which never goes out, and which no cold can chill" (*W*, V, 167), as he puts it in "A Winter Walk." Or it may be likened to a breathing, living animal, as in "The Thaw," or to an immortal plant, as in the prose poem to autumn from the *Week*.

The fields are reaped and shorn of their pride, but an inward verdure still crowns them. . . . Behind the sheaves, and under the sod, there lurks a ripe fruit, which the reapers have not gathered, the true harvest of the year, which it bears forever, annually watering and maturing it, and man never severs the stalk which bears this palatable fruit. [*W*, I, 404][18]

The idea of nature as a living organism is, I have earlier indicated, a very old one. Thoreau, however, would give it conscious emphasis and assent, more so than Emerson or Coleridge or even Wordsworth. In the readings he did as Emerson's student he kept on its track. In 1840 he read Ralph Cudworth's *True Intellectual System of the Universe,* a large seventeenth-century compendium of cosmological speculation from earlier times, which leads into the author's own Christian-organicist conception of

[18] This prose poem appears as rough verse in Thoreau's manuscript journal. Carl Bode conjectures that the date of the verse is September 1, 1842—see *Collected Poems,* pp. 136, 313, 362.

"plastic nature." Thoreau was especially drawn to fragments Cudworth quotes of an Orphic Hymn to Zeus. The chief point of the hymn, as Cudworth remarks, is that "the whole world is represented as one animal, God being the soul thereof."[19] Thoreau retranslated these fragments effectively, then used hints Cudworth supplied to locate the entire hymn, which he also translated.[20]

This living organism of nature Thoreau generally conceived, like Emerson and even more like Goethe, as evolving with infinite gradualness.

Nature never makes haste; her systems revolve at an even pace. The bud swells imperceptibly, without hurry or confusion, as though the short spring day were an eternity. [*J*, I, 92]

The great events to which all things consent, and for which they have prepared the way, produce no explosion, for they are gradual, and create no vacuum which requires to be suddenly filled; as a birth takes place in silence, and is whispered about the neighborhood, but an assassination, which is at war with the constitution of things, creates a tumult immediately. Corn grows in the night. [Feb. 26, 1840—*J*, I, 124].

This last is a favorite sentence of Thoreau's and the germ of other sentences. His first variation is in a journal entry for January 23, 1841, "We grow like corn in the genial dankness and silence of the night" (*J*, I, 174). I would here single out a difference from Emerson, who wrote, we remember, "I expand and live in the warm day like corn and melons."[21] Thoreau's original sentence stresses the thing itself, not the man who perceives it. Thoreau's implication in the variation is that growth takes place in the hidden recesses of nature, perhaps most secretly and certainly in swamps, or in the "genial dankness and silence" of man's uncon-

---

[19] Ralph Cudworth, *The True Intellectual System of the Universe* (London: Priestley, 1820), II, 90.

[20] See Cameron, *The Transcendentalists and Minerva*, pp. 289–290.

[21] Emerson, *Works*, I, 59.

scious. He is drawn to the mystery and danger of night. *Walden's* "I grew in those seasons like corn in the night" (*Walden,* p. 111) is of course closer to Emerson. It suggests Thoreau's wish to liken his own growth to a natural process, to show that he corresponds in his inner development to a potent and sensitive plant native to Concord.

An advantage in the concept of nature as an immortal organism is that it provided Thoreau, as it also did Emerson and Whitman, with an answer to death. When his brother John died of lockjaw in January 1842, Thoreau was terribly shaken—to the extent that he suffered a while from sympathetic lockjaw himself! His journal is empty for one month, and uncertain of its bearings for the next. Then in March he turned for solace to the idea of growing nature. From March 8 to March 13 he is preoccupied with death, trying to convince himself that nature does not die.

The death of the flea and the elephant are but phenomena in the life of nature. [March 8, 1842—*J,* I, 324]

There is no continuance of death. It is a transient phenomenon. Nature presents nothing in a state of death. [March 12—*J,* I, 328]

If we see Nature as pausing, immediately all mortifies and decays; but seen as progressing, she is beautiful. [March 13—*J,* I, 328]

Thus Thoreau would think of nature as becoming, *Werden,* an unending grand circulation. He would feel it paradoxically as both alive and immortal.

Yet there are difficulties in this rationalization. At times, we shall learn, Thoreau sees nature as the scene of mortification and decay and wishes to be free of it, sees the principle of death implicit in nature along with the principle of growth.

While meditating on his brother's death, Thoreau is prone to disappear in nature. He is no longer the poet who stands apart or the speculative critic of *kosmos;* instead he imagines himself as a passive feature of the landscape.

I live in the perpetual verdure of the globe. I die in the annual decay of nature. [March 8—*J*, I, 324]

I must receive my life as passively as the willow leaf that flutters over the brook. . . . I will wait the breezes patiently, and grow as Nature shall determine. . . . We may live the life of a plant or an animal, without living an animal life. This constant and universal content of the animal comes of resting in God's palm. I feel as if I could at any time resign my life and responsibility of living into God's hands, and become as innocent, free from care, as a plant or stone. [March 11—*J*, I, 326–327]

His wish to be a plant or stone is similar to his wish to be a zephyr in "Nature" or to participate in the melting of the snow in "The Thaw." Thus we find him, as he contemplates the great whole of nature, coming back to a desire to merge himself with it, involve himself in that sense. Yet this wilfully unconscious passivity is only temporary, one end of a spectrum of moods Thoreau will experience in confronting nature.

Two Episodes

To sum up thus far: Thoreau is elementally attracted to nature; both its violence and its calm set up inner reverberations in him; he gets strength from his contact with it. When he is so attracted he writes of the here-and-now, and natural details crowd his pictures that mean more to him than his own consciousness. Yet just as fundamental is his recognition that he is detached from ordinary natural processes; his human attribute of reflectiveness separates him from the contact he desires. As a reflective man he is even aware of the danger of losing control, of giving himself up to the nature within and the nature without. Much of his thinking is devoted to reconciling his wish for involvement and the fact of his separation. He defines the poet as a man who stands reverently apart from nature, who can be detached from it and yet involved in it. As he describes the landscape he knows, he tries to give nature a formal structure, a personality, and a spirit, so that he may imagine a meaningful relation with it. Yet despite the intensity of his wish for a relation, an intermittent skepticism tends to erode his faith in a combining imagination and prompts him to look for truth in utter factuality, in potato-blows and yellow primroses "as they are."

I want now to discuss briefly two episodes in which the young Thoreau seeks to come into relation with the spirit in nature. The second of the two belongs among his "Excursions"—Thoreau's word for his travel essays—and the first is also an excursion in that a man goes out from his own human world and for a limited time explores the foreign world of nature. Both episodes contain conflicting attitudes toward nature; thus they reflect Thoreau's uncertainty in finding a single appropriate attitude. Both indicate a drift in Thoreau's mind from a speculative concern with the spiritual and ideal to an observant focusing on things in themselves. Driven by his compulsive concern for evidence and accuracy, Thoreau tries to relate his dream of nature to the facts before him.

The first episode is the fox-chase in "Natural History of Massachusetts."

I tread in the steps of the fox . . . with such a tiptoe of expectation as if I were on the trail of the Spirit itself which resides in the wood, and expected soon to catch it in its lair. I am curious to know what has determined its graceful curvatures, and how surely they were coincident with the fluctuations of some mind. I know which way a mind wended, what horizon it faced, by the setting of these tracks, and whether it moved slowly or rapidly, by their greater or lesser intervals and distinctness; for the swiftest step leaves yet a lasting trace. [*W*, V, 117]

In his free movements and in his mysterious wildness, the fox is an appropriate embodiment of the Spirit of the wood. And Thoreau thinks of the fox-chase first as a means by which to catch that Spirit. He is for the moment following his idealist bent: the fox's spirit is the expression of some mind. But very quickly the fox becomes more than a correspondence. As Thoreau's attention centers on the fox he shifts his emphasis from the mind that created its graceful curvatures to the mind of the fox, which plans it own tracks. The fox, tracing its designs in the snow, is inhuman, other, not "packed in my mind" but with a mind of its own. Recognizing and admiring the fox's separate beauty, Thoreau would even allow that nature is its province, not his. "When I see a fox run across the pond on the snow . . . I give up to him sun and earth as to their true proprietor. He does not go in the sun, but it seems to follow him, and there is a visible sympathy between him and it" (*W*, V, 117).

Thoreau has adopted an appropriate stance for a poet who would be Nature's brother. He feels humility and wonder before a creature so at harmony with sun and earth, mingled with regret that he himself is less in touch with them. But in the journal version of the episode, Thoreau adopts a quite different persona to express different feelings.

Yielding to the instinct of the chase, I tossed my head aloft and bounded away, snuffing the air like a fox-hound, and spurning the world and the Humane Society at each bound. It seemed the woods rang with the hunter's horn, and Diana and all the satyrs joined in the chase and cheered me on. . . . When he doubled I wheeled and cut him off, bounding with fresh vigor, and Antaeus-like, recovering my strength each time I touched the snow. Having got near enough for a fair view, just as he was slipping into the wood, I gracefully yielded him the palm. [*J*, I, 186–187]

The published version departs almost wholly from the journal. In a study of Thoreau's mental economy, however, both versions may be brought together. They are opposites which may be reconciled; they do not cancel, but complement each other. Surely Thoreau felt both the hunter's joy and the humble spectator's awe, the joy of touching the earth and the awe of contemplating it. Both feelings are necessary in his confrontation with the fox, who is a perfect symbol of a nature that is strange and elusive, yet sensuous and beautiful. The poet must be aggressive if he is to broach the fox's wild realm at all, but must feel guilt for his aggressiveness if he loves what he pursues.

Having presented their separate pictures of Thoreau's state of mind, both versions turn to an accurate and sympathetic description of the fox as he moves before the eyes of his pursuer.

Notwithstanding his fright, he will take no step which is not beautiful. His pace is a sort of leopard canter, as if he were in no wise impeded by the snow, but were husbanding his strength all the while. When the ground is uneven, the course is a series of graceful curves, conforming to the shape of the surface. He runs as though there were not a bone in his back. [*W*, V, 118]

There is an interplay of all our modes of relating to nature in the fox episode. Thoreau is a hunter chasing a fox, a poet in touch with his spirit, and a calm observer of his form. He seeks involvement in that he aggressively enters the woods and imagines himself as a fox-hound—only thus can he come close to the fox with his senses. Once in the woods, however, he looks on the fox with poetic detachment; the distance between the two becomes a fixed esthetic distance. He ceases to think of himself as a pagan animal and becomes a poet, the fox's human brother, not his fellow beast and antagonist. Thus humanly reflective, he is interested in fitting the isolated phenomenon of the fox into a total framework of nature. He tries to see what laws govern the fox's movements, and what role the fox plays in the Concord *kosmos*. Finally, the episode evolves imperceptibly from a posing of idealist questions into a sustained act of simply seeing, as if the joy of seeing were enough to dispel all questions.

"A Walk to Wachusett," which appeared in the *Boston Miscellany* in 1843, also exhibits Thoreau's uncertainty of approach to nature, an uncertainty not hidden this time in his journal but displayed before the public. I find in it two Thoreaus, two narrators for the same excursion. The first is a Tasso-like poet, above the mundane earth and its rudimentary citizens and in touch

with a deeper harmony. The second is a factually inclined surveyor of the *kosmos*. The resulting conflict remains in uneasy
balance at the heart of the essay. Thoreau has two purposes in
climbing Wachusett, to discover in the lofty mountain a natural
symbol of purity and grandeur, and to see what is palpably there,
how the mountain actually fits into the scheme of nature. The
two purposes conflict from the start. For Thoreau in Concord
before the climb, Wachusett is a feature of his revery; by observing it at close hand he will call what he has imagined into question. "At length, like Rasselas, and other inhabitants of happy
valleys, we resolved to scale the blue wall which bounded the
western horizon, though not without misgivings that thereafter
no visible fairyland would exist for us" (*W*, V, 135). When he
writes, after another sentence, "In the spaces of thought are the
reaches of land and water, where men go and come. The landscape lies far and fair within, and the deepest thinker is the farthest traveled," he seems to be protesting too much. He will not,
in parts of the essay, be describing the within but the hardly
modified without. If he explores a mind, it will be the mind of
that other, nature.

For much of "A Walk to Wachusett" is the chronicle of a
rather plain landscape, one that is organized but hardly spiritualized. Thoreau gets up on the top of a mountain in order to see
how nature fits together. For this purpose, the high point of the
essay is the moment when Thoreau wakes the second morning
and looks out over Massachusetts. The atmosphere is so clear that
he can survey the scene precisely, but what he looks at is an array
of distinct objects; little is left to the imagination with its appetite
for mystery.

There was little of the sublimity and grandeur which belongs to
mountain scenery, but an immense landscape to ponder on a summer's day. We could see how ample and roomy is nature. As far as
the eye could reach there was little life in the landscape; the few
birds that flitted past did not crowd. . . . On every side, the eye
ranged over successive circles of towns, rising one above another,

like the terraces of a vineyard, till they were lost in the horizon. Wachusett is, in fact, the observatory of the State. There lay Massachusetts, spread out before us in its length and breadth, like a map. [*W*, V, 146–147]

Thoreau is on a surveyor's bent. His tone is matter-of-fact; he picks out exact details and describes them. Following the above passage, he gives a surveyor's description of the lay of the land—though his poetic attention is arrested by the imposing spectacle of Monadnock which, he writes, "will longest haunt our dreams" (*W*, V, 148). The intention of this geographical description is to illustrate the structure of nature.

We could at length realize the place mountains occupy on the land, and how they come into the general scheme of the universe. When first we climb their summits and observe their lesser irregularities, we do not give credit to the comprehensive intelligence which shaped them; but when afterward we behold their outlines in the horizon, we confess that the hand which moulded their opposite slopes, making one to balance the other, worked round a deep centre, and was privy to the plan of the universe. So is the least part of nature in its bearings referred to all space. [*W*, V, 148]

Thus empirically Thoreau is working out his conception of nature as one and continuous, systematic and creative. Wachusett is part of the system; it belongs to Appalachia. From the vantage point of his observatory, Thoreau can see that mountain ranges, rivers, the coastline and even the clouds in eastern America run from north-east to south-west and have direction and meaning within nature as a whole. The resulting total structure exists in and for itself in this part of the essay. The immense landscape is Thoreau's center of attention, not the man who ponders it. Human beings appear on the road as tiny objects, not as souls. Thoreau's visible fairyland has become an observatory. Except for the bow to Monadnock, there are no intrusions of his imagination on nature's separate world.

Yet if at times in the essay Thoreau concentrates on an objective presentation of observable facts, at other times he is on an errand that is exclusively and even antinaturally imaginative. He has another approach to Wachusett. Early in his writing, Thoreau already feels that mountains are places of "Noble Purity."[22] There one can discover "the source of song" to which "we look back and upward," "whose crystal stream still ripples and gleams in the clear atmosphere of the mountain's side" (*J*, I, 284). Such a reflection is a bit of allegory. We look "back and upward" at mountains because we may discern there traces of our pure, ideal, preconscious, Golden Age past. And when Thoreau climbs such a mountain he will be in touch with an ideal realm, standing "alone without society" (*W*, V, 135), close to the sun and stars, and exalted like Moses on Pisgah (a favorite image) above things and men.

Whoever has had one thought quite lonely, and could contentedly digest that in solitude, knowing that none could accept it, may rise to the height of humanity, and overlook all living men as from a pinnacle. . . .

A greater baldness my life seeks, as the crest of some bare hill, which towns and cities do not afford. I want a directer relation with the sun. [*J*, I, 248]

His pilgrimage to Wachusett is in this sense an enactment of his fantasy of poetic withdrawal and a quest for celestial loftiness and purity. Thoreau is preoccupied with a selected, purified nature already on the first morning of his journey.

As we passed through the open country, we inhaled the fresh scent of every field, and all nature lay passive, to be viewed and traveled. Every rail, every farmhouse, seen dimly in the twilight, every tinkling sound told of peace and purity, and we moved happily along the dank roads, enjoying not such privacy as the day leaves when it withdraws, but such as it has not profaned. . . . But anon, the sound of the mower's rifle was heard in the fields, and this, too, mingled with the lowing of kine. [*W*, V, 136]

[22] See Emerson's Graveside Address, *Works*, X, 484.

The landscape Thoreau walks out into has the same suspended life we find in Wordsworth's "Seen from Westminster Bridge." We infer in both instances a wish that time would stop at this perfect point. Just as Wordsworth is less pleased by London when its mighty heart comes to life,[23] so Thoreau expresses a tinge of regret when the mowers enter the scene. As in "The Cliffs and Springs," nothing else in nature can seem quite as good after one has experienced the ecstasy of revery. The day cannot be perpetually as pure as its beginnings; the next morning it must again be "hallowed by the night air" (W, V, 141). Thoreau has been suffering from the heat of nature's summer. "The air lay lifeless between the hills, as in a seething caldron, with no leaf stirring, and instead of the fresh odor of grass and clover, with which we had before been regaled, the dry scent of every herb seemed merely medicinal" (W, V, 140).

Before the travelers begin their climb, they gather raspberries as if for a ritual. Thoreau imagines the gathering as a sacrament signifying his separation from the lower earth. (I would point out in passing how consciously fanciful Thoreau is. These thoughts are expressed with far more rhetorical appeal but with less evident plain speaking than his observations of Massachusetts from the camp on the top.)

We fancied that that action was consistent with a lofty prudence; as if the traveler who ascends into a mountainous region should fortify himself by eating of such ambrosial fruits as grow there, and drinking of the springs which gush out from the mountain-sides, as he gradually inhales the subtler and purer atmosphere of those elevated places. . . . The gross products of the plains and valleys are for such as dwell therein; but it seemed to us that the juices of this berry had relation to the thin air of the mountain-tops. [W, V, 142]

The separation from earth is complete when they reach the sum-

[23] See David Ferry, *The Limits of Mortality* (Middletown, Conn.: Wesleyan University Press, 1959), p. 13.

mit, which is "infinitely removed from the plain" (*W*, V, 142).
(Thoreau recorded it as a thousand feet higher than it actually
is![24]) The phrase sticks in his mind and he uses it with a new significance a page later. "Before sunset, we rambled along the ridge
to the north, while a hawk soared still above us. It was a place
where gods might wander, so solemn and solitary, and *removed
from all contagion with the plain*" (*W*, V, 144—my italics).

Thoreau has thus separated the mountain from the rest of nature, just as he has separated the morning from the rest of the
day and his companion and himself from the rest of mankind.
But if he feels Wachusett as apart from ordinary nature, he cannot also feel it as a feature of the geological structure of the Eastern United States. His desire to discover the ideal on a mountain
is thus at variance with his desire to understand nature as a
whole, whose structure can be observed empirically. The former
requires an exclusion of parts of nature, the latter the inclusion
of all of it.

This conflict works under the surface in "A Walk to Wachusett"; Thoreau will be more bothered by it in the *Week*. He here
displays his wish for the ideal and his appetite for the actual without squaring them off against each other. The whole essay is so
suffused with cheerfulness that the conflict hardly matters, though
it is evident enough. His strategy is not to exhibit a self-conscious
polarity but rather to make glancing gestures of reconciliation between heaven and earth, the ideal and the natural, and himself
and society. While the morning on the summit dawns, he thinks
of "the white villages" as answering to "the constellations of the
sky" (though in the *Week* he seems to have been disillusioned
with this very perception: "When we come down into the distant village, visible from the mountaintop, the nobler inhabitants
with whom we peopled it have departed, and left only vermin in
its desolate streets" [*W*, I, 405]). The birds that migrate from the
southwest are earthly creatures in touch with the ideal: they are

---

[24] Lauriat Lane, "Thoreau at Work: Four Versions of 'A Walk to
Wachusett,'" *Bulletin of the New York Public Library*, 69 (1965), 10–11.

guided "in their course by the rivers and valleys; and who knows but by the stars, as well as the mountain ranges, and not by the pretty landmarks which we use" (*W*, V, 149). Thoreau himself returns to the contagious plain, and he ends his narrative at home in Concord, thankful for the hospitality of an Acton farmer and his wife.

ᘒ 4

The *Week:* A Journey through
New England and Beyond

Thoreau's first book, *A Week on the Concord and Merrimack Rivers,* baffled its first readers and is indeed a baffling subject for critical reflection. On first glance its principle of organization would seem to be haphazardness itself; it seems "a happy fortuity of a book," as Lowell wrote in an early review,[1] a compendium of sentiments and memories gathered together during the 1840's and hung loosely on a narrative thread. Though it is organized in seven "Days," not all of these are felt by the reader as evident formal units. The structure of the book is not apparent in pervasive metaphors or designs; the separate essays from which it is composed are too disconnected for an easy apprehension of unity. Perhaps, then, a different approach, directed toward a reading of Thoreau's consciousness of nature, will be useful in allowing us to see meaning and artistic expression in the *Week.*

Thoreau does have specific intentions as he presents nature in the *Week.* First, he means to give a full representation of the *kosmos* of the Concord and the Merrimack, describing not only its geography, botany and animal biology, but also its history and—as much as may be imagined—its mythology. Thus he establishes and reinforces over and over a sense of place, makes his audience repeatedly familiar with the mystery of a changing

---

[1] Quoted in the introductory note to the *Week, W,* I, xliv.

place (for the landscape itself changes before our eyes and assumes the hues of autumn on the day of Henry and John's return home). The desire to perceive and represent a living *kosmos* informs the *Week* profoundly. It is not, however, my subject here, and I will not linger over it.

Second, Thoreau has in mind to write a deliberately loose, and therefore a more natural book. Thoreau was glad afterwards that he had made it a *"hypaethral* or unroofed book, lying open under the ether and permeated by it, open to all weathers, not easy to be kept on a shelf" (*J*, II, 275). He means not only that the book is about the outdoors but also that he has tried to imitate in it the fecundity, variety, and secret inner unity of nature itself. He has tried to make more natural a book that represents his mind, as a way of blending its might with nature's. He wants to whole book to stand for the kindly interchange and balance between the poet and nature. He will therefore give due attention at times to nature, at other times to his more exclusively poetic or intellectual interests. His design is to create a rich and variegated impression of Man Thinking on a particular voyage through a particular landscape.

Related to this loose design is Thoreau's third intention, which is to combine or reconcile his human imagination and nature, doing justice to both. With this intention I will be principally concerned. Occasionally in the *Week* Thoreau's effort at reconciliation appears in a passage like the fox episode in "Natural History of Massachusetts," where he seeks out an affectionate balance with nature, an I-Thou relation. For example, as he looks out over the river before the voyage, he and nature are clearly distinct from each other, yet he enjoys the difference. Affectionately he observes and names the logs, chips, weeds and pebbles of the river scene.

I had often stood on the banks of the Concord, watching the lapse of the current, an emblem of all progress, . . . the weeds at the bottom gently bending down the stream, shaken by the watery wind, still planted where their seeds had sunk, but ere long to die and go down likewise; the shining pebbles, not yet anxious to better their condition, the chips and weeds, and occasional logs and stems of trees that floated past, fulfilling their fate, were objects of singular interest to me, and at last I resolved to launch myself on its bosom and float whither it would bear me. [*W*, I, 11]

Yet an "I-Thou relation" suggests a gentler and easier combination between imaginative man and nature than is generally characteristic of the *Week*. Indeed, they are often in conflict. I wish to show here not only where Thoreau succeeds in his intentions of combination but also where he fails, and where he is on the straining edge of failure. The strain of combination is evident, as it frequently is in Thoreau, in his use of polarities. The chief organizing polarity in the book is between the poet's desire for imaginative scope and his hardly compatible insistence on concrete, natural particularity. In several essays and episodes this polarity takes the form of a dialectical or narrative pattern. These passages—which are among the most spirited in the *Week*—have enough in common so that they can be understood as voiced and enacted by a single persona. This persona, this Thoreau, acts out a pattern of changing attitudes toward nature, in which his tone changes correspondingly from that of a sober observer to that of a reckless enthusiast and back again, somewhat altered by the passage between. In these episodes Thoreau begins by being involved in nature, then feels imaginatively limited by it and wants to get free, and finally returns to it as a solace and a discipline. What is especially characteristic of the *Week* is the extravagant expression of the desire for freedom from local and ordinary nature. Nowhere else does Thoreau so often allow himself such imaginative expansion, even if, like Ishmael on his masthead, he then focuses back on common things, as if to safeguard himself against the excesses of his heady Platonism.

The conflict dramatized in this pattern can be expressed in voyage imagery. The *Week* is, like "A Walk to Wachusett," a journey on two levels: into the circumscribed realm of New England nature and into the boundless realm of private thought. Thoreau's destination on his historical voyage in 1839 was Mt. Washington; and in the course of the book he relates another mountain trip, taken in 1844 to Saddleback Mountain in the Berkshires. Both excursions are narratives not only of actual events, but also of symbolic approaches to an ideal realm. The river on which Thoreau travels is equally a double symbol. It literally helps bind the New England *kosmos* together, from the White Mountains to Plum Island and Concord. The river is emphatically material in Thoreau's first presentation:

The sluggish artery of the Concord meadows steals thus unobserved through the town, without a murmur or a pulse-beat, its general course from southwest to northeast, and its length about fifty miles; a huge volume of matter, ceaselessly rolling through the plains and valleys of the substantial earth with the moccasined tread of an Indian warrior. [*W*, I, 9–10]

Yet once he and his brother are launched on it, he can say, "We seemed to be embarked on the placid current of our dreams, floating from past to future as silently as one awakes to fresh morning or evening thoughts" (*W*, I, 17).

More emphatically and more often than in "A Walk to Wachusett," the two journeys in the *Week* are felt as existing in incongruous tension alongside each other. Throughout the book we find a tendency to make the gap between man and nature as wide as possible and then bridge it forcefully and spasmodically. In single sentences or paragraphs or poems, Thoreau will join the human and the natural in a swift conjunction. "The Universal Soul, as it is called, has an interest in the stacking of hay, the foddering of cattle, and the draining of peat-meadows" (*W*, I, 131). The *discordia concors* here has the epigrammatic abruptness of metaphysical poetry—though the distinct things yoked together are opposites in a romantic framework. Goethe and Schelling, Wordsworth and Coleridge would join them by gentler methods. The allusion to Thoreau's metaphysical style points up his comparative unsmoothness, which accompanies his truculent fondness for sharp juxtaposition and antisentimental terseness. A concise example of this specifically Thoreauvian maneuver of combination is the second poem he uses as a rubric to introduce and characterize the *Week:*

> I am bound, I am bound, for a distant shore.
> By a lonely isle, by a far Azore,
> There it is, there it is, the treasure I seek,
> On the barren sands of a desolate creek. [*W*, I, 2]

This is Thoreau's double journey epitomized in a radical image, the common element of which is his romantic interest in both these disparate goals. The cheerful and adventurous tension in the lines is characteristic of the *Week* as a whole. On the one hand, Thoreau will make an imaginative effort to enjoy and exaggerate the pleasures of the local scene; on the other hand, as he travels down the desolate creek he dreams of the far Azores. And he shifts demonstratively from one opposite pole to the other, in an energetic and overweening effort to know both as simultaneously as possible.

ii

Let us turn in detail to Thoreau's desire for involvement as it appears in the *Week*. This desire dominates the first two chapters of the book. There is a long passage placed in the middle of the introductory chapter, "Concord River," that might be an enlargement on "Surely joy is the condition of life."

It is worth the while to make a voyage up this stream, if you go no farther than Sudbury. . . . Many waves are there agitated by the wind, keeping nature fresh, the spray blowing in your face, reeds and rushes waving; ducks by the hundred, all uneasy in the surf, in the raw wind, just ready to rise, and now going off with a clatter and a whistling straight for Labrador, flying against the stiff gale with reefed wings, or else circling round first, with all their paddles briskly moving, just over the surf, to reconnoitre you before they leave these parts; gulls wheeling overhead, muskrats swimming for dear life, wet and cold, with no fire to warm them by that you know of, their labored homes rising here and there like haystacks; and countless mice and moles and winged titmice along the sunny, windy shore; cranberries tossed on the waves and heaving up on the beach, their little red skiffs beating about among the alders;— such healthy natural tumult as proves the last day is not yet at hand. And there stand all around the alders, and birches, and oaks, and maples, full of glee and sap, holding in their buds until the waters subside. [*W*, I, 5–6]

With such stimulus, who would not enter nature, at least as far as Sudbury? Thoreau is glorying in "the huge volume of matter" and in the sensuous joys of a present life that arise in the stir of a spring freshet. He is expressing his "yearning toward all wildness," his lust for the creative tumult.

Thoreau's narrative of his journey begins with this mood of sensual expectancy. At the opening of "Saturday" he evokes the presence of creative Nature, a hulking goddess who, after "dripping and oozing from every pore" following the summer rains, now respires "more healthily than ever" (*W*, I, 12). This is Nature as Phusis, a mythical personification of all that Thoreau had felt in the glee and sap of the river scene. She seems to be "maturing some scheme of her own," and the brothers would be part of her gradual plan. They would leave behind the quiet village they know to face the vast strangeness.

As they pitch camp for their first night seven miles from Concord, they are already enveloped in nature's other world.

To the right and left, as far as the horizon, were straggling pine woods with their plumes against the sky, and across the river were rugged hills, covered with shrub oaks, tangled with grape-vines and ivy, with here and there a gray rock jutting out from the maze. The sides of these cliffs, though a quarter of a mile distant, were almost heard to rustle while we looked at them, it was such a leafy wilderness; a place for fauns and satyrs, and where bats hung all day to the rocks, and at evening flitted over the water, and fireflies husbanded their light under the grass and leaves against the night. [*W*, I, 38–39]

The landscape is dense, astir, a bit ghostly. Consider the details: straggling pines, a maze and tangle of trees against shadowing hills, bats and fireflies among the rocks and leaves. We are reminded of Thoreau's turning around in *Walden* and feeling himself in strangeness—this is what the brothers have done a day's journey from home by penetrating the darkness of the woods. Yet Thoreau's penchant for finding a balance between the roving, inquiring mind and nature asserts itself even here for a moment. The hillside is a place for fauns and satyrs, for creatures of the poetic, European imagination, as well as for wholly natural, American animals. As the brothers sit looking out over the scene, their attention is drawn to "our lonely mast on the shore just seen above the alders, and hardly yet come to a standstill from the swaying of the stream; the first encroachment of commerce on this land. There was our port, our Ostia. That straight, geometrical line against the water and the sky stood for the last refinements of civilized life" (*W*, I, 39). The picture is an emblem for much of Thoreau's art: not Wallace Stevens's shapely jar placed in a slovenly wilderness, but an upright hewn mast, a single line of definition that orders but hardly alters the dense mystery surrounding it. Just so much human intervention is necessary to establish a brotherly relation with nature; more will tend to crowd nature out.

The mast against the woods, however, is only a picture in time, a transient balance. Thoreau's wish on Saturday evening is to get into the natural, away from the town. As he and his brother enter the wilderness, they imagine themselves not as men of commerce but as water rats.

Now, having passed the bridge between Carlisle and Bedford, we see men haying far off in the meadow, their heads waving like the grass which they cut. In the distance the wind seemed to bend all alike. As the night stole over, such a freshness was wafted across the meadow that every blade of cut grass seemed to teem with life. Faint purple clouds began to be reflected in the water, and the cowbells tinkled louder along the banks, while, like sly water-rats, we stole along nearer the shore, looking for a place to pitch our camp. [*W,* I, 37–38]

Thoreau would think not only of himself and his brother but also of the haymakers as involved in nature, blended with the grass and in touch with its secret life. That night he chooses to attend not to the civic commotion caused by a fire in Lowell but to the more natural noise of housedogs. His eulogy of barking is a good example of his reaching out in sympathy toward nature. It culminates in the wish to "be a dog and bay the moon" (*W,* I, 40) —in a denial of the human and an exaltation of the animal.

When Thoreau lards his prose liberally with comparisons between humans and animals, he is stressing such a romantic conceit partly to awaken his neighbors to the possibility that their ancestry goes back farther than the the Puritans. Casually he says of one spot on the Merrimack, "This ferry was as busy as a beaver dam, and all the world seemed anxious to get across the Merrimack River at this particular point" (*W,* I, 122). But behind these comparisons is not only his pleasure in provoking his audience, but also his rooted desire to flee the human and institutional and merge with nature. Out of the same impulse, he shows sympathy for animal-like, natural men. Already, in "Concord River," he brags of the River farmers as greater than Homer, Chaucer, or Shakespeare. Thoreau's deference to such types is a kind of self-elimination, at least a temporary whimsical abandonment of the pretensions of a poet. The farmers are not men of imagination, but men unconcerned with the affairs of the mind, and Thoreau fancies them as giant delvers in the earth, relics of a more natural time. He will come close to them by means of a determined and exaggerated sympathy, a willed negative capability.

Most of the encounters in the book that provoke his imagination are with such men: with the brawny New Hampshire locks-

man at Cromwell Falls, who is as untouched by the cares of consciousness as "a maple of the mountain" (*W,* I, 211); or with
Rice, the Connecticut Valley misanthrope who, despite his in-
civility, pleases Thoreau as "a singular natural phenomenon"
(*W,* I, 217). Thoreau's appreciation of the animal in man is
most extreme and surprising in his recollection of the Concord
Cattle Show. Of the coarse farm-hands there he writes: "I love
these sons of earth, every mother's son of them, with their great
hearty hearts rushing tumultuously in herds from spectacle to
spectacle" (*W,* I, 359); and "I love to see the herd of men feeding heartily on coarse and succulent pleasures, as cattle on the
husks and stalks of vegetables" (*W,* I, 361). Thoreau's didactic
intention is to dare his readers to enlarge their scope and to risk
sympathizing with such uncivilized behavior. But the spokesman
for coarse Concord Fair sensations is a strange bedfellow with
the spokesman for Noble Purity. Here too, Thoreau's interest is
mixed with critical disgust. Immediately before this last passage
he presents "the more supple vagabond" who "dearly loves the
social slush," who "empties both his pockets and his character
into the stream, and swims in such a day" (*W,* I, 361). Thoreau's diatribe and his subsequent manic rush to share the day's
succulent pleasures are, seen together, typical of his tendency to
express as pointedly as possible each polarized value that he
entertains.

Another way in which Thoreau imagines himself involved in
nature is habitually to see human artifacts as features of the landscape. He will blend, even submerge, art in nature. As a symbolic
link to nature, the brothers paint their boat green for water and
blue for sky. Thoreau is happy to see the river-locks that have
weathered in the sun and appear "like natural objects in the
scenery" (*W,* I, 252). He admires the cabins on the Merrimack:
"Strange was it to consider how the sun and the summer, the
buds of spring and the seared leaves of autumn, were related to
these cabins along the shore; how all the rays which paint the
landscape radiate from them, and the flight of the crow and the

gyrations of the hawk have reference to their roofs" (*W*, I, 245).
Such perceptions give rise to the esthetic principle that art should
reflect a balance between human and natural elements. When
Thoreau writes, "Man's art has wisely imitated those forms into
which all matter is most inclined to run, as foliage and fruit" (*W*,
I, 340), he means that man contributes his wisdom and matter
its inclination to shaping a beautiful form. But the tendency to
see art as nature can also lead to Thoreau's denunciations and
imagined annihilations of art. "The works of man are everywhere
swallowed up in the immensity of nature" (*W*, I, 336). The
sentence can be understood not only as a generally evident truth,
but also as the expression of a wish. It is consonant with the wish
for destruction we saw in the early journal. Another time he
writes:

> What though the traveler tell us of the ruins of Egypt, are we so
> sick or idle that we must sacrifice our America and to-day to some
> man's ill-remembered and indolent story? Carnac and Luxor are
> but names, or if their skeletons remain, still more desert sand and
> at length a wave of the Mediterranean Sea are needed to wash
> away the filth that attaches to their grandeur. Carnac! Carnac! here
> is Carnac for me. [*W*, I, 266–267]

He is not only angrily showing his partisanship for "America and
to-day" in this passage, but is also enjoying the prospect of art
being swallowed up by a wave of the sea. And since art in general
aspires toward permanence and grandeur, much or all art is potentially included in Thoreau's condemnation. When he is on this
tangent, getting close to nature means preferring Concord farmers to great poets: "Homer and Shakespeare and Milton and
Marvell and Wordsworth are but the rustling of leaves and
crackling of twigs in the forest, and there is not yet the sound of
any bird. The Muse has never lifted up her voice to sing" (*W*,
I, 328). The generosity, fullness, particularity, and wild formless-
ness of nature are preferred to the form, limitation, civility, and
control of art. Art is imposed on nature by a measuring con-

sciousness. When Thoreau pushes his quest for the natural to this extreme, he has no use for art.

iii

At least as often in the *Week,* Thoreau's balance with nature is lost in an imaginative flight from it. Imagination, we remember, is a faculty of the mind, the power of consciousness to invest experience with heightened significance. This power seems to pull two ways in Thoreau, toward nature and away from it toward "the ideal," the realm of the separated, mentally-created, self-delighting soul. On the one hand, the events that stimulate imagination in him generally occur in nature. The whole effort to blend with nature is itself an imaginative effort, an attempt to give new significance to nature by means of in-sights and in-scapes. He reaches out in sympathy toward nature as if to say, "Man is like nature; therefore nature is meaningful and man is at home in it." The likeness between man and nature is reinforced over and over in individual images and metaphors in the *Week,* in the boat painted in nature's colors, in the cabin roofs reflecting the flight of hawks, in the natural men who resemble beasts and trees. The extreme of this tendency is reached when Thoreau manages, by means of imaginative distortion, to think of himself as dissolved in nature, selfless.

Sometimes a mortal feels in himself Nature,—not his Father but his Mother stirs within him, and he becomes immortal with her immortality. From time to time she claims kindredship with us, and some globule from her veins steals up into our own.

> I am the autumnal sun,
> With autumn gales my race is run; . . .
>   I am all sere and yellow,
>   And to my core mellow.
> The mast is dropping within my woods,
> The winter is lurking within my moods,

> And the rustling of the withered leaf
> Is the constant music of my grief. [*W*, I, 404]

Yet Thoreau acknowledges typically that this merging is possible for him only *sometimes,* and we may infer that he has other imaginative needs besides the need of nature. His total involvement is a distortion, an exaggeration. The man of imagination is not always the man of nature. He cannot be permanently swallowed up in sensuous richness, nor can the autumnal sun be a man, and can only be made to seem so by the rhetorical feat of an exaggerating consciousness.

The exaggeration is a sign of Thoreau's wish to make more of ordinary nature than is there. He recognizes at moments how insufficient nature is for his imaginative demands on it. His latent dissatisfaction with nature becomes articulate in a passage from "Tuesday." While the morning is shrouded in fog, he reflects on the advantages of omitting to see:

The most stupendous scenery ceases to be sublime when it becomes distinct, or in other words limited, and the imagination is no longer encouraged to exaggerate it. The actual height and breadth of a mountain or a waterfall are always ridiculously small; they are the imagined only that content us. Nature is not made after such a fashion as we would have her. [*W*, I, 202]

An interesting admission! We are reminded of Thoreau's wish to preserve Wachusett as a "visible fairyland," of his slip in recording its height, of his observing from its summit so little grandeur and sublimity in the distinct scene. New England nature must seem limited at times, and then it fails to satisfy Thoreau. It does not always seem so limited: The grand circulation of the Concord and the wildness of the hillside near Billerica are features of nature he can exaggerate for his own imaginative delight. He makes his river trip precisely because he wants to get beyond local limits and because he can find in nature variety and power. In the *Week,* the mark of his imagination, as of his style, is restlessness. He can be content neither with ordinary, untransformed nature nor with castles-in-air whose foundation he has not checked.

Nevertheless, Thoreau is most strongly attracted in the *Week* to experiences in nature that he can identify with the ideal. These he describes in a sentence from "Concord River." The sentence appears without logical connection with what comes before and after it, and is interjected to balance the naturalist bent of that chapter. "As yesterday and the historical ages are past, as the work of to-day is present, so some flitting perspectives and demi-experiences of the life that is in nature are in time veritably future, or rather outside to time, perennial, young, divine, in the wind and rain which never die" (*W*, I, 7). For such "flitting perspectives and demi-experiences . . . outside to time" Thoreau is imaginatively on the look-out. ("The Cliffs and Springs" gives a picture of one such experience.) He would suggest that we can receive these illuminations only in the context of concrete natural sensation, such as the enjoyment of nature's glee and sap in spring. We shall find, however, that if his illuminations begin in nature, they then prompt him to separate himself from body, matter, earth, air, wind, and water. As he describes them here, he hovers between the realms of spirit and matter, fusing both in a beautiful, momentary, unstable balance.

The nub of Thoreau's problem in relating the poet in himself to nature is that, despite his romantic naturalist inclinations, his imagination is constituted differently from nature and therefore works differently. Nature is regular, repetitive, gradual; its production is constant and predictable. Thoreau's imagination in the *Week* has a different rhythm. It is volatile one moment and quiet the next. Its time scheme differs from nature's. It has moments of demi-divine experience and then long stretches when nothing happens.

Whole weeks and months of my summer life slide away in thin volumes like mist and smoke, till at length, some warm morning, perchance, I see a sheet of mist blown down the brook to the swamp, and I float as high above the fields with it. [*W*, I, 314]

Nature doth have her dawn each day,
  But mine are far between;
Content I cry, for, sooth to say,
  Mine brightest are, I ween.

For when my sun doth deign to rise,
  Though it be her noontide,
Her fairest field in shadow lies
  Nor can my light abide. [*W*, I, 302]

Here nature and the poet are more strange than kin. For the moment, Thoreau wants only the ideal experience of a brightest dawn; the moderate, continuous success of nature is not enough. The context of the poem is the "Friendship" essay. Friendship seems to mean for Thoreau not an erotic or natural relation, but the arm's-length communication of two idealists. When it works, the experience of friendship is the mutual recognition of the ideal, and is regarded by Thoreau in his idealist moments as better than the experience of nature. In friendship the poet feels himself exalted above the village and the plain, enveloped in a private, exclusive atmosphere. The poem continues:

Sometimes I bask me in her day,
  Conversing with my mate,
But if we interchange one ray,
  Forthwith her heats abate.

Through his discourse I climb and see,
  As from some eastern hill,
A brighter morrow rise to me
  Than lieth in her skill. [*W*, I, 302]

In another poem, however, Thoreau compares unfavorably his own temporary barrenness to nature's constant fecundity.

THE POET'S DELAY

In vain I see the morning rise,
In vain observe the western blaze,

Who idly look to other skies,
Expecting life by other ways.

Amidst such boundless wealth without,
I only still am poor within,
The birds have sung their summer out,
But still my spring does not begin. [*W*, I, 366]

We might surmise that Thoreau professed so vocally his intention
not to write an Ode to Dejection in *Walden* because he was per-
sonally familiar with the feelings evoked and the questions raised
in Coleridge's poem. For Thoreau the passion and the life within
will not necessarily follow the regular pattern of the seasons,
much as he might wish them to.

The concept of time is a focal point for the conflict in Thoreau between naturalism and idealism. In a nature that renews
itself after the year's slumber, time does not matter. Nature is an
immortal organism, with an eternal fire within. Or, as Thoreau
puts the idea more extensively in the *Week:*

There is, indeed, a tide in the affairs of men . . . and yet as things
flow they circulate, and the ebb always balances the flow. All streams
are but tributary to the ocean, which itself does not stream, and the
shores are unchanged, but in longer periods than man can measure.
Go where we will, we discover infinite change in particulars only,
not in generals. [*W*, I, 128]

In natural circumstances, eternity is simply time lengthened out,
a "natural eternity," the infinitely extended periods in which nature gradually evolves. Nature changes as slowly as the pressed
grass in the Concord mud, which still at the end of the voyage
shows the imprint of the boat removed from it for the Week. The
mortal Thoreau who would blend with nature goes to it repeatedly for assurances of its stability. In so far as he is part of it
and like it he can share that stability. "When my thoughts are
sensible of change, I love to see and sit on rocks which I *have*
known, and pry into their moss, and see unchangeableness so

established. I not yet gray on rocks forever gray, I no longer green under the evergreens. There is something even in the lapse of time by which time recovers itself" (*W*, I, 374). Yet there is a fundamental ambiguity in Thoreau's "eternity." In his idealist moods he uses the word in an opposite sense, not as a length of time but as an element in consciousness. In a meditation on astronomy—of which I shall have more to say later—he speaks of "those faint revelations of the Real which are vouchsafed to men from time to time, or rather from eternity to eternity" (*W*, I, 411). He means here a mystic's eternity, a moment of illumination when he feels free of both tides and circulations.

Thoreau's disturbed sense of the disparity between imagination and nature reminds us of the Emerson who wrote, "We distrust and deny inwardly our sympathy with nature." This sentence in "Prospects" is a temporary discord in Emerson's affirmative peroration. His more common theme is that nature is there to be worked and experienced; it presents us with no fundamental difficulties because it exists around us for our own use, and we continually create and transform it as men of mind—poets or philosophers or scientists. Just as Thoreau's involvement in nature is more concretely realized than Emerson's, so is his distrust and denial of it. (This is not to take away from the grandeur of Emerson's condensed and abstract formulations.) When Thoreau echoes the Emersonian sentiment that the poet creates nature, he tends to couple it with his recognition that the imagination works apart from nature. A passage that begins, "This world is but canvas to our imaginations" continues, "there is a life of the mind above the wants of the body, and independent of it. Often the body is warmed, but the imagination is torpid" (*W*, I, 310). An imagination that is above the body and independent of it can hardly be content always with the sluggish matter of nature. At times it will demand more scope than this world's canvas can offer it.

While Emerson, the practical evangelist, subdues and dominates his landscape in *Nature*, Thoreau, the daemonic solitary, is restless with his in the *Week*. Left alone to his reflections during his homeward journey, Thoreau turns to the problem of nature's meagreness. First he thinks:

If there is nothing new on the earth, still the traveler always has a resource in the skies. They are constantly turning a new page to view.

There is another reason for a poet's resorting to the sky. Celestial phenomena are not only interesting in themselves, he writes later in "Friday," but also in that "they chiefly answer to the ideal in man" (*W*, I, 418). Here, however, even the corresponding sky does not long satisfy his appetite for variety:

These continents and hemispheres are soon run over, but an always unexplored and infinite region makes off on every side from the mind, further than to sunset.

Nature provides no lasting satisfaction unless it can be imaginatively transformed, seen again as if through mist:

Sometimes we see objects as through a thin haze, in their eternal relations.

Yet even this position is not idealist enough for Thoreau once he is on this mental tangent. He concludes:

If we see the reality in things, of what moment is the superficial and apparent longer? What are the earth and all its interests beside the deep surmise which pierces and scatters them? [*W*, I, 383]

The sentiment derives from Emerson. Yet the way Thoreau phrases it suggests not only the aggressiveness of his mind but his willingness at moments to disparage his beloved earth.[2]

[2] For a different perspective on Thoreau's attitude toward the plain earth and the ideal sky, see Jonathan Bishop's stimulating article, "The Experience of the Sacred in Thoreau's *Week*," *Journal of English Literary History*, 33 (1966), pp. 66–91. Bishop argues that Thoreau treats distant natural objects as sacred, objects near at hand as profane. But he does not give as much emphasis to the conflict between these two kinds of perception as I do.

iv

The sequence of feelings in this passage on the sky is a truncated example of a recurrent psychological and imaginative pattern which, as I have indicated, appears in a number of key spots in the *Week*. The pattern begins in involvement, in the concrete observation and enjoyment of a natural scene such as the Concord River near Sudbury. Thoreau will on occasion be not merely concrete, but minutely factual, listing and classifying his fishes, weeds, and wild flowers. In the midst of this concreteness he rises to a "flitting perspective"—it may be a response to some overpowering beauty in nature, or an insight into the unity of nature, or a recognition of the balance between himself and nature, or all three together. Thoreau, like Goethe, generally feels that a generalized insight is valid only when it arises organically from a mass of specific perceptions.[3]

Thoreau's tendency at this point—I might say, in terms of his naturalist values, his temptation—is to want to rise still further to a state of trans-natural ecstasy. But in the passages I shall now discuss, he will feel after a spasm of imaginative flight that so to divorce himself from ordinary concrete natural experience is both hubristic and narrow-minded. He will thus return, as if to start fresh, to his narrative. His unspoken moral commitment to nature enforces his return; and his scrupulous skepticism makes him cautious about these flights and acts as a gravitational bond on him.

My examples of how this pattern works itself out in the *Week* will be arranged according to the degree to which Thoreau is

[3] Goethe's view of the development of insight from detailed observation is one aspect of his principle of *Steigerung* ("enhancement"). According to this principle, all nature develops in a process of gradual, undramatic growth that is marked occasionally by significant and clearly evident ascending steps (*Steigerungen*). See E. M. Wilkinson, " 'Tasso— ein gesteigerter Werther' in the Light of Goethe's Principle of 'Steigerung,' " in E. M. Wilkinson and L. A. Willoughby, *Goethe: Poet and Thinker* (London: Arnold, 1962), pp. 185–214.

stimulated by nature to go beyond it. The last examples are at least in part "antinaturalist"; they show him tempted to thrust aside his much-pondered and hard-earned balance with nature. But in the first example he stays very close to nature's limits. It is that carefully contrived illustration of proper combination between ideal and natural, the description of the "natural Sabbath" in "Sunday."

The expression "natural Sabbath" is itself a conscious, not to say sacrilegious paradox. The New England sabbath is an occasion for men to withdraw from woods and fields into churches. From Thoreau's perspective, it is usually a perversion of nature and an imposition on it. On this occasion, however, he is of a mind to have nature agree to a sabbath and do kindly offices for it. Thoreau's whimsically sacramental scene rises out of a texture of ordinary narrative. He has been classifying the trees seen on his morning voyage, when he moves swiftly and suddenly onto naturally enchanted ground. I quote at length in order to give a sense of the episode as a whole.

As we thus dipped our way along between fresh masses of foliage overrun with the grape and smaller flowering vines, the surface was so calm, and both air and water so transparent, that the flight of a kingfisher or robin over the river was as distinctly seen reflected in the water below as in the air above. The birds seemed to flit through submerged groves, alighting on the yielding sprays, and their clear notes to come up from below. We were uncertain whether the water floated the land, or the land held the water in its bosom. . . .

For every oak and birch . . . growing on the hilltop, as well as for these elms and willows, we knew that there was a graceful ethereal and ideal tree making down from the roots. . . . The stillness was intense and almost conscious, as if it were a natural Sabbath, and we fancied that the morning was the evening of a celestial day. The air was so elastic and crystalline that it had the same effect on the landscape that a glass has on a picture, to give it an ideal remoteness and perfection. The landscape was clothed in a mild and quiet light, in which the woods and fences checkered and partitioned it with new regularity, and rough and uneven fields stretched away with lawn-like smoothness to the horizon, and the clouds, finely distinct and picturesque, seemed a fit drapery to hang over fairyland. . . .

Two men in a skiff, whom we passed hereabouts, floating buoy-antly amid the reflections of the trees, like a feather in mid-air, or a leaf which is wafted gently from its twig to the water without turning over, seemed still in their element, and to have very deli-cately availed themselves of the natural laws. Their floating there was a beautiful and successful experiment in natural philosophy, and it served to ennoble in our eyes the art of navigation; for as birds fly and fishes swim, so these men sailed. It reminded us how much fairer and nobler all the actions of man might be, and that our life in its whole economy might be as beautiful as the fairest works of art or nature.

The sun lodged on the old gray cliffs, and glanced from every pad; the bulrushes and flags seemed to rejoice in the delicious light and air; the meadows were a-drinking at their leisure; the frogs sat meditating, all Sabbath thoughts, summing up their week, with one eye out on the golden sun, and one toe upon a reed, eying the wondrous universe in which they act their part; the fishes swam more staid and soberly, as maidens go to church; shoals of golden and silver minnows rose to the surface to behold the heavens, and then sheered off into more sombre aisles; they swept by as if moved by one mind, continually gliding past each other, and yet preserving the form of their battalion unchanged, as if they were still em-braced by the transparent membrane which held the spawn. [*W,* I, 44–49]

Thoreau is trying to present a scene in which the gap between man and nature will seem virtually closed. He not only natural-izes the human, but also (rather singularly for him) humanizes the natural. The trees have an ideal as well as a natural aspect; the scene's stillness is "almost conscious"; while at the same time the boatmen and the bridges are imagined as features of the landscape. All things and men are for the moment on their good behavior. It is a moment of romantic utopia he has framed for us and, as a utopia (no place)', a rare Thoreauvian fiction, an illustration of an imaginative possibility for his skeptical neighbors. The tone hovers between that of a serious rhapsody and that of a lyrical tall story. Those church-going fish are chaste only by whimsical fiat, and that frog, with his head in the air and one foot on the watery ground, is a picturesque, playfully conceived emblem of combination.

As fiction, the episode is no longer an exact representation of nature. Moreover, not only is Thoreau's fable an imaginative departure from nature, but some of the details of his description are made to emphasize the ideal aspect of the scene. His landscape is covered, as it were, by a glass that sets it apart from the poet, just as a thin haze idealizes objects for him in the sequence on the sky. Though elsewhere distinctness in nature means imaginative limitation, here the checkered, regular fields captivate his imagination. He feels free to exaggerate the landscape into a fairyland, which has been momentarily given him before he moves on to scrubbier pastures. The brothers' fancy that this is the evening of a celestial day suggests (in the allusion to Genesis) that they feel in the presence of a creative god whose work is good; in that moment morning and evening are natural images representing an eternal vision in which instances of time are seen as flitting perspectives of delight. And in the sentence, "We were uncertain whether the water floated the land, or the land held the water in its bosom," we get a flickering feeling of a mythical Wordsworthian landscape with an inland sea and islands, where land and water are composed and combined, "married."[4]

Yet though Thoreau feels strongly the pull of the ideal, he does not here give in to it so as to disregard the natural. He does not allow us to lose for long the sense of the underlying presence of

---

[4] One might think here of Wordsworth's "spousal verse," of Isaiah's Beulah (the married land), and of a favorite stanza of Thoreau's from Herbert's "Virtue":

> Sweet day, so cool, so calm, so bright,
> The bridal of the earth and sky;
> The dew shall weep thy fall tonight,
>   For thou must die.

abundant, chaotic nature. The detail is too rich for an exclusively idealized portrait. The birds flitting through "submerged groves" suggest the circulating life that comes up from the earth below. The golden and silver minnows, surrounding the boat in swarms, are perfectly ideal and natural (they anticipate the swarms of shining perch dimpling the smooth surface of Walden Pond). Thoreau adopts the style of a working naturalist briefly as he thinks of their still swimming in the membrane that holds the spawn; yet this laboratory observation in no way distracts us from the pervasive sense of nature's unity, but rather enhances it. In their profusion the minnows yet move as if guided by one mind. Thoreau is asserting and demonstrating the existence of a *phuendos kosmos,* a structured world constantly creating itself.

A natural Sabbath cannot last; it is but a fragile moment of peace that soothes the restless travelor. Nor does it answer all Thoreau's imaginative needs; he approaches nature with many different desires and designs. At other times he will want his Saturday evening wilderness or his Tuesday morning fog, his moments of involvement in the chaos and his moments of abstraction from it. The book would hardly be so hypaethral, so unpredictable, if it were but a succession of perfectly balanced descriptions. Yet the natural Sabbath episode, by representing the idea of balance, is a focus for Thoreau's concern with this idea. It is set in the *Week* like a jewel accidentally-intentionally placed among variegated pebbles in a landscape with indefinite borders.

v

A fuller example of our pattern is the excursion up Saddle-back, narrated while Thoreau waits behind that object-blurring fog on Tuesday. In his narrative of this voyage into the New England hinterland, Thoreau strains by turns to be factual and idealist. He first saunters forth into nature, full of cheerful and religious anticipation.

It seemed a road for the pilgrim to enter upon who would climb to the gates of heaven. Now I crossed a hayfield, and now over the

brook on a slight bridge, still gradually ascending all the while with
a sort of awe, and filled with indefinite expectations as to what kind
of inhabitants and what kind of nature I should come to at last.
[*W*, I, 190]

But if the pilgrim's expectations are indefinite, his practice in
the woods is precise. With prudent resourcefulness he deals with
each natural circumstance as it arises. He navigates his own path
up the mountain; takes bearings on trees every ten feet; digs his
own well with sharp stones he finds for the occasion; cooks his
supper and eats it with a wooden spoon he has whittled; and
passes the night covered by a board he has unearthed. The narrator is enamored of the facts he meets. He gives the impression
that he would leave nothing out. He cherishes the irregular, unpredictable terrain and enjoys the very names of commodities he
reads of in an old newspaper at his camp-site, wishing only that
he might read some thoughts as good to balance the things. By
the time he comes to the climax of the narrative on the final
morning, we feel we know the detailed texture of the mountain
—its paths and by-ways, trees and thickets, newspapers and water
sources. From this texture then comes a "sudden and steep . . .
transition . . . to an infinitely expanded and liberating [view of
things]" (*W*, I, 413).

I was up early and perched upon the top of this tower to see the
daybreak, for some time reading the names that had been engraved
there, before I could distinguish more distant objects. An "untamable fly" buzzed at my elbow with the same nonchalance as on a
molasses hogshead at the end of Long Wharf. Even there I must
attend to his stale humdrum. But now I come to the pith of this
long digression. As the light increased, I discovered around me an
ocean of mist, which by chance reached up exactly to the base of
the tower, and shut out every vestige of the earth, while I was left
floating on this fragment of the wreck of a world, on my carved
plank, in cloudland; a situation which required no aid from the
imagination to render it impressive. As the light in the east steadily
increased, it revealed to me more clearly the new world into which

I had risen in the night, the new *terra firma* perchance of my future life. There was not a crevice left through which the trivial places we name Massachusetts or Vermont or New York could be seen, while I still inhaled the clear atmosphere of a July morning,—if it were July there. . . . It was such a country as we might see in dreams, with all the delights of paradise. . . . As there was wanting the symbol, so there was not the substance of impurity, no spot nor stain. It was a favor for which to be forever silent to be shown this vision. The earth beneath had become such a flitting thing of lights and shadows as the clouds had been before. It was not merely veiled to me, but it had passed away like the phantom of a shadow, σκιᾶς ὄναρ, and this new platform was gained. As I had climbed above storm and cloud, so by successive days' journeys I might reach the region of eternal day, beyond the tapering shadow of the earth. . . .

But, alas, owing, as I think, to some unworthiness in myself, my private sun did stain himself, and . . . I sank down again into that "forlorn world," from which the celestial sun had hid his visage. . . .

In the preceding evening I had seen the summits of new and yet higher mountains, the Catskills, by which I might hope to climb to heaven again, and had set my compass for a fair lake in the southwest, which lay in my way, for which I now steered, descending the mountain by my own route, on the side opposite to that by which I had ascended, and soon found myself in the region of cloud and drizzling rain, and the inhabitants affirmed that it had been a cloudy and drizzling day wholly. [*W*, I, 197–200]

Even up to the moment when he is standing above the fog, the narrator remains preoccupied with the mental process of meticulously discerning objects. And even then he does not escape at once into his cloudland, but instead explains empirically how it happens that the land beneath him is obscured from sight. Once he can no longer scrutinize what he sees, however, he abandons his factual style with a rush. The routine of ordinary nature, as represented by the fly's "stale humdrum," becomes swiftly distasteful to him. Such a nature "is not made after such a fashion as we would have her." In the mountains, for once, he claims to find a natural scene sufficiently impressive without the aid of imaginative exaggeration. But his narrative belies this very claim; here too, the imagined only contents him; he presents not the scene but his manic reaction to it. Stimulated by a natural event, his imagination looses itself from nature and riots in its ebullience. His rhapsody includes not only the succession of paradisaical images that appear in my excerpt, but images of voyages to distant lands (he looks out on "some unimagined Amazon or Oronoco"), classical allusions ("The dazzling halls of Aurora," "the rosy fingers of the Dawn," "the far darting glances of the god"), and rapturous fragments from the celestial imaginings of other poets.

At the same time as the narrator presents his own glorious feelings, he cheerfully continues to belittle ordinary nature. The world hardly exists any more—it is "this fragment of the wreck of a world," "the phantom of a shadow." He exults like a soldier-idealist in nature's nonexistence. In other references he sees nature as unimportant, or impure: Massachusetts, Vermont, and New York are "trivial places." While the shrouded summit is unstained, the drizzly land beneath it corresponds appropriately to its inhabitants. Thoreau has effected a separation between himself and the rest of nature similar to that we saw in "A Walk to Wachusett," but more extreme.

How do the two parts of "Saddleback" accord with each other? What does the juxtaposition tell us about Thoreau's mind? First, we may see in both parts an instance of his not quite controlled tendency to go to extremes. The narrative of the approach is not merely factual; it is *gründlich,* thorough from the ground up in its coverage of the narrator's practical problems and successes. And the account of the summit experience is not merely an attempt to be imaginative; it is a wilful presentation of imagination leapfrogging over itself. Literary images are used to make his response more dazzling; he searches for language that will express his momentary belief in another world with sufficient extravagance; he is bold enough to claim words for a wordless sublime.

Second, "Saddleback" shows how Thoreau's mystical and practical tendencies can be in conflict with each other in a single incident. We have seen how from his idealist viewpoint he casts repeated doubt on the reality of the earthly world. At the same time, his instinctive skepticism toward all ideas not empirically grounded quietly manifests itself and deflates his idealism. The transition between trying to "distinguish distant objects" and "floating on this fragment of a wreck of a world" is too sudden for our easy acceptance. When he writes "I discovered around me an ocean of mist, which by chance reached up exactly to the base of the tower, and shut out every vestige of the earth," we feel that he is precisely reporting a not uncommon occurrence in nature, the capricious but normal activity of mist on mountains. Though we may admire his imaginative gymnastics after this, they amount to a rhetorical extravaganza in which his belief seems equivocal. There is one Wordsworthian expression of faith in the rhapsody: "It was a favor for which to be forever silent, to be shown this vision." The rest is metaphor, allusion, exaggeration. The exaggeration—the assertion of partial truth as total— here fails to eclipse completely our awareness (which Thoreau has just provided) that he is standing by the Williams College Observatory, surrounded for good reasons by fog, on a mountain he has carefully climbed and reconnoitered. His facts do not support his vision, as they do in the "natural Sabbath," but coexist with it incongruously.

I have not dealt with one meaning Thoreau tries to assign to the entire digression, including the summit passage, which is that a man who relies on his own wits and takes the trouble to make his own way into nature may be happily reconciled to it, may derive unlooked for imaginative pleasure and encouragement with little discomfort. On the summit, this practical moral is at odds with Thoreau's temporarily stronger wish to be transported to another world, and is thus lost in shimmering, nebulous prose. The result is that we respond to "Saddleback" not as to a parable of romantic combination, but as to a self-revealing narrative in two parts, that displays two opposed tendencies of mind. The unresolved conflict between them runs like an underground fissure through the episode, gives it its complexity and nervousness, and makes it more than just an exuberant illustration of the rewards of self-reliance.

vi

"Saddleback" is comparable to three texts Paul de Man has chosen to illustrate the necessary tension between nature and imagination in early European romanticism. In all three texts, the Simplon Pass episode from *Prelude* VI, the twenty-third letter of Rousseau's *Nouvelle Héloise,* and the opening stanzas of Hölderlin's "Heimkunft," as in "Saddleback," the poet-protagonist tells of his feelings of transcendence, freedom, and peace in the high mountains, contrasting them with the greater sense of difficulty and resistance he has felt facing nature lower down. De Man writes: "Each of these texts describes the passage from a certain type of nature, earthly and material, to another nature which could be called mental and celestial, although the 'Heaven' referred to is devoid of specific theological connotations."[5] I have been describing just such a transition from the "earthly and material" to the "mental and celestial" in "Saddleback." The celestial landscape in which Thoreau finds himself is similar to the Alpine landscapes of Wordsworth, Hölderlin, and Rousseau in that for him also "matter, objects, earth, stones, [and] flowers"[6] are excluded from his perception. In his new access of power, Thoreau chooses like Wordsworth to regard the nature below as a "blank abyss"—in other words to disregard it. Moreover, his many images of paradise are the imaginal overflow of a newly achieved state of mind, a romantic, not a Christian, revelation.

The chief difference between "Saddleback" and these passages

[5] Paul de Man, "Intentional Structure of the Romantic Image," in Harold Bloom, ed., *Romanticism and Consciousness: Essays in Criticism* (New York: Norton, 1970), p. 75.
[6] De Man, p. 76.

is that Thoreau feels still more strongly than the other romantics what de Man calls "the nostalgia for the object," and has difficulty passing from it convincingly to what we might call "the nostalgia for the celestial beyond."[7] De Man describes how poetry at the beginnings of romanticism becomes increasingly literal, how poets like Wordsworth, Goethe, and Hölderlin, in their desire to be in touch with natural sources of feeling, tend to exlude all metaphor. Instead, they present the names of things, in the forlorn hope that their records of consciousness may have the permanence and stability of natural objects. In his effort to be close with his senses to nature, Thoreau has to an extreme the romantic fascination with naming. The names of the commodities he reads of in his abandoned newspaper—"Lumber, Cotton, Sugar, Hides, Guano, Logwood"—are poetic to him, "as suggestive as if they had been inserted in some pleasing poem" (W, I, 195)`. Yet, as de Man points out, the romantic poet's interest in objects in themselves is in necessary conflict with his interest in his illuminations. A natural object is stable and permanent, arising according to a specific law of growth from a specific original structure. An illumination is fortuitous and ephemeral, arising out of nothing, but then eclipsing nature in its "brightest dawn." Hölderlin writes hopefully in "Brot und Wein":

> nun aber nennt er sein Liebstes,
> Nun, nun müssen dafür Worte, wie Blumen entstehn.[8]

> (But now he names what he loves best,
> Now, now words for it must, like flowers, come to life.)

Words and images, however, do not arise like things, but come to the poet in the sudden effusions of the imagination.

De Man regards the conflict between the desire for concrete objectification and the desire for imaginative vision as a crucial

---

[7] De Man, p. 70. Cf. also p. 76.

[8] Friedrich Hölderlin, *Sämtliche Werke und Briefe,* ed. Günter Mieth (Munich: Hanser, 1970), I, 312.

element in romantic writing about landscape: "An abundant imagery coinciding with an equally abundant quantity of natural objects, the theme of imagination linked closely to the theme of nature, such is the fundamental ambiguity that characterizes the poetics of romanticism. The tension between the two poles never ceases to be problematic."[9] This tension between the desire to cling to nature and the desire to escape from it is particularly pronounced in "Saddleback," but pervades all I would discuss of the *Week* in this chapter. It is a creative tension that Thoreau would use and hide throughout his writing.

vii

A third example of our pattern is the rhapsody on music and sound at the end of "Monday." It begins with a characteristic transition from the observation of things to an imaginative combination with them. The travelers pitch camp on a bank north of Nashua, spread their map upon the ground, and read in the Gazeteer, a compendium of "bald natural facts" from which (Thoreau says elsewhere) "we extracted the pleasure of poetry" (*W*, I, 92).

Then, when supper was done and we had written the journal of our voyage, we wrapped our buffaloes about us and lay down with our heads pillowed on our arms, listening awhile to the distant baying of a dog, or the murmurs of a river, or to the wind . . . or half awake and half asleep, dreaming of a star which glimmered through our cotton roof. Perhaps at midnight one was awakened by a cricket shrilly singing on his shoulder, or by a hunting spider in his eye, and was lulled asleep again by some streamlet purling its way along at the bottom of a wooded and rocky ravine in our neighborhood. It was pleasant to lie with our heads so low in the grass, and hear what a tinkling, ever-busy laboratory it was. [*W*, I, 180–181]

This is the same laboratory of earth as in "Concord River" and "Surely joy is the condition of life." Here Thoreau is alert to it

[9] De Man, p. 66.

at nighttime, and his response is the more subjective. After a day of traversing obstacles he is itching to get to his ecstasy. The natural signal for it is in itself insignificant, "Some tyro beating a drum" (*W*, I, 181); but the drumbeat ushers in a condition of enthusiasm sustained through the rest of the chapter. Nothing more happens outside Thoreau's consciousness; we are treated to successive waves of solipsistic joy. The activity of his consciousness may be likened to that of a tethered horse pawing the ground excitedly—the horse stands for Thoreau's aggressive imagination, the post to which it is tied for nature.

The chief question that Thoreau variously and continuously confronts in this rhapsody is whether his joy takes place as an apprehension of nature or as part of a mystical, supernatural experience. He vacillates several times between the two alternatives. Naturalistically, he asserts:

That ancient universe is in such capital health, I think undoubtedly it will never die. Heal yourselves, doctors, by God I live.

> Then idle Time ran gadding by
> And left me with Eternity alone;
> I hear beyond the range of sound,
> I see beyond the verge of sight,—

I see, smell, taste, hear, feel, that everlasting Something to which we are allied, at once our maker, our abode, our destiny, our very Selves; the one historic truth, the most remarkable fact which can become the distinct and uninvited subject of our thought, the actual glory of the universe. [*W*, I, 181–182]

He would argue that his mystical apprehension of "that everlasting Something" is identical to his natural appreciation of "the actual glory of the universe," because both are nothing other than heightened sense experience contributing to our physical-imaginative health. Yet his language reveals how equivocal is this combining of realms. In the quatrain above on "idle Time" and "Eternity," eternity is clearly mystical (the timeless moment of illumination), not natural (time lengthened out). In the verse, if not in the prose, Thoreau would be left alone with his bliss, apart from nature as well as from time.

The way he talks about music illustrates his vacillation. He finds images for music that persuade us it is a purely natural phenomenon, in this lovely sentence: "It is the flower of language, thought colored and curved, fluent and flexible, its crystal fountain tinged with the sun's rays, and its purling ripples reflecting the grass and the clouds" (*W*, I, 182–183). Yet in the very next sentence he associates a strain of music with "the idea of infinite remoteness," explaining that "to the senses that is farthest from us which addresses the greatest depth within us" (*W*, I, 183). In this second reflection music tends to lead away from immediate sense experience and suggests a more transcendent realm. The polarized inconsistency of these two views also appears in Thoreau's quotations. According to Plutarch, Plato surmised that the gods gave men music so "that the discordant parts of the circulations and beauteous fabric of the soul, and that of it that roves about the body, and many times . . . breaks forth into many extravagances and excesses, might be sweetly recalled and artfully wound up to their former consent and agreement" (*W*, I, 184). Music helps regulate the circulation and thus restores the health and balance of a man, whose body and soul are here conceived as organically related. Plato's opinion is used to underscore Thoreau's commitment to nature as one and continuous. But the next quotation suggests a dualistic view.

According to Jamblichus, "Pythagoras . . . extended his ears and fixed his intellect in the sublime symphonies of the world, he alone hearing and understanding, as it appears, the universal harmony and consonance of the spheres, and the stars that are moved through them, and which produce a fuller and more intense melody than anything effected by mortal sounds." [*W*, I, 184–185]

The music of Pythagoras is the music of a visionary, so "infinitely remote" from ordinary ears that it cannot be heard at all.

If these are the celestial sounds the ears are made to hear, they are but tenuously identical to the shrill singing of a cricket and the booming of a drum.

We recall how music sometimes starts for Thoreau as "the sound of the circulation in nature's veins," the tinkling laboratory, but then becomes a stimulus to wildness, heroism, and the annihilation of matter. A similar progression occurs in this rhapsody. At the end of it Thoreau loosens his tether and allows himself to feel heroical, wild, and idealist, primed for mental fight: "Still the drum rolled on, and stirred our blood to fresh extravagance that night. The clarion sound and clang of corselet and buckler were heard from many a hamlet of the soul, and many a knight was arming for the fight behind the encamped stars" (*W,* I, 185–186). Plato had felt that music might "sweetly recall" the "extravagances and excesses" of body and soul. But Thoreau will not be toned down or recalled; he will be extravagant. He will set out for an infinitely distant battleground behind the stars, not here.

Thoreau follows this clarion call first with a quotation from a cosmic simile in Milton's *Paradise Lost,* an important poem for him of otherworldly imagination, and then with an apocalyptical poem of his own. "Away! away!" may be an impertinent extravagance artistically, but it is instructive in terms of our pattern. It is a more extreme and unqualified version of "I am bound, I am bound for a distant shore," an expression of Thoreau's wish to be away from ordinary circumstances in the infinite regions of his private imagination.

> Away! away! away! away!
>   Ye have not kept your secret well,
> I will abide that other day,
>   Those other lands ye tell. . . .
>
> Ye skies, drop gently round my breast,
>   And be my corselet blue,

Ye earth, receive my lance in rest,
    My faithful charger you;

Ye stars, my spear-heads in the sky,
    My arrow-tips ye are;
I see the routed foemen fly,
    My bright spears fixèd are.

Give me an angel for a foe,
    Fix now the place and time,
And straight to meet him I will go
    Above the starry chime.

And with our clashing bucklers' clang
    The heavenly spheres shall ring,
While bright the northern lights shall hang
    Beside our tourneying.

And if she lose her champion true,
    Tell Heaven not despair,
For I will be her champion new,
    Her fame I will repair. [*W*, I, 186–187]

In exclaiming "Away! away!" Thoreau would free himself from Concord, from nature, from decorum, and from his literary predecessors. The "ye" in the second line of the poem seems to stand for "ye poets," writers such as Milton who present images of heroism in visionary landscapes without connecting them sufficiently to life. Thoreau would be a soldier-hero himself, not just a reader of heroic literature. He writes, "'Tis sweet to hear of heroes dead, / To know them still alive, / But sweeter if we earn their bread, / And in us they survive" (*W*, I, 186). Yet his turning away from Milton to celebrate himself is itself literary and visionary, a piece of exuberant solipsism; in the last five stanzas he revels in a grandiose imaginative self-projection. He dispenses almost entirely with "the poetry of the actual"—yet still would use the earth as his steed and illuminate his apocalyptic joust (appropriately) with the northern lights of New England. But he has quite abandoned his stance of curious, unselfish sympathy with nature; rather he would possess skies, earth, stars, and heavens for himself alone. He would slaughter the angel of heaven and then take his place as "her champion." The prevailing image is of a giant soldier-idealist, striding aggressively through the universe.[10]

The natural explanation of all this excitement is inevitably a sobering comedown. "There was a high wind this night, which we afterwards learned had been still more violent elsewhere, and had done much injury to the corn-fields far and near; but we only heard it sigh from time to time, as if it had no license to shake the foundations of our tent" (*W*, I, 187). The narrator would suggest that this is not the point to get carried away any further. Yet the poem stands as an epitome of the young Thoreau's desire for an extreme vision, one that untransformed nature can never give him.

[10] For such a wild poem a Freudian interpretation may not be out of place. As Raymond Gozzi argues, "Nature" is a surrogate mother and/or sister for Thoreau. (Thoreau himself was aware of these not very surprising identifications. In the first version of "Solitude" he wrote, "Shall I not have intelligence with the earth? Am I not partly leaves and vegetable mould myself? God is my father & my friend—men are my brothers —but nature is my mother & my sister" [Shanley, *The Making of Walden,* p. 169]. Later he canceled the last sentence.) In "Away! Away!" "heaven" seems to have replaced nature as mother; but we need not separate heaven and nature here—both are to be possessed by the young hero. The angel may be thought of as an emissary from a fatherly authority in an Oedipal triangle; the speaker would slay him and replace him as "her champion new." The possible significance of this idea is as follows: Thoreau's stance of detached sympathy toward nature may be thought of as the result of a restraint he places on himself. Insofar as nature stands for mother in his imagination, his secret wish is to intrude on her and possess her. This unexpressed wish is perhaps behind his more apparent wish for "involvement."

viii

The attempt to hammer a consistent doctrine out of his conflicting tendencies and to include his mystical experience in his idea of nature informs the essay in "Friday" which begins:

Men nowhere, east or west, live yet a *natural* life, round which the vine clings, and which the elm willingly shadows. Man would desecrate it by his touch, and so the beauty of the world remains veiled to him. He needs not only to be spiritualized, but *naturalized,* on the soil of earth. Who shall conceive what kind of roof the heavens might extend over him, what seasons minister to him, and what employment dignify his life! Only the convalescent raise the veil of nature. An immortality in his life would confer immortality on his abode. The winds should be his breath, the seasons his moods, and he should impart of his serenity to Nature herself. [*W,* I, 405]

This is the last extended essay in the *Week* and is, I judge, meant as a significant epitome of what Thoreau wished to say in the book. Much of it is extraordinary writing, intentionally more dynamic, less desultory in style than other essays. The passage quoted above, for example, skirts the frontiers of intelligibility in each sentence, in an extra-vagant effort to reach by successive casts toward that realm of illuminated nature we now perceive so faintly. What Thoreau is speaking for in the essay is a romantic combination of the spiritual and the natural, realized through a naturalized imagination and through spiritualized, or purified senses. As elsewhere, this effort, central to the *Week,* is not felt to be easy but strenuous and exciting—thence the elliptical dynamism of the style. Through much of the essay Thoreau is mindful of the poles of spirit and nature, moving rapidly back and forth between them. Nevertheless, his larger general movement is again away from nature toward disembodied aspiration.

Thus the essay follows approximately our typical pattern, except that it begins with the expression of the desire for nature, rather than the recollection of experience within it. The *"natural life"* projected in the opening sentences is a pastoral, sensuous life in harmony with nature as *phusis*. Thoreau suggests that it is possible for man to share his moods with nature as with an intimate relation. It is here in the book that he makes his most general statement of his pleasure in natural men. He prefers in this frame of mind their natural expression to the more intelligible words and arguments of poets and philosophers.

We love to hear some men speak, though we hear not what they say; the very air they breathe is rich and perfumed, and the sound of their voices falls on the ear like the rustling of leaves or the crackling of the fire. . . . Their eyes are like glowworms, and their motions graceful and flowing, as if a place were already found for them, like rivers flowing through valleys. [*W*, I, 406]

In his enthusiasm for natural things, feelings, and men Thoreau is temporarily ready to opt for present sensation: "Here or nowhere is our heaven"—"We can conceive of nothing more fair than something which we have experienced"—"We have need to be earth-born as well as heaven-born" (*W*, I, 405–406). Nevertheless, the polarizing activity of Thoreau's mind is at work even in these declarations of faith in the natural world, distinguishing between heaven and earth, naturalized and spiritualized, and suggesting that we require both opposites for full health and awareness.

The first hint of a movement away from nature is contained in the following sentence:

When I consider the clouds stretched in stupendous masses across the sky, frowning with darkness or glowing with downy light, or gilded with the rays of the setting sun, like the battlements of a city in the heavens, their grandeur appears thrown away on the meanness of my employment; the drapery is altogether too rich for such poor acting. [*W*, I, 407]

This is a glorious combining of earth and heaven. Yet the image of a heavenly city is already suggestive of another world, a suggestion Thoreau will quickly take up. The more ethereal things he names now—music, echoes, the "painted [imaginatively transformed] fruits" of earth—are representative not of nature alone but of the intercourse between the man of imagination and nature. The conclusion he draws from these examples of experience suggests that the reader's concept of "here" must be stretched if it is to include the new heaven Thoreau envisions. "These things imply, perchance, that we live on the verge of another and purer realm, from which these odors and sounds are wafted over to us" (*W*, I, 407).

How are we to enter these "Elysian fields adjacent"? The proposal Thoreau makes is perhaps the central statement in an essay full of central statements, full of exuberant sententious redundancy.

We need pray for no higher heaven than the pure senses can furnish, a *purely* sensuous life. Our present senses are but the rudiments of what they are destined to become. . . . Every generation makes the discovery that its divine vigor has been dissipated, and each sense and faculty misapplied and debauched. The ears were made, not for such trivial uses as men are wont to suppose, but to hear celestial sounds. The eyes were not made for such groveling uses as they are now put to and worn out by, but to behold beauty now invisible. May we not *see* God? Are we to be put off and amused in this life, as it were with a mere allegory? Is not Nature, rightly read, that of which she is commonly taken to be the symbol merely? [*W*, I, 408]

Thoreau would tie his intimations of the heavenly and eternal fiercely to this world. Nature is the "here" not only of objects but also of divine sensations; the sensations come directly from the experience of objects and there is no separation. Nature is thus a word for the unbroken continuum between material and spiritual; things and human intimations of the divine belong together in a great organic Whole. Nature is divine of itself and needs no human transformation, only human participation; no images or symbols need be drawn from what is already sufficient. Vanquished and banished is the problematical tension between image and object.

Yet Thoreau's triumph is momentary and rhetorical; the further development of his thought belies it. The phrase "a *purely sensuous life*" is itself a problematical paradox, indicating that he is not a writer with settled or comfortable views but one committed to forcing together opposites in the hope that they will mesh. In the above passage he does not answer his bold and, indeed, unanswerable questions, nor does he afterwards stay with his program to explain it. The hectoring tone of his prose is a sign of the precariousness of his noble plea. By means of extra-vagance he has made forcefully clear his conviction that the senses need to be educated, but how this is to be accomplished or for what ultimate end he can hardly say; for he is probing not evident sensations but faint intimations. Indeed, he closes out this part of the essay in a gentle demurral that balances and qualifies his assertiveness. With a self-effacing quotation from oriental authority, he implicitly acknowledges the difficulty of reading Nature and seeing God. "A Hindoo sage said, "As a dancer, having exhibited herself to the spectator, desists from the dance, so does Nature desist, having manifested herself to soul. Nothing, in my opinion, is more gentle than Nature; once aware of having been seen, she does not again expose herself to the gaze of soul" (*W,* I, 409). His Hindoo sage suggests that Nature is an elusive mystery, a winged joy not to be bound nor understood with certainty by an aggressive Yankee yea-sayer.

In the rest of the essay Thoreau does not write of sensuous nature but of "a nature behind the ordinary" (*W,* I, 409) and distinct from it, nor only of the five senses but also of "a sense which is not common, but rare in the wisest man's experience" (*W,* I, 413), nor of the here and now but of "that OTHER WORLD which the instinct of mankind has so long predicted" (*W,* I, 412). As he contemplates the process of illumination, he describes it not as sense experience but as something that goes on apart from the material and terrestrial. This shift from naturalism to idealism is complete in the meditation on astronomy, which corresponds in its place in the typical pattern to the summit vision on Saddleback and to "Away! away!" at the end of the rhapsody on sound. Thoreau, like Emerson, is affected by "the anecdotes of modern astronomy" (*W*, I, 411).[11] Yet Thoreau puts astronomy to a different use from Emerson. For Emerson, it is a sublime example of how human thought orders the vastness of nature. It is a worthwhile study because it demonstrates the human power to subject facts to laws. In the course of his meditation, Thoreau entertains this Emersonian view briefly: He remembers how Copernicus conceived the true principle of planetary motion before Galileo saw Venus through his telescope. But Thoreau has no lasting interest in echoing his mentor. Astronomy is valuable for him only because it encourages the poetic mind to enlarge its scope. Once encouraged, the poet discards astronomy. In his restless eagerness to "see beyond the range of sight," he becomes impatient with astronomers, whom he regards as too exclusively concerned with celestial phenomena as phenomena. Their sights are limited; the poet's are boundless.

In what inclosures does the astronomer loiter! His skies are shoal, and imagination, like a thirsty traveler, pants to be through their desert. The roving mind impatiently bursts the fetters of astronomical orbits, like cobwebs in a corner of its universe, and launches itself to where distance fails to follow, and law, such as science has discovered, grows weak and weary. [*W*, I, 413]

In this climactic passage, Galileo and Copernicus, whom Thoreau has just so warmly appreciated, are shunted aside as mere materialists. Again we see the movement toward idealism in Thoreau as one also toward intoxicated solipsism—toward a purely private ecstasy. When he enjoys his own imaginative thirst and power, he has no further need for the concrete, nor any need for intellectual assistance from the historical community of artists and thinkers. The meditation ends in the dismissal of astronomy.

[11] See Paul, *Emerson's Angle of Vision*, pp. 82–84.

"I know that there are many stars, I know that they are far enough off, bright enough, steady enough in their orbits,—but what are they all worth? . . . I have interest but for six feet of star, and that interest is transient. Then farewell to all ye bodies, such as I have known ye" (*W*, I, 413).

Yet even as Thoreau rejects matter he quietly acknowledges its possible use. The last sentence alludes to the ideal of a purely sensuous life. It means not only "Farewell ye bodies; my concern is imagination," but also "Farewell my body; I will replace you with a purified body." But though Thoreau here nods back at his naturalism, he ends the essay by echoing his own words in an exclusively idealist quotation. Then he returns to the narrative of his material voyage, writing characteristically as if nothing had happened to take him away from nature.

> In the life of Sadi by Dowlat Shah occurs this sentence: "The eagle of the immaterial soul of Shaikh Sadi shook from his plumage the dust of his body."
> Thus thoughtfully we were rowing homeward to find some autumnal work to do, and help on the revolution of the seasons. Perhaps Nature would condescend to make use of us even without our knowledge, as when we help to scatter her seeds in our walks, and carry burs and cockles on our clothes from field to field. [*W*, I, 415]

Once again, and swiftly, he has become not a man alone and apart but a seed carrier, a thoughtful dust-shaker, a friend and servant of nature, an agent of ecological change.

In the description of evening that follows, however, the last description of the book, Thoreau, it seems, would achieve at this resting place a perfectly harmonious balance between man and nature. His return to familiar waters brings back the mood of the "natural Sabbath": The river is still, the travelers silent and thoughtful, the banks alive and fertile—"fragrant and blooming" —the fields clothed in a light that transforms them. "Though the shadows of the hills were beginning to steal over the stream, the whole river valley undulated with mild light, purer and more memorable than the noon" (*W*, I, 416). Even as Thoreau describes the perfect moment, he indicates with a last reminder that it is passing him by; he can take his balanced stance toward it only for that moment. The pure, mild light emanates from a sunset that reminds us of the natural-apocalyptical sunset in the previous essay, though here the tone is deliberately quieter for a final balance. The flight of two herons is used beautifully to represent the total meaning of the voyage of two brothers.

Two herons . . . with their long and slender limbs relieved against the sky, were seen traveling high over our heads,—their lofty and silent flight, as they were wending their way at evening, surely not to alight in any marsh on the earth's surface, but, perchance, on the other side of our atmosphere, a symbol for the ages to study, whether impressed upon the sky or sculptured amid the hieroglyphics of Egypt. Bound to some northern meadow, they held on their stately, stationary flight . . . and disappeared at length behind the clouds. Dense flocks of blackbirds were winging their way along the river's course, as if on a short evening pilgrimage to some shrine of theirs, or to celebrate so fair a sunset. [*W*, I, 416–417]

The herons are sensuous symbols of the spiritual. Their flight is from Concord toward the boundless unknown—or toward a northern meadow. They link the poet Thoreau not only with nature but also with that ideal realm which he too, perchance, has glimpsed. Lest the herons seem too exalted and traditional a symbol, Thoreau adds also to his sunset picture the flocks of blackbirds—humbler and less selected birds from nature's store that yet have their own spiritual pilgrimage.

In his desire for a final wholeness, Thoreau would be reconciled with the human endeavor he has earlier attacked extravagantly. He uses the herons in part to show that he would make his provisional peace with art and tradition, even with the hieroglyphics of Carnac and Luxor. In a similar spirit he qualifies his criticism of astronomy as he watches the evening sky, praising the "rare imagination which first taught that the stars are worlds" (*W*, I, 417).

Thus in much of the *Week* an important use of nature is to set the stage for the roving mind's antics of self-delight. Yet there are signs even here that idealism is a promising froth for Thoreau, while nature is his daily bread. It is ironic that he should write in the meditation on astronomy of "the interval between that which *appears* and that which *is*" (*W*, I, 413), meaning that the real is the ideal and the apparent the material; while he feels compelled over and over in the *Week* to speak of his visions and imaginings as if they were but appearances or possibilities: "We seemed to be embarked on the placid current of our dreams." "We fancied that the morning was the evening of a celestial day." "These things imply, perchance, that we live on the verge of another and purer realm." His uncertainties regarding the ideal are particularly striking in the summit vision from Saddleback. Ecstatic in tone, the passage is carefully guarded in factual statement. And after the *Week,* Thoreau reaches for the ideal more cautiously. The *Week* remains his boldest attempt to see man, nature, and the ideal as part of a great continuum, to understand the life of sensations and that of thoughts as one life—with different emphases and exaggerations at different times and places perhaps, but with a unity nevertheless radiating through the whole and all.

༐ 5

"Ktaadn": The Wanderer in *Phusis*

"Ktaadn," Thoreau's account of his first voyage to the Maine woods in 1846, and "The Shipwreck," his account of two visits to the Cohasset beach in 1849 and 1851, represent points of stress in Thoreau's career as a romantic naturalist.[1] Because he is under stress in the experiences he narrates, his relation to nature is in each case temporarily unbalanced, though part of the significance of both essays is that he recovers his romantic balance. Thus in their disturbed drama the essays are by no means typical of Thoreau. Nevertheless, they are important for my interpretation of him, first because they contain some of his most highly charged and daring writing, and second because they show in what ways he is willing under stress to depart from his usual perspective. His extra-vagances, which show him capable of unexpected thought, can sometimes be more illuminating than his repetitions, which confirm what we knew before. In these essays he is confronted by difficulties and prospects he need not reckon with from day to day in Concord. In "Ktaadn" he writes about the potential insolence and destructiveness of man in the wild, and of the hidden, dark power of nature. In "The Shipwreck" he writes about

---

[1] "Ktaadn" was published serially in the *Union Magazine* from July through November, 1848. After Thoreau's death it appeared as the first part of *The Maine Woods* (Boston: Ticknor and Fields, 1864). "The Shipwreck" was published in *Putnam's Monthly Magazine* for June, 1855. It later became the first chapter of *Cape Cod* (Boston: Ticknor and Fields, 1865).

death, as caused by nature's power. Whereas in the *Week* he is sometimes distracted away from nature by a desire for imaginative expansion, in these two essays he feels fear and uncertainty *in* nature, in the experience of a "direct intercourse" with it.

"Ktaadn" dramatizes a tension latent in Thoreau's work whenever he writes about himself as an enterprising wanderer making his way into nature. He wants to push forward, but he feels at the same time that he threatens the passive world he encroaches on. Where this tension occurs in the *Week* or in *Walden,* it appears as a temporary mood of the speaker's mind; it is not allowed to become so dramatically vivid as in "Ktaadn." But in both these books and often elsewhere Thoreau is preoccupied with contrasting impulses toward heroism and adventure and toward self-restraint and repose.

The ambivalent wanderer is a common type in the literature of romantic naturalism—Goethe's Werther and Egmont, for example, or the speaker in Wordsworth's "Nutting." Goethe, like Thoreau, is throughout his career both an adventurer and a reflective guardian of his own psychic and artistic life. In their fine book on Goethe, Elizabeth Wilkinson and L. A. Willoughby describe how he represents this contrast by means of the opposed images of *Wanderung* and *Hütte*—"wandering" and "cabin."

Early and late this image [*Wanderung*] is a symbol for expressing every conceivable manner and mode of his "wandering," from the simple impulse to roam in space, through the urge to dalliance and philandering, or the limitless aspiration of individual striving, to every variation of self-fulfillment, including that soaring of the human mind which we call poetic vision. But with him the complementary image of *"Hütte"* is never far away. The one impulse at once calls forth its corresponding opposite, its regulative counterforce. *"Hütte"* represents the other pole of man's being, and symbolizes an equally wide range of experience: the comfort of home, the cramping ties of domesticity, the irksomeness, but also the fulfilment, of self-limitation.[2]

[2] Wilkinson and Willoughby, *Goethe: Poet and Thinker,* pp. 35–36.

This is of course a sympathetic description of Goethe and no one else. Nevertheless, "wandering" and "cabin" are also appropriate images for two opposed tendencies in Thoreau, and I will gratefully borrow them. The pattern of his artistic life is a continual oscillation between wandering on excursions and withdrawing to cabins and homes. In his writing he soars and exaggerates, but also revises, hedges, and qualifies. For both Thoreau and Goethe, withdrawal, detachment, simplicity are necessary to balance a marked propensity to overexuberance and self-assertiveness.

These two opposed tendencies take form in the *Week* as elsewhere in Thoreau. He meditates frequently in that book on the opposition between enterprise and detachment, balancing the human needs for both. In his narrative also, he must deal occasionally with his own aggressiveness toward a passive nature. The *Week* was begun before "Ktaadn" and finished after it. Thus I will have another look at it; it can give us a context for thinking about "Ktaadn."

ii

Most men, Thoreau argues in the *Week*, realize their humanity inadequately because they are either forceful Yankees or serene Hindus, rather than wise and inventive combinations of the two. The limitation of the New Englander, and of the European generally, is that he places too exclusive a reliance on self-assertive enterprise and on the mastery of nature. One result is that he lays waste wild nature even as he plants his civilization in its midst. Thoreau's narrative of the coming of the white man to the new world reads like a balance sheet of things accomplished and things destroyed.

[He] persuaded the civil apple-tree to blossom next to the wild pine and the juniper, shedding its perfume in the wilderness. . . . He culled the graceful elm from out the woods and from the riverside, and so refined and smoothed his village plot. He rudely bridged the stream, and drove his team afield into the river meadows, cut the wild grass, and laid bare the homes of beaver, otter, muskrat, and with the whetting of his scythe scared off the deer and the bear. . . . The white man's mullein soon reigned in Indian corn-fields, and sweet-scented English grasses clothed the new soil. Where, then, could the red man set his foot? . . .

The white man comes, pale as the dawn, with a load of thought, with a slumbering intelligence as a fire raked up, . . . dull but capable, slow but persevering, severe but just, of little humor but genuine; a laboring man, despising game and sport; building a house that endures, a framed house. He buys the Indian's moccasins and baskets, then buys his hunting-grounds, and at length forgets where he is buried and plows up his bones. [*W*, I, 52–53]

The white man has been destructive of nature because he has been so doggedly single-minded in the pursuit of his virtuous goals. There is a tragic inevitability about his history that Thoreau chronicles with disinterested regret. Thoreau's (and Emerson's) juggling of polar opposites is a way of avoiding "tragic inevitability," a method of scrutinizing any rigidity of doctrine or life-style, and thus a form of freedom. Thoreau suggests that we may be free by being double-minded, by making room for both the otter and for sweet-smelling grains in our lives and imaginations.

The Hindus, by contrast, are incomplete in their "sublime conservatism" because they fail to account for human restlessness. "Their speculations never venture beyond their own tablelands, though they are high and vast as they. Buoyancy, freedom, flexibility, variety, possibility, which also are qualities of the Unnamed, they deal not with" (*W*, I, 141). Men are so broadly constituted that they require the qualities represented in both protestant Christianity and mystical Hinduism. "There is an orientalism in the most restless pioneer, and the farthest west is but the farthest east" (*W*, I, 157).

Once, in the *Week*, Thoreau seems for a moment to have found a human pattern based on a synthesis of East and West, in the pastoral life of those who dwell by the New Hampshire rivers.

I have not read of any Arcadian life which surpasses the actual
luxury and serenity of these New England dwellings. For the out-
ward gilding, at least, the age is golden enough. As you approach
the sunny doorway, awakening the echoes by your steps, still no
sound from these barracks of repose, and you fear that the gentlest
knock may seem rude to the Oriental dreamers. The door is opened,
perchance, by some Yankee-Hindoo woman, whose small-voiced
but sincere hospitality, out of the bottomless depths of a quiet nature, has traveled quite round to the opposite side, and fears only to
obtrude its kindness. . . . We thought that the employment [of
the inhabitants] would be to tend the flowers and herds, and at
night, like the shepherds of old, to cluster and give names to the
stars from the river banks. [*W*, I, 256–257]

But in this extravagant idyll, the New Hampshire woman who
feeds the traveler is a Western American only by virtue of her
place and origin, distinctly a pastoral Oriental in her literary
character. Hers is an Oriental cabin to which Thoreau has been
temporarily attracted and from which he soon restlessly makes his
way. It is not typical of Thoreau to be long content with resolu-
tions for his polarized conflicts. As he finds it a lifetime's work to
maintain a vital balance between restlessness and indolence,
wandering and living at home, he does not expect anyone else to
manage it. Earlier he says, in shifting remarks about the lives of
this same pastoral people:

They were contented to live, since it was so contrived for them, and
where their lines had fallen.

> Our uninquiring corpses lie more low
> Than our life's curiosity doth go.

Yet these men had no need to travel to be as wise as Solomon in all
his glory, so similar are the lives of men in all countries. [*W*, I,
226–227]

A use of nature is that it provides an environment for the free
play of the opposite impulses toward *Wanderung* and *Hütte*.

Thoreau observes the boundless variety, yet formal simplicity of the American linden: "As we sailed under this canopy of leaves, we saw the sky through its chinks, and, as it were, the meaning and idea of the tree stamped in a thousand hieroglyphics on the heavens. *The universe is so aptly fitted to our organization that the eye wanders and reposes at the same time*" (*W*, I, 166–167 —my italics). In Emerson's teaching also, the universe corresponds to all our moods and needs. Nature displays an endless tableau of impressions and scenes in which a broadly constituted man can find the different sides of himself.

If nature were no more than an agreeable and varied background for wandering and reposing, Thoreau could use it innocently to relieve the stress of living with other men—and at times he does so use it. But as he regards it as a living organism, even as a friend or sister or mother, his relation with it is more intimate and difficult. Nature cannot simply be construed as a spectacle for our enlightenment and enjoyment, as Emerson construes her. She is herself a "Thou," whom man must be careful not to offend. Any wandering, any human probing into nature is felt as an encroachment upon her territory. In the *Week,* the mere act of setting forth on the river seems aggressive to Thoreau in one frame of mind. By their very presence the brothers interfere with the perfect harmony of the natural Sabbath. "It required some rudeness to disturb with our boat the mirror-like surface of the water, in which every twig and blade of grass was so faithfully reflected" (*W*, I, 47). A man can stand in proper relation to nature only by following the purest, humblest, and most circumspect style of life. Otherwise, we remember from the essay on "a *purely* sensuous life," he will "desecrate it by his touch," with the result that "the beauty of the world remains veiled to him" (*W*, I, 405)'.

The sense that he is disturbing nature in his wanderings causes Thoreau to seek ways to minimize the affront. This is an additional reason for his converting human artifacts into natural objects, or for his imagining himself as a feature of nature. In

"Natural History of Massachusetts" he is pleased that the seines of flax placed in the river by Concord fishermen "are no more *intrusions* than the cobwebs in the sun" (*W*, V, 119—my italics). At the beginning of "Wednesday" in the *Week*, he claims that a river provides an innocent passage into nature. "Other roads do some violence to Nature, and bring the traveler to stare at her, but the river steals into the scenery it traverses without intrusion, silently creating and adorning it, and is as free to come and go as the zephyr" (*W*, I, 249).

A man, however, cannot be so innocent as the river he travels. Thoreau continues "Wednesday" by observing the small bittern, "the genius of the shore," peacefully minding a business that is about to be disturbed by the approach of the *voyageurs*. "Now away he goes, with a limping flight, uncertain where he will alight, until a rod of clear sand amid the alders invites his feet; and now our steady approach compels him to seek a new retreat" (*W*, I, 249). Once Thoreau has recognized that he has encroached on the solitude of the bittern, his reaction is to regard it all the more tenderly. The bittern is of primeval race, more deeply in harmony with nature than we late-coming trespassers ever can be. Thoreau would abandon his aggressive humanity; he would be the bittern:

What a rich experience it must have gained, standing on one leg and looking out from its dull eye so long on sunshine and rain, moon and stars! What could it tell of stagnant pools and reeds and dank night-fogs! It would be worth the while to look closely into the eye which has been open and seeing at such hours, and in such solitudes its dull, yellowish, greenish eye. Methinks my own soul must be a bright invisible green. [*W*, I, 250]

If a man has only to watch out not to intrude on nature, he may solve his problem by acting as a pacifist-quietist in her presence. Thoreau's I-Thou stance of sympathetic detachment, as in the published version of the fox-chase, is in fact a quietest solution, and his deliberate and protracted effort to purify the senses and live as an ascetic close to nature is another. In his vital work, at least through *Walden,* however, though it is full of peaceful moments, Thoreau never gets far away from his perception that his relation with nature is essentially aggressive. As a creature of *phusis,* involved with it and loving it, man not only feeds on its sensual richness and circulating life, he also participates in its creative-destructive cycle. Sensitive to nature's stimulus, he enjoys the destructiveness of freshets, storms, and hunters. At times he revels in natural aggressiveness, including his own against nature. Indeed, by adopting a predatory role he becomes more animal (he feels himself a fox-hound in the journal version of the fox-chase) and therefore, paradoxically, more natural. Yet at the same time he is aware of his own power to desecrate nature, to destroy with Yankee natural energy the life that sustains him. Thus those passages that describe hunting, fishing, and wilderness-living are persistently ambivalent in Thoreau. When he exercises his animal spirits he feels a blend of wanton natural joy and guilt for the offense against nature. "Tuesday" begins: "Long before daylight we ranged abroad, hatchet in hand, in search of fuel, and made the yet slumbering and dreaming wood resound with our blows" (*W,* I, 188). Thoreau expresses both pleasure at the axe resounding exuberantly in the natural forest and sadness at the forest's passive suffering.

Thoreau's ambivalence regarding man's aggressive potential is still more obvious in a hunting episode from the *Week.* Though the wood pigeons he meets on Tuesday are images of fecund natural joy, delighting the river-listener with "their gentle, tremulous cooing," he nonetheless slays, plucks, broils, and eats one of them, "heroically" persevering in the operation as in the execution of a ritual of nature. "Heroically" suggests not only "with resolution, despite our aversion," but also "like a man, a warrior-hero." When Thoreau concludes that "we are double-edged blades, and every time we whet our virtue the return stroke straps our vice" (*W,* I, 236), his "virtue" is almost *virtus*—manly, pagan courage and hardihood, while his "vice" is, from a quietist point of view, the inevitable consequence of the exercise of such virtue. He who lives self-reliantly off the land is bound to commit crimes against it.

After eating the pigeons, however, Thoreau, with his brother, decides to forego some squirrels they have killed, abandoning the carcasses "in disgust, with tardy humanity" (*W*, I, 237). In these two successive incidents he acts out his polarized desires for an aggressive involvement in nature and a poetic, peaceful relation to it. The entire episode is an example of another psychological and dramatic pattern that we find on several occasions in his work, not the pattern of "Saddleback," but a pattern similar to that of Wordsworth's "Nutting." Thoreau enters nature as wanderer, hunter, or woodsman; he rejoices in the vigorous life he confronts, but he also feels sympathy for that life and senses its vulnerability; he then either comes into loving relation with natural creatures and things, as when he thinks of himself as treading the steps of the fox in "Natural History of Massachusetts" and when he reflects on the eye of the bittern in the *Week*, or he feels himself a guilty intruder. Sometimes, as in the above episode, his writing expresses both guilt and sympathy. Involvement is thus followed in this pattern not by the impatient wish to detach oneself from nature and rove beyond it, but by an aggressive desire for possession coupled with guilt and fear on the part of the intruder.

If Thoreau as wanderer persists in his aggressiveness he may find himself consciously opposed to nature. Nature, we know, does not always appear peaceful and innocent to such a probing romantic; on occasion the face it presents is ominous, inhuman, potentially destructive. Then the pattern alters: aggressive involvement is followed not so much by an access of sympathy as by a hesitant withdrawal—a reluctant, not a free-spirited, detachment. The wanderer's main thought is to save his human identity. Such a disconcerting development occurs in "Ktaadn."

There Thoreau takes on nature only to regret it, though at last he reaches an accommodation with it.

iii

In "Ktaadn," Thoreau goes out of his way to enter an intractable wilderness and affirm a more difficult nature than he normally meets. The excursion is a more daring *Wanderung,* a more perilous involvement than a trip on the Merrimack. Nature in Maine is conspicuously hostile, as well as kindly. "Ktaadn" is, in large part, a narrative of conflict between man and nature.

Thoreau's first recorded public mention of "Ktaadn" is in a letter to Emerson for January 1848, where he writes that "It contains many facts and some poetry" (*Correspondence,* p. 204). As well as a romantic voyage, then, it is also a travel essay, written for a lecture audience, with a mass of heterogeneous facts that the Maine traveler might find useful. But the "poetry" that runs through it is almost wholly concerned with the relation between a thoughtful romantic and nature. Thoreau's thematic emphasis is on one question: How can a man who is conscious of his separation from wild nature approach it and preserve himself?

Just as the narrative of "Ktaadn" is more straightforward than that of the *Week* or *Walden,* the persona of the narrator is less guarded, less constructed, more apt to reveal his contrasting feelings about nature. This narrator is comparatively without rhetoric or pretension. More intent on the narrative itself, he is thus more involved in the experience of nature.

The nature that Thoreau confronts in "Ktaadn" is nature-as-wilderness. In his revisions, as Robert Cosbey shows, Thoreau focused on the theme of the wilderness. He "added passages describing the feelings of a civilized man confronted with savage nature on Katahdin" and added also the important "conclusion summarizing the wilderness experience."[3] The wilderness for Tho-

---

[3] Robert C. Cosbey, "Thoreau at Work: The Writing of 'Ktaadn,' " *Bulletin of the New York Public Library,* 65 (1961), 24.

reau is a form of *phusis,* of nature-as-growth, but one that threatens man with its vastness and power. The salient cheerful fact about it is its unhindered growth; the last words of "Ktaadn" are: "sixty miles above [Bangor], the country is virtually unmapped and unexplored, and there still waves the virgin forest of the New World" (*The Maine Woods,* p. 83). As a pure expression of nature, the wilderness grows organically without the man-made divisions that interfere with its natural form in civilized communities. Yet it is not easy to approach, at least for the white man. This landscape has never been humanized. It is part of the "dark continent" of which Thoreau also speaks at the end (*The Maine Woods,* p. 78), that unexplored America that is yet wilder to the imagination than a Concord cranberry swamp, though it speaks to the same desire for the unformed, uncolonized earth. To venture into it requires more aggressiveness than does a river voyage. On the mountain itself, for the first time in Thoreau's work, nature is felt to oppose the wanderer's intrusion. The straining attempt to humanize the wilderness suddenly fails; on Katahdin the wilderness present an irreducibly natural face. Thoreau the narrator is left nonplused by the spectacle of intractable matter.

"Ktaadn" seems a particularly clear example of Thoreau's conscious use of a polarity, his characterization of the wilderness as alternately savage and lovable. My own examination of the manuscript of the first draft of "Ktaadn" (from Thoreau's unpublished 1846 Journal) strongly suggests that in the process of composition he became conscious of this polarity and used it thematically to give the essay structure. His revisions indicate his increasing awareness of it. It informs the summary of the wilderness experience added to the first draft at the end of "Ktaadn," where Thoreau asks, "Who shall describe the inexpressible tenderness and immortal life of the grim forest?" (*The Maine Woods,* p. 81). The tenderness of the forest would seem unreal, or at least insipid, without its grimness. In the very last paragraph, the area north of Bangor ("the virgin forest of the New World") is also

called "night," "the howling wilderness," "a desolate island and
No-Man's land" (*The Maine Woods,* pp. 82, 83). Early in the
excursion, while still confined in the stagecoach, Thoreau observes the woods with an eye for both the sensuous and the sublime.

> The beauty of the road itself was remarkable. The various ever-
> greens, many of which are rare with us,—delicate and beautiful
> specimens of the larch, arbor-vitae, ball spruce, and fir-balsam, from
> a few inches to many feet in height, lined its sides, in some places
> like a long front yard, springing up from the smooth grass-plots
> which uninterruptedly border it, and are made fertile by its wash;
> while it was but a step on either hand to the grim untrodden wilder-
> ness, whose tangled labyrinth of living, fallen, and decaying trees,
> —only the deer and moose, the bear and wolf, can easily penetrate.
> [*The Maine Woods,* p. 11][4]

The familiar beauty of nature's abundance is contrasted with the
unknown beauty of the forest, set apart from the man-made
road. A man must be fellow in some degree to the moose or the
bear in order to enter that forest.

The first morning in the woods, when Thoreau and his cousin
George Thatcher "leap . . . over a fence" and set out with a
wanderer's freedom on "an obscure trail" (*The Maine Woods,*
p. 16), Thoreau contemplates the prospect of his adventure with
joy and yet with a kind of determined apprehension. The details
he notices suggest that hardly controllable excitement that appears in his writing when he is faced with impressions of wild,
sparsely settled America. "The roar of the rapids, the note of a
whistler-duck on the river, of the jay and chickadee around us,
and of the pigeon-woodpecker in the openings, were the sounds
that we heard." The comment that follows this first moment in

[4] In the manuscript (Journal, 1846, p. 103), the clause beginning "while
it was but a step to the grim untrodden wilderness"—in a slightly different form—is closely written above the text in a different ink. Thus this
clause, which establishes the polarity, was a second thought. Quotations
from the manuscript are by permission of the Henry W. and Albert A.
Berg Collection, The New York Public Library, Astor, Lenox and Tilden
Foundations.

the woods, however, differs significantly from his usual simply enthusiastic reaction to *phusis*; nevertheless, it accords well with his double emphasis on the grimness and tenderness of the wilderness. "This was what you might call a bran new country; the only roads were of Nature's making, and the few houses were camps. Here, then, one could no longer accuse institutions and society, but must front the true source of evil" (*The Maine Woods*, p. 16).[5]

The last sentence does not logically conclude its paragraph, in which the emphasis is wholly on youthful expectation; rather, by means of a paradoxical and surprising twist, it provides a balance for that spirit of expectation. Joy and evil are both inherent in the wilderness. Thoreau, I think, is probing for uncomfortable insight when he uses "evil" (an unusual word in his vocabulary). He does not mean moral evil in a Christian sense. Rather, he is searching for a romantic redefinition of evil, according to which evil is understood as embedded in nature. He wants a word that will suggest the opposite of "joy" in nature, an opposite factor that is another "condition of life." In his own secretive way he is "striking the uneven balance," as Melville put it in his review of Hawthorne's *Mosses*.[6] Thoreau will meet the evil he seeks on the climb to the summit of Katahdin; perhaps he will also meet a corresponding evil and darkness in the barbarism of men who live in the wilderness in a natural state. In "Ktaadn" he is trying to reach a nature beneath the crust of civilization, whose otherness he here anticipates. He will plunge into a darker reality than in his earlier writings, a reality which, we infer from *Walden*, will have an element of "meanness."[7]

Brooding seriousness and cheerful anticipation, attraction to-

[5] Both the sympathetic description of wild nature and the stern resolve to "front the true source of evil" appear in the manuscript, though the opposites in this polarity of stern-and-gentle are not so clearly set off against each other as in the published text (Journal, 1846, pp. 115, 116).

[6] *The Works of Herman Melville*, ed. Raymond W. Weaver (London: Constable, 1924), XIII, 129.

[7] See *Walden*, p. 91.

ward the wilderness and fear of it are combined in Thoreau's narrative of his first night in the woods. As he watches his companions stir themselves from bed to feed the fire, he sees them as "grotesque and fiend-like forms," a phrase that reminds us how he enjoyed discovering ominous images in the Billerica cliffside on Saturday evening in the *Week*. The forms of his companions blur into the wilderness at night and are emblematic of it. Aroused himself, he rambles by the Penobscot in search of a moose or a wolf, and observes:

The little rill tinkled the louder, and peopled all the wilderness for me; and the glassy smoothness of the sleeping lake, laving the shores of a new world, with the dark, fantastic rocks rising here and there from its surface, made a scene not easily described. It has left such an impression of stern yet gentle wildness on my memory as will not soon be effaced. [*The Maine Woods,* p. 40]

"Stern yet gentle wildness" might stand as an appropriate description for the subject matter of "Ktaadn."[8] The passage balances affection for the placidity of slumbering nature with uneasy attraction for its wild and dark creations.

In order to enter the wilderness, Thoreau must become involved, literally and symbolically, with natural men. He travels three times to Maine partly in order to live a woodsman's life and to get acquainted with the Indian. In "Ktaadn," he writes of the native boatmen Tom Fowler and "Uncle George" McCauslin as he does of the men in the *Week,* abandoning his stance of poetic detachment in deference to them. Moreover, he joins with them in their natural, predatory pursuits: chopping, fishing, hunting, and meat-eating. Yet, though he thus throws himself into a natural life, he wants at the same time to be a poet and humanizer in nature's midst. He will on occasion detach himself from his companions and indulge in "poetry," or he may criticize them

---

[8] The phrase is not yet present in the manuscript, where the last sentence of the passage reads only, "It had such a smack [?] of wildness as I had not tasted before" (Journal, 1846, p. 157).

from a more civilized viewpoint. At moments he leaves them to pursue his own thoughts and poetic purposes. The most striking example of this humanist withdrawal in *The Maine Woods* occurs in "Chesuncook," the narrative of his 1853 journey to Maine. After a bloody moose hunt, Thoreau reflects in solitude on the natural horror he and his fellow hunters have caused. He acknowledges his own difference from them, but still feels himself implicated. Specifically at this point he adopts the role of the poet, whom he praises as the man who best sympathizes with the pine tree.

Is it the lumberman then who is the friend and lover of the pine—stands nearest to it, and understands its nature best? Is it the tanner who has barked it, or he who has boxed it for turpentine, whom posterity will fable was changed into a pine at last? No! no! it is the poet; he it is who makes the truest use of the pine—who does not fondle it with an axe, nor tickle it with a saw, nor stroke it with a plane. [*The Maine Woods,* p. 121]

The poet loves the pine from a near distance, with a chaste love; he respects its separate spirit. "It is the living spirit of the tree, not its spirit of turpentine, with which I sympathize, and which heals my cuts" (*The Maine Woods,* p. 122). Thoreau seeks again in an I-Thou relation with nature to avoid the destructiveness, brutishness, and sensuality of men caught in the natural cycle.

Thoreau creates an image for the life of natural men in his sketch of a logger's camp on the Penobscot. The camp is a symbol of the loggers' immersion in nature. It is fitted to nature like the cabins beside the Merrimack, but differs from them as the wilderness life in Maine differs from the pastoral life of long-settled New Hampshire communities. The scenery about it is "drear and savage"; and it is nestled close into the woods "without a" civilizing or poetic "thought for the prospect." "The logger's camp is as completely in the woods as a fungus at the foot of a pine in a swamp." Thoreau thinks of these houses in the woods as natural outgrowths of the loggers inside them.

They are very proper forest houses, the stems of the trees collected together and piled up around a man to keep out wind and rain: made of living green logs, hanging with moss and lichen, and with the curls and fringes of the yellow-birch bark, and dripping with resin, fresh and moist, and redolent of swampy odors, with that sort of vigor and perennialness even about them that toad-stools suggest. [*The Maine Woods,* p. 20]

The nature that surrounds the Maine woodsman is rich, dense, erotic. There is no talk of a resemblance between the house roof and such an ideal symbol as a hawk in flight; instead the camp is like a fungus or a toadstool. Fungi, toadstools, and swamps are all, according to Raymond Gozzi, sexual symbols in Thoreau's imaginative world,[9] and it seems that he lights on such imagery here because he is on a masculine adventure in Maine. The loggers at the camp are represented as rude, primitive men living in grand and simple houses, building huge fires, devouring huge meals, and proving their mettle in the vast and fertile forest. All these facts concerning their habits and their environment suggest their sexual prowess. Thoreau's withdrawal from the company of natural men, a withdrawal also evident in *Walden,* can be conceived on one level as a retreat from unthinking masculine sexuality.

With McCauslin and Fowler, Thoreau's movements of withdrawal are only evident in his private-voiced, subdued comments on their activities; the general stress in "Ktaadn" is on the joy of the adventure. Yet these private reactions represent the emergence of Thoreau's critical sensitivity in the midst of his narrative of facts. While he assists the boatmen in "warping up" a river rapid, he is partly detached even as he admires and imitates them. He thinks of them as magnificent animals, men of great courage, keenness, and physical skill:

[9] Gozzi, "Tropes and Figures," pp. 190–198. Thoreau himself noted and reflected on the phallic appearance of some fungi. See *J,* III, 255, and the incident of the giant toadstool, *J,* V, 270–275.

While the sternman obstinately holds his ground, like a turtle, the bowman springs from side to side with wonderful suppleness and dexterity, scanning the rapids and the rocks with a thousand eyes; and now, having got a bite at last, with a lusty shove which makes his pole bend and quiver, and the whole boat tremble, he gains a few feet upon the river. [*The Maine Woods,* p. 49]

But the rocks in the river oppose their progress, "lying in wait, like so many alligators, to catch [the poles] in their teeth, and jerk them from your hands, before you have stolen an effectual shove against their palates" (*The Maine Woods,* p. 49). Nature in the river is itself imagined as a hostile and dangerous beast with which the boatmen must do battle in order to secure a passage.

On the return downstream, Thoreau feels that the boatmen have won their battle, but for him something has been lost.

After such a voyage, the troubled and angry waters, which once had seemed terrible and not to be trifled with, appeared tamed and subdued; they had been bearded and worried in their channels, pricked and whipped into submission with the spike-pole and paddle, gone through and through with impunity, and all their spirit and their danger taken out of them, and the most swollen and impetuous rivers seemed but playthings henceforth. I began, at length, to understand the boatman's familiarity with and contempt for the rapids. [*The Maine Woods,* p. 77]

The poet in Thoreau wants to keep "spirit and danger" in the river. While the boatmen are subduing nature he is keeping it alive, imagining the presence of "some river monster amid the eddies." He regrets the passing of the woods and streams as a fairy-and-monster land for the imagination.

Similarly, as Thoreau fishes with his companions in a mountain pool, we infer his compassion for nature from the tone of his description of the dying trout.

While yet alive, before their tints had faded, they glistened like the fairest flowers, the product of primitive rivers; and he could hardly trust his senses, as he stood over them, that these jewels should have swum away in that Aboljacknagesic water for so long, so many dark ages;—these bright fluviatile flowers, seen of Indians only, made beautiful, the Lord only knows why, to swim there! [*The Maine Woods,* p. 54]

The beautiful colors of the trout are expressive of a life that they create within themselves. Their beauty, like that of flowers and of all living things, is not fixed or permanent, but the result of a continuous process of joyful self-creation. Natural beauty and life are vulnerable to human desecration. Yet, in order to discover them, Thoreau must make his way through the wilderness as a natural man. He cannot spend all his time loving colors and imagining monsters. He is again a double-edged blade, destroying nature, like Goethe's Egmont, while he draws sustenance from it.

Thoreau's mixed feelings toward men more natural than he show themselves in a disjointed paragraph toward the end of "Ktaadn," which in the manner of its disjointedness is typical of the workings of his mind. His party has just dropped off Tom Fowler at his house on the Millinocket, and Thoreau reflects on the merits of a woodsman's life.

Thus a man shall lead his life away here on the edge of the wilderness, on Indian Millinocket stream, in a new world, far in the dark of a continent, and have a flute to play at evening here, while his strains echo to the stars, amid the howling of wolves; shall live, as it were, in the primitive age of the world, a primitive man. Yet he shall spend a sunny day, and in this century be my contemporary; perchance shall read some scattered leaves of literature, and sometimes talk with me. Why read history then if the ages and the generations are now? [*The Maine Woods,* pp. 78–79]

Thoreau's effort to act as a natural man is here turned about. He is trying to think of the woodsman as *like himself,* and thus bring him closer. The woodsman is balanced between nature and civilization; he plays the flute and reads literature, yet lives as a primitive man in an ancient, natural style; he spends sunny days on a dark continent—he experiences the wilderness in both its polarized aspects. Above all, he may "sometimes talk with me." Thoreau is reaching out for his friendship, not by a self-dissolving effort of sympathy, but in a fantasy of mutual accommodation. But though Thoreau's whole work is a balancing act, he is uncomfortable in adjusting to the shifting and precarious balance in another person. He would see persons as clearly defined symbolic types, not as confused combinations like himself. And so he turns abruptly in this paragraph from the woodsman to the Indian, whom he describes with atmospheric relish as simple, aboriginal, wild, and wholly untouched by transcendental longings. At the same time he changes the subject from a personal search for a friend to "history" in all its generality. The woodsman, he continues,

lives three thousand years deep into time, an age not yet described by poets. Can you well go further back in history than this? Ay! ay! —for there turns up but now into the mouth of Millinocket stream a still more ancient and primitive man, whose history is not brought down even to the former. In a bark vessel sewn with the roots of the spruce, with horn-beam paddles he dips his way along. He is but dim and misty to me, obscured by the aeons that lie between the bark canoe and the batteau. He builds no house of logs, but a wigwam of skins. He eats no hot-bread and sweet-cake, but musquash and moose-meat and the fat of bears. He glides up the Millinocket and is lost to my sight, as a more distant and misty cloud is seen flitting by behind a nearer, and is lost in space. So he goes about his destiny, the red face of man. [*The Maine Woods*, p. 79]

The highly rhetorical description of the Indian diverts our attention from the fact that the speaker has just expressed his wish for companionship. He would obscure that personal note. The structure of the paragraph, with its hortatory beginning and end surrounding a middle expressive of a wistful private hope, is a paradigm of one aspect of Thoreau's mind. The surface persona of much of his work is a grandiloquent and rhetorical public speaker, while sometimes another persona emerges from within who is more subtle, scrupulous, hesitant, and lonely. In *Walden,* we shall see, Thoreau will play these two sides of himself off against each other with the self-conscious intention of creating a structural balance.

iv

In his account of the ascent of Katahdin, Thoreau is not concerned with his relation to his fellows, but with the challenge of the mountain. He does his climbing by himself, and his narrative becomes his own personal excursion: these pages on Katahdin constitute a self-contained digression within the whole. Thoreau presents himself in it as a man who tries his strength against nature. He has left his companions to accomplish his Yankee intrusion alone. As on Wachusett and Saddleback, he wants his own moment of personal, poetic eminence.

The landscape here, however, is more obstructive than in his previous mountain escapades, and grimmer than in the rest of "Ktaadn." The camp ground from which the final ascent is made is "savage and dreary," "even a more grand and desolate place for a night's lodging than the summit would have been" (*The Maine Woods,* p. 62). The trees near by are so "evergreen and sappy"—so entirely natural—that they will hardly burn for the comfort of the wanderers. Nature is becoming distinct from man, no longer kindly. For the moment, however, Thoreau revels in these obstacles. In his evening climb, like Wordsworth on Snowden, he bends his strength "as if in opposition set / Against an enemy."[10] The natural things he meets in his walk are sublime and wonderful, but hardly gentle. His ascent is up great rocky steps beside a mountain torrent, on the tops of "ancient black spruce trees, old as the flood"[11] (Thoreau is traveling back in

[10] Wordsworth, *Prelude,* XIV, 29–30.

[11] I think it likely that Thoreau has in the back of his mind here the seventeenth-century divine Thomas Burnet's Sacred Theory of the Earth, according to which mountains are conceived as magnificent deformities brought about by a second creation at the time of the flood. The expecta-

time, prying into the secrets of nature's past), and over "dark and cavernous regions" where "bears were even then at home"—which Thoreau is not (*The Maine Woods,* pp. 60, 61). The landscape is alien, unpastoral, with rocks and trees so old and hard one can have no easy relation to them, and clouds that block the saunterer's view and bound his walk. It is an Aeschylean or Shelleyan landscape that Thoreau has stumbled into, expressive of power and strangeness. Nevertheless, he maintains a cheerful, matter-of-fact tone in his narrative. He still has an appetite for wildness, for new, incommensurable impressions that will feed his imagination. Yet when he observes his surroundings, he feels the mountain as hostile.

Having slumped, scrambled, rolled, bounced, and walked, by turns, over this scraggy country, I arrived upon a side-hill, or rather side-mountain, where rocks, gray, silent rocks, were the flocks and herds that pastured, chewing a rocky cud at sunset. They looked at me with hard gray eyes, without a bleat or a low. This brought me to the skirt of a cloud, and bounded my walk that night. But I had already seen that Maine country when I turned about, waving, flowing, rippling, down below. [*The Maine Woods,* pp. 61–62]

He has made here an explicit division between Katahdin and the rest of the Maine country "down below," between a nature that is hard and unfriendly and one that is in circulation, "waving, flowing, rippling." The polarity that gives organic tension to the wilderness as a whole is splitting into spacially separated parts. The forest is tender; the rocks are grim. The Katahdin landscape has its own slow growth, but one must make a still greater effort of imagination to come into relation with it than with the rest of the wilderness.

---

tions of eighteenth- and nineteenth-century English travelers in the Alps— including Wordsworth and Shelley—were influenced by the Burnet tradition. In another of Thoreau's descriptions of the Katahdin summit, quoted below on page 200, the landscape looks to him "as if sometime it had rained rocks." See Marjorie Nicolson, *Mountain Gloom and Mountain Glory* (Ithaca, N.Y.: Cornell University Press, 1959).

The next morning Thoreau sets out for the summit over a similar landscape.

I climbed alone over huge rocks, loosely poised, a mile or more, still edging toward the clouds—for though the day was clear elsewhere, the summit was concealed by mist. The mountain seemed a vast aggregation of loose rocks, as if sometime it had rained rocks, and they lay as they fell on the mountain sides, nowhere fairly at rest, but leaning on each other, all rocking-stones, with cavities between, but scarcely any soil or smoother shelf. They were the raw materials of a planet dropped from an unseen quarry, which the vast chemistry of nature would anon work up, or work down, into the smiling and verdant plains and valleys of earth. [*The Maine Woods*, p. 63]

Thoreau's instress on "rock" is characteristic. He involves himself in the sense experience of rocks and impresses the word on us by repetition; but suddenly he becomes detached, and recovers his balance and aplomb by punning on it ("rocking-stones"); then he changes his perspective with typical flexibility from that of a man involved with nature to that of a poetic scientist. His speculation on the function of these rocks in the "vast chemistry" of the *kosmos* recalls Goethe's organicism. (Such a theory was obviously in the air, but Goethe and Thoreau are alike in entertaining it as naturalists and using it as poets.) Goethe thought that granite was the basic organic material out of which the surface of the earth was formed; and we have seen how in "Harzreise im Winter" he speaks of mountains much as Thoreau does here, as nourishing the fertile glory of the surrounding plain. Thoreau, in his momentary appreciation of nature's chemistry, also feels the mountain as an organic part of what he loves.

Soon, however, "the smiling and verdant plains and valleys" are forgotten—they have no bearing on this experience. Thoreau is "deep within the hostile ranks of clouds" (*The Maine Woods*, p. 63). On Katahdin, even a sparrow he sees is compared to a "fragment of the gray rock blown off by the wind" (*The Maine Woods*, p. 65). *Phusis* has grown stony-faced. For once, Thoreau is disconcerted by the terrible sublime in nature. The mountain reminds him

of the creations of the old and epic dramatic poets, of Atlas, Vulcan, the Cyclops, and Prometheus. Such was Caucasus and the rock where Prometheus was bound. Aeschylus had no doubt visited such scenery as this. It was vast, Titanic, and such as man never inhabits. Some part of the beholder, even some vital part, seems to escape through the loose grating of his ribs as he ascends. He is more lone than you can imagine. There is less of substantial thought and fair understanding in him, than in the plains where men inhabit. His reason is dispersed and shadowy, more thin and subtle like the air. Vast, Titanic, inhuman Nature has got him at disadvantage, caught him alone, and pilfers him of some of his divine faculty. [*The Maine Woods*, p. 64]

Except in a few passages in *Cape Cod* there is nothing in the rest of Thoreau quite like this personal alienation from nature. Elsewhere, he may "soon get through with Nature"; here he has too much of it. The literary allusions that he uses profusely in this part of the narrative seem meant in part to create a saving distance between the writer and his terrific experience. The customary "buoyancy, flexibility, freedom" in his style and temper vanish for the moment, like the vital part escaping through his ribs. The wanderer feels not exalted, but very small.

There is a significant twist in calling the top of Katahdin "vast, inhuman, Titanic." Sometimes in Thoreau the human *is* the Titanic, or should be. "We have need to be earth-born as well as heaven-born, γηγενεῖς, as was said of the Titans of old, or in a better sense than they" (from the essay on "a *purely* sensuous life"—*W*, I, 406). In such a pronouncement Thoreau urges that in order to live naturally we should act as if we were strong as nature herself, much as the young Goethe recommends during his own period of *Titanismus*. This is Thoreau's implied message in his early essays on heroism, in his praise of heroic farmers, loggers, and boatmen, and in his self-portrait as a self-reliant, self-sufficient intimate of nature. Elsewhere in the *Week*, in the same

vein, he urges his readers to be encouraged by this image of a
giant-man which he quotes from Phineas Fletcher's *Purple Island:*

> Mountains he flings in seas with mighty hand;
>   Stops and turns back the sun's impetuous course;
> Nature breaks Nature's laws at his command;
>   No force of Hell or Heaven withstands his force.
>   [*W*, I, 415]

A good deal of submerged giant imagery is present in the early
Thoreau. He seems to have been haunted by the archetypal image
of giants dwelling in the earth and mysteriously guiding our des-
tinies. In a revealing early poem, "Tell me ye wise ones if ye
can," he expresses both his contempt for ordinary men—"the
titmen of their race"—and his wish to imitate these huge mythical figures who have power over us.

> These elder brothers of our race
> By us unseen with larger pace
> Walk oer our heads, and live our lives
> Embody our desires and dreams
> Anticipate our hoped for gleams. . . .
>   [*Collected Poems*, p. 158]

Mountain-climbing in particular Thoreau regards as a Titanic
pursuit. When we go forth to meet these "elder brothers," he
writes in the same poem, "we stand" for a moment "Astonished
on the Olympian land." The fantasy of meeting giants in mountains is in line with a tradition of the collective imagination.
"Mountains, according to the general testimony of the imagination, are fallen heroes: they have giants in or below them. Atlas
stares mutely out of Mt. Atlas. The Titans groan under Mt.
Aetna."[12] Writing of his evening climb up the Katahdin stream-
bed, Thoreau likens his path to "a giant's stairway" (*The Maine
Woods*, p. 60) and pictures himself as Milton's Satan finding his

---

[12] Hartman, *Wordsworth's Poetry*, p. 49.

way through Chaos. The myth behind this personal excursion, in other words, is that of a would-be Titan setting himself to confront other Titans in their mountain homes. Lurking in the myth is a prospective combat between Titans, a combat between an aggressive romantic and the nature he invades.

Thoreau's Titanism is a fantasy of self-glorification, of *hubris*. His extreme reaction to the landscape near the summit of Katahdin seems the result of the deflation of his adventurous ambition. The narrative of "Ktaadn" at this point seems to be recording an experience of personal and metaphysical shock. His response to this shock is to carry out a markedly quietist withdrawal. He who had set out to stand grand and solitary over nature and society now feels "more lone than you can imagine." His thrust into the unknown parts of nature now seems a piece of individual insolence.

The tops of mountains are among the unfinished parts of the globe, whither it is a slight insult to the gods to climb and pry into their secrets, and try their effect on our humanity. Only daring and insolent men, perchance, go there. Simple races, as savages, do not climb mountains—their tops are sacred and mysterious tracts never visited by them. [*The Maine Woods*, p. 65]

Thoreau is on a tack of self-belittlement. Just as in the *Week* he is sorry to have disturbed the bittern, here he feels guilty as the party passes by a mountain tarn and through a meadow that properly belong to the moose, for it to "browse and bathe, and rest in peace" (*The Maine Woods*, p. 69).

Thus on Katahdin Thoreau has renounced entirely the role of a Titan, who is properly an amoral, pagan, tremendous, earth-born, animal-like man. Thoreau now rejects all of these attributes. He talks like a Christian about his "reason" and his "divine faculty." He asserts his difference from the rocks, his separation from the Indian, his loss of contact with the earth. He is no longer eager to measure up to the giants of his fantasy. His crisis is fully represented in the following well-known passage, in which he describes his feelings while descending the "wild and desolate" slopes of Katahdin.

Perhaps I most fully realized that this was primeval, untamed, and forever untamable *Nature,* or whatever else men call it, while coming down this part of the mountain. . . . I found myself traversing [it] familiarly, like some pasture run to waste, or partially reclaimed by man; but when I reflected what man, what brother or sister or kinsman of our race made it and claimed it, I expected the proprietor to rise up and dispute my passage. It is difficult to conceive of a region uninhabited by man. We habitually presume his presence and influence everywhere. And yet we have not seen pure Nature, unless we have seen her thus vast, and drear, and inhuman, though in the midst of cities. Nature was here something savage and awful, though beautiful. I looked with awe at the ground I trod on, to see what the Powers had made there, the form and fashion and material of their work. This was that Earth of which we have heard, made out of Chaos and Old Night. Here was no man's garden, but the unhandselled globe. It was not lawn, nor pasture, nor mead, nor woodland, nor lea, nor arable, nor waste land. It was the fresh and natural surface of the planet Earth, as it was made forever and ever, —to be the dwelling of man, we say,—so Nature made it, and man may use it if he can. Man was not to be associated with it. It was Matter, vast, terrific,—not his Mother Earth that we have heard of, not for him to tread on, or be buried in,—no, it were being too familiar even to let his bones lie here—the home this of Necessity and Fate. There was there felt the presence of a force not bound to be kind to man. It was a place for heathenism and superstitious rites,—to be inhabited by men nearer of kin to the rocks and to wild animals than we. We walked over it with a certain awe, stopping from time to time to pick the blueberries which grew there, and had a smart and spicy taste. Perchance where *our* wild pines stand, and leaves lie on their forest floor in Concord, there were once reapers, and husbandmen planted grain; but here not even the surface had been scarred by man, but it was a specimen of what God saw fit to make this world. What is it to be admitted to a museum, to see a myriad of particular things, compared with being shown some star's surface, some hard matter in its home! I stand in awe of my body, this matter to which I am bound has become so strange to me. I fear not spirits, ghosts, of which I am one,—*that* my body might,—but I fear bodies, I tremble to meet them. What is this Titan that has possession of me? Talk of mysteries!—Think of our life in nature,—daily to be shown matter, to come in contact with it,—rocks, trees, wind on our cheeks! the *solid* earth! the *actual* world! the *common sense! Contact! Contact! Who* are we? *where* are we? [*The Maine Woods,* pp. 69–71—Thoreau's italics]

What is Thoreau's view of nature in this remarkable outburst, and what does it mean for his work as a whole? I will isolate two strains in the paragraph. First, even this experience he tries to accommodate to his organicism: in some sentences he takes the stance that he is investigating the original matter out of which the lovely earth is made, probing actively into nature as no laboratory or museum scientist can, enjoying the direct experience of a Goethean *Anschauung.* Yet the overriding strain is not a wandering naturalist's optimism but a threatened private pessimism. In Thoreau's total scheme, the experience on Katahdin represents the possibility, always inherent in the scheme, that his relation with nature may fail. This relation, we have seen, is inevitably precarious, as it is the willed joining of two disparate worlds, the poet's and nature's, in generous interchange. When nature ceases utterly to seem generous, when nothing in nature corresponds to any feature in man's soul, then all contact is broken and Thoreau is homeless in nature's world. He may properly ask, *"where* are we?" In these rocks these is no perceptible circulation, growth, or structure; there is only force and Necessity, as in Shelley's "Mont Blanc"—awesome and inhuman "Powers." The romantic combinations (or contacts) Thoreau ordinarily makes use of are split apart at such a time: There is no further relation between man and nature, subject and object, spirit and matter. This matter on Katahdin is only "vast, terrific"; no formal principle may emerge from it as from the New England hills around Wachusett or from the "huge volume of matter" that finds its shape in the

Musketaquid. Most strikingly, Thoreau feels his soul split apart from his body. In his usual scheme, we remember, the soul and the body enjoy a mutual generosity akin to the relation between man and nature. "Good for the body is the work of the body, good for the soul the work of the soul, and good for either the work of the other. Let them not call hard names, nor know a divided interest" (*J*, I, 174). If man's whole duty, according to Thoreau, is to make his body perfect, his program to purify the senses in the *Week* is an effort to seek that perfection and to fit the body for the soul's hope of seeing God immediately and corporeally. In *"Contact! Contact!"* on the other hand, the body is not a magnificent expression of the active soul, but a formless matter that the narrator trembles to inhabit. He is more at ease with disembodied ghosts. He thinks of himself as a spiritualized collection of ribs and bones, the opposite of a Titan.

Thus an antinaturalist idealism, a preference for mind over nature, emerges once more out of Thoreau's involvement, not the idealism of a soldier who would destroy or a mystic who would ignore nature, but that of a lonely wanderer who feels threatened by it. Thoreau again wishes to be free of his body and to emphasize his spiritual capacities, but with an anxious, not an exuberant emphasis. He prefers—indeed, he feels impelled—to think of himself as a man of mind, not of nature.

Though Thoreau may elsewhere question the value of sensuous experience in nature, this is the only occasion I know of when he indicates uneasiness about the word: "primeval, untamed, and forever untamable *Nature,* or whatever else men call it." He means to express by this hesitation that the world he has known and loved, the verdant surface with its variety and structure, appears from the vantage point of the Katahdin rocks no more than a surface to cover the hard matter of a star. If the earth is indeed this hard matter, then he must feel it not as Mother Earth, but as a stray feature of a universe in which man is an infinitesimal titman. Though the rocks are "untamed," they are not to be identified with the wild forest, which is full of diversified, erotic growth. If the rocks represent the reality at the heart of nature, then nature is radically different from Thoreau's usual conception of it.

Contact! Contact! is an example of Thoreau's drawing back from nature and humbling himself after a deep involvement, a passage in which he overturns his usual assumptions about the relation between man and nature. Yet such a description does violence to "Ktaadn" as a whole. To treat *Contact! Contact!* as the anagnorisis in a tragedy of which Thoreau is the disillusioned protagonist is to be false to the spirit and style of his nature writing, which is, we remember, "epic without beginning or end" (*J*, I, 284). The summit experience is but an incident in that epic; I may have even exaggerated and oversimplified its drama. Even as Thoreau meditates on its awesome meaning, he chooses to tell how he stopped to pick and taste blueberries. After it he quite recovers his balance and his stance. When he comes down off the mountain he continues his narrative in the same vein as before the ascent, a factual narrative with geographical details, descriptions of local customs, humorous sallies, and poetic footnotes. His attitude toward nature and natural men shows no discernible change—he is full of ready appreciation for the Titan boatmen. The wanderer is no longer frightened, but cheerfully pleased, as after Wachusett, that he has accomplished so arduous a journey.

The final summary, moreover, contains no reference to the crowning incident of "Ktaadn." It is as if Thoreau were using a strategy of deliberately appearing to forget his experience of metaphysical shock to show its relative unimportance. Having made an emphatic statement of what disturbs him in nature, he proceeds to ignore it because he knows that nature is fundamentally life-giving and health-restoring. The summary itself is a convincing description of nature in abundant health. It is an eloquent expression of faith, as the account of the summit is a still more powerfully eloquent expression of doubt. Thoreau begins it by reasserting the basic polarity of "Ktaadn." The forest is even more grim and wild than you had anticipated, a damp and intricate wilderness, in the spring everywhere wet and miry. The aspect of the country indeed is universally stern and savage, excepting the distant views of the forest from hills, and the lake prospects, which are mild and civilizing in a degree. The lakes are something which you are unprepared for: they lie up so high exposed to the light, and the forest is diminished to a fine fringe on their edges, with here and there a blue mountain, like amethyst jewels set around some jewel of the first water,—so anterior, so superior to all the changes that are to take place on their shores, even now civil and refined, and fair, as they can ever be. [*The Maine Woods*, p. 80]

Nature is once more a theatre for the reconciliation of opposites. The civilizing lakes are set off against the savage forest. If the balance is imperfect (if the lakes are still partly wild), Thoreau is reporting the imbalance in being true to nature, where symmetries are shifting rather than permanent. And though the wilderness is difficult to penetrate, the stress Thoreau places on the beauty of the lakes suggests that his epiphanies there are worth the trudging and portaging it takes to reach them. In the next paragraph, his emphasis shifts to the virginal gentleness of the forest, thus creating the effect of an overall balance of opposites in the summary.

It is a country full of evergreen trees, of mossy silver birches and watery maples, the ground dotted with insipid, small red berries, and strewn with damp and moss-grown rocks—a country diversified with innumerable lakes and rapid streams, peopled with trout and various species of *leucisci*, with salmon, shad and pickerel, and other fishes; the forest resounding at rare intervals with the note of the chickadee, the blue jay, and the woodpecker, the scream of the fish-hawk and the eagle, the laugh of the loon, and the whistle of ducks along the solitary streams; and at night, with the hooting of owls and howling of wolves; in summer, swarming with myriads of black flies and mosquitoes, more formidable than wolves to the white man. Such is the home of the moose, the bear, the caribou, the wolf, the beaver, and the Indian. Who shall describe the inexpressible tenderness and immortal life of the grim forest, where Nature, though it be mid-winter, is ever in her spring, where the moss-grown and decaying trees are not old, but seem to enjoy a perpetual youth; and blissful, innocent Nature, like a serene infant, is too happy to make a noise, except by a few tinkling, lisping birds and trickling rills? [*The Maine Woods,* pp. 80–81]

Thoreau has recovered his feeling for sensuous nature. Again he is inviting us to enjoy a fruitful chaos swarming with all manner of living things. Nature is not a "stepmother" as she was on Katahdin, but an innocent infant. Yet hers is a pagan, savage innocence, symbolized in the inhuman vitality of black flies and mosquitoes and in the sounds of blue-jays, fish-hawks, loons, owls, and wolves.

It is perhaps significant that both *Contact! Contact!* and the final summary were added after the first draft of "Ktaadn" was completed.[13] I surmise that the two passages were consciously de-

---

[13] In the "Ktaadn Journal," a short version of *Contact! Contact!* is present, not in its proper chronological place in the narrative, but rather between the sketchy preliminary notes of meals, weathers, and geographical details and the rest of the narrative. Thoreau seems to have had what he wanted to say in *Contact! Contact!* very much on his mind, for he evidently wrote a draft of it before writing the rest of "Ktaadn"; but he took a while to learn how to say it and to decide on its structural role. The manuscript version, as far as I can decipher it, follows. Note the Goethean use of "Demonic."

It is difficult to conceive of a region uninhabited by man. We habitually presume his presence and exaggerate his influence everywhere. —And yet we have not seen pure Nature unless we have since seen her thus vast and grim and drear whether in the wilderness or in the midst of cities.

Perhaps I first most fully realized that this was untamed primeval Demonic Nature, or whatever else men call it, while coming down the mt. The nature primitive Titanic aweful and yet beautiful, untamed forever. We were passing over burnt lands burnt by lightening perchance with occasional strips of timber crossing it, and low poplars, springing up—open and pasture-like—with patches of blue berries sloping away down toward the Penobscot—for our convenience. I found myself traversing it familiarly like some pasture run to waste

signed to balance each other. Thoreau is again juxtaposing extreme statements to express both sides of a mixed truth. He is saying: here are two faces of nature; I present and accept them both. He thus makes the Maine woods both grim and tender not only in individual sentences, but in the deployment of his contrasting reflections.

v

The Katahdin experience seems to have had little direct effect on Thoreau's youthful romantic point of view.[14] Although Thoreau does seem more skeptical of and less interested in his capacity to combine imaginatively with nature as a living whole in his very late essays, this change does not seem directly related to his vision on the summit. The *Week* and *Walden*, both thoroughly romantic in conception, were both completed and published after the writing of "Ktaadn," *Walden* seven years after. It is a seldom noted fact that Thoreau was working on "Ktaadn," the *Week,* and the first version of *Walden* all during his stay at the pond. (The 1846 Journal that contains most of the first draft of "Ktaadn" also has material for the two books.) It is likely then that Thoreau had all three works very much on his mind at approximately the same time. But the style and temper of each work is radically different from the other two, and in each Thoreau de-

---

or partially reclaimed by man—but when I reflected what a man—what a brother or sister or kindred of our race made it and claimed [it] I expected the proprietor to rise up and dispute my passage. But only the moose and the deer browsed and the bear skulked—and the black partridge fed here on the berries and the weeds [?]. Thus Nature primitive titanic but so beautiful as awful and sublime.

The passage appears with a number of crossed-out false starts, and with a few scarcely decipherable pencilled jottings that may or may not have represented Thoreau's later intentions. He seems at first to have wanted to stress man's presumptuousness in imagining that he "overtops" nature. Later he seems in two places to suggest that Katahdin is the home of giants, "a playing-ground for giants" (Journal, 1846, pp. 79–81).

[14] For a contrary opinion, see Leo Stoller, *After Walden* (Stanford, Calif.: Stanford University Press, 1957), pp. 45–47.

velops his relation to nature differently. Thus, I infer, Thoreau was not committed in this period to one view of nature, but was capable of consciously entertaining different and even opposing views, and he felt compelled to present each view in a manner appropriate to it. After "Ktaadn" Thoreau has few occasions for such an openly doubtful view as he adopts in the summit excursion. He regards external nature as markedly unfriendly only in a few isolated passages in *Cape Cod* (to be discussed in the next chapter); and he questions the self-reliant man's adequacy in the face of nature only once at any length, in an extraordinary letter to Harrison Blake of April 10, 1853. According to this letter, Thoreau, like Blake, is a "spiritual foot-ball,—really nameless, handleless, homeless . . . —a mere arena for thoughts and feelings; definite enough outwardly, indefinite more than enough inwardly. . . . mastered, and not wholly sorry to be mastered, by the least phenomenon. . . . A dandelion down that never alights,—settles,—blown off by . . . some divine boy in the upper pastures." In such a mood Thoreau may be content with existence from moment to moment, but he lacks all sense of his own centrality and significance. "I would like to ask you if you know whose estate this is that we are on? For my part I enjoy it well enough, what with the wild apples and the scenery; but I shouldn't wonder if the owner set his dog on me next" (*Correspondence,* pp. 302, 303). The "divine boy" and "the owner" may be associated with the "elder-brothers of our race" in "Tell me ye wise ones if ye can," and with the "proprietor," the "Powers," and the "force not bound to be kind to man" in *Contact! Contact!* Thoreau ends the letter, however, by assuring Blake that he is an exaggerator, and never erupts in the same strain again.

My judgment is that Thoreau deposited the memory of Katahdin's grimmer aspects in some recondite compartment of his mind and kept it there to be exploited carefully and very occasionally. In October 1857, eleven years after the excursion, the memory curiously surfaces. He records in his journal a recurrent dream of ascending a mountain that he imagines to be in "the easterly part of our town (where no high hill actually is)." His phrasing of the dream experience recalls the narrative of the evening ascent up the stream bed in "Ktaadn."

My way up used to lie through a dark and unfrequented wood at its base . . . and then I steadily ascended along a rocky ridge half clad with stinted trees, where wild beasts haunted, till I lost myself quite in the upper air and clouds, seeming to pass an imaginary line which separates a hill, mere earth heaped up, from a mountain. . . . What distinguishes that summit above the earthy line, is that it is unhandselled, awful, grand. It can never become familiar; you are lost the moment you set foot there. You know no path, but wander, thrilled, over the bare and pathless rock, as if it were solidified air and cloud. [*J*, X, 142]

In a letter to Blake written soon afterward, Thoreau patently echoes the thought and expression of *Contact! Contact!*

You must have been enriched by your solitary walk over the mountains. . . . You must ascend a mountain to learn your relation to matter, and so to your own body, for *it* is at home there, though *you* are not. It might have been composed there, and will have no farther to go to return to dust there, than in your garden; but your spirit inevitably comes away, and brings your body with it, if it lives. Just as awful, really, and as glorious, is your garden. See how I can play with my fingers! . . . Where did they come from? What strange control I have over them! *Who* am I? What are they?—those little peaks—call them Madison, Jefferson, Lafayette. What is *the matter*? [*Correspondence*, p. 497]

On first glance this is a complacent, avuncular reduction of a more disturbing original. As literature it has indeed lost its force. But the import is much the same as in *Contact! Contact!* A man is made aware on a mountain top that his soul is separate from his body and that there is a division between his soul or spirit and all matter. True, Thoreau would add consolingly that a man is still mysteriously connected to his body, to his garden, to the earth. The separation is for the time being healed when he returns to the valleys. Nevertheless, it is still there, and death will finally establish it.

Perhaps, then, Thoreau brooded over the problem and even the phrasing of *Contact! Contact!* for years. But he did not let this segregated brooding interfere with his other thoughts. Indeed, in *Walden* and the later journals he is finding new ways of getting close to nature. His later references to Katahdin are infrequent and casual. The one extended reference illustrates his pride and pleasure in the accomplishment of writing "Ktaadn." In a letter to George Thatcher for August 24, 1848, Thoreau calls it "that everlasting mountain story" and asserts that if it had been published as a whole instead of in five parts, "it would have gone down at one dose by its very gravity" (*Correspondence,* p. 229). Far from feeling intimidated by his experience, he seems happy to have written of something so exciting, and sure enough of his story to pun on its "gravity." Perhaps he would even suggest that his contact is now stronger for his having probed nature so adventurously. He has, at least on the surface, recovered his balance and with it his ideology. And he has managed his recovery clearly in this case by turning experience into art. "Ktaadn" is another instance of Thoreau's combination of art and the truth of nature, his bringing together "many facts and some poetry." It is, on the one hand, a personal narrative, a sincere and at moments a driven expression of strange feelings in response to untoward circumstances. But because Thoreau has also shaped his narrative into "an everlasting mountain story," he can regard it with detachment even after he has told it in the first person.

We may more properly regard Thoreau's concept of nature not chronologically, as a gradual development, but spatially, as a self-contained universe of ideas. Within that universe there is room for maneuver, for contradictions, qualifications, and refinements. For Thoreau to "develop" by making permanent concessions to the point of view expressed in *Contact! Contact!* would be to give up the whole structure of his romantic naturalism. Either one regards nature as an impersonal chaos not bound to be kind to man or one accepts nature as a generous source, but a romantic naturalist cannot compromise. Thoreau's solution to this quandary is to be a romantic naturalist most of the time and a man disillusioned with nature on special occasions. There is, it is true, a diminishing focus on the romantic notion of sympathy with a generous nature in his later work, but it is simplistic to attribute this change to any one cause. It is more a drift than a development. And in "Walking," a paper he revised critically for publication shortly before his death, he is the same old would-be romantic Titan, as cunning, as self-assertive, and as insistent on his kinship with nature as in any of his work.

Postscript: A Note on "Forgetting"

A key tenet of romantic naturalism is that when a man re-enters nature as *phusis,* he forgets the confusion and falsehood engendered by social intercourse and intellectual hyperactivity. Many of us will feel this in a general way; as Emerson put it, "in the woods, we return to reason and faith."[15] But such a feeling becomes the occasion for a strategy and a principle in Thoreau, Wordsworth, and Goethe. Even if a romantic naturalist suffers for his own fault or as the result of his own moral sensitivity, nature will comfort him in his afflictions, and he is justified in forgetting what troubled him. Thus Thoreau forgets the political outrage of the remission of Anthony Burns to slavery in contemplating a white water-lily (see "Slavery in Massachusetts"). Wordsworth forgets the possibilities and the discontents suggested by syllogistic reasoning when he remembers nature, and he thereby recovers his simpler and truer self (see *Prelude,* XIII). Goethe's Faust even forgets his guilt feelings for his betrayal of Gretchen: he is visited by nature spirits who benevolently induce his forgetfulness while he is sleeping and dreaming in "a pleasant

[15] Emerson, *Works,* I, 10.

region" (see "Anmutiger Gegend," in *Faust*, II).[16] In all these works, the return to *phusis* brings an access of health and gratitude to the vexed wanderer. The "forgetting" that takes place in "Ktaadn" may seem different in that Thoreau forgets one part of nature by returning to another. But he too is reviving his health by thinking of nature as growth rather than as intractable matter; and he is leaving behind him not only the burnt lands on Katahdin, but also the metaphysical anxiety that swept over him as he experienced the mountain.

[16] For Goethe's use of forgetting (*Vergessen*) as an emotional and artistic strategy, see Staiger, *Goethe* I, 302; III, 274. For an instance in which Goethe dismisses the unpleasant in nature by focusing on nature's power to bring health, see "Der Wanderer," in Goethe, *Gedenkausgabe,* I, 378–384.

~ 6

"The Shipwreck":
A Shaped Happening

"The Shipwreck," the first chapter of *Cape Cod,* represents another meeting with inhuman nature, another occasion when the individual mind finds itself bereft and confused in the external world. More specifically, it is an occasion in which Thoreau confronts the fact of human death in the wild landscape of the seashore. As we have seen in the early journal, when Thoreau meditates on death, he recognizes—albeit reluctantly—a difference between man and other natural beings. The creatures and creations of *phusis* do not experience death in the same way that humans do, in that plants and animals lack the consciousness that they are going to die or that death takes place around them. They thus lack any conception of the morbid; whereas a romantic naturalist so reflective as Thoreau is inevitably aware of the possibilities of decay and nothingness in nature; and this awareness again separates him from nature.[1]

Thoreau handles his uncomfortable awareness of death in several ways when it intrudes in his writing on nature. We have already seen him try to rid himself of it as if it were a disease of the mind that could nevertheless be cured or at least made tolerable by proper intercourse with naturally dying and becoming

[1] See Ferry, *The Limits of Mortality,* ch. ii, for a treatment of this conflict in Wordsworth.

things. When he writes, "I not yet grey on rocks forever gray. I no longer green under the evergreens," he is in a mood to accept his mortality as a mere "phenomenon in the life of nature." But Thoreau will not bask in this tranquil, mollified mood for long; his professions of indolence are but provisional. Like the Puritans he comes back and back to the question of what it is to be truly human, truly regenerate, truly absolved of mortality in a more than natural sense, and when he is in this neo-Puritan state of mind he exhibits reservations about "natural eternity." For example, as he reflects in the *Week* on the pigeons he and John have killed, he generalizes their fate: "They must perish miserably; not one of them is translated" (*W*, I, 237). Thoreau shows here obliquely but clearly that he has not renounced the human hope to be "translated," to be removed in death to a realm of happy eternity where souls do not die. The impersonal, unending circulation of an ever-progressing nature is insufficient to satisfy such a hope.

Sometimes, Thoreau sees death in nature not as a mere stage in the endless natural cycle but as a prospect that is a good deal more threatening. Death becomes at moments not a phenomenon in an organic process of recreation but rather a phenomenon of *disorganization,* in which things that die lose their structure and become formless, and the human observer is estranged from the disorder in nature that he now sees in the spectacle of death. This sense of death such writers as Thoreau and Goethe fought with all the strategies at their command, including the strategy of omitting to talk about it. But Thoreau at least on occasion also has the courage to articulate his sense of death-as-disorganization and to try to allow it its place in the totality of his work. One such occasion is "The Shipwreck."

Readers who dismiss Thoreau's imaginative concern with death as abnormal and distasteful, untypical of a healthy-minded naturalist, may miss some of the excitement of his skirmishes with morbidity. He does not allow himself to be comfortably in love with death, as Whitman might, but in his images of death one sometimes feels a surge of controlled, dangerous energy coming into his writing, for example when he wishes for self-dissolution in "The Thaw" or when he invites the reader in *Walden* to look hard at "reality," and feel the bliss of suicide in the perception of the real: "If you stand right fronting and face to face to a fact, you will see the sun glimmer on both its surfaces, as if it were a cimeter, and feel its sweet edge dividing you through the heart and marrow, and so you will happily conclude your mortal career" (*Walden*, p. 98). Here "the nostalgia for the object" is carried to extremes indeed! Such a startling conceit is a fine incidental thought in "Where I Lived and What I Lived For," a fragmentary felicity in the poetry of extra-vagance. Often Thoreau's meditations on death are like this. They are brief excursions into a realm of thought he prefers to visit only briefly, but they are also honest exhibitions of what he perceives there. They are examples of his willingness to cherish a perception or inspiration even if it runs counter to the ordinary grain of his thought.

Thoreau saunters around the problem of death in *Walden*, giving it occasional glancing recognition and engaging it profoundly only by indirection. He reserved most of his more explicit meditations on death for the privacy of his journal. The source of the power of "The Shipwreck," on the other hand, is that he is wrestling with his thoughts and feelings about human and natural death openly and in public, presenting them in their natural incoherence but reflecting on them as a deliberate artist. He tries both to expose his reactions and to shape them artistically, so that they will point the way toward some cumulative meaning, and so that the occasion which prompts them will become a significant episode, will take on the quality of a truthful if obscure recollection of intense experience.

I focus on "The Shipwreck" for three reasons. First, it is another, more effectively shocking encounter between Thoreau and the estranging otherness of nature. Like Keats, Thoreau "saw too far into the sea," and the conclusion to which this seeing leads him in the chapter is less "forgetful," more pessimistic than the final summary of "Ktaadn." Second, it is a rare direct and sustained recognition that the wild nature he desires is the scene and even the cause of death for men and animals. Third, it is a brief but complex example of Thoreau's method in drawing art from the chaos of nature, including the nature of his own mind. I have written of several shaped episodes in his work, among them "Saddleback," "A Walk to Wachusett," and the summit climb in "Ktaadn." All three of these, though they are forceful and engaging narratives, contain conscious or unconscious inconsistencies in Thoreau's attitude toward nature. Yet I do not feel that these inconsistencies necessarily mar the episodes; on the contrary, they may add to the dense liveliness of the narrative, may reflect Thoreau's rash or brave willingness to be double-minded for the sake of a more encompassing truth. "The Shipwreck" is an extreme example of Thoreau's wilful but purposeful inconsistency. He seems to throw himself into the encounter and let it guide his reactions. Both the narrative of the events on Cohasset beach and the thoughts that accompany this narrative have the character of a "happening"—a cluster of linked observations, presented seemingly unmodified as they occur to him on the scene. Thoreau does not take one attitude toward the sea, but a succession of different attitudes. Thus he becomes, even more than usually, the speaker or narrator in a dramatic meditation. He responds feelingly to each new thought, and tries by shifts of feeling, not by normal logic, to come to terms with nature and death. He arrives at no final answers—the shipwreck is too compelling and inscrutable an event for that. Instead he throws out solutions, and then finally comes to a definite stance, which he maintains till the end of the chapter but no longer.

"The Shipwreck" is not, however, a chaotic, formless rumination. There is a residue of uncertainty in it; it presents a man caught in the cross-currents of his own thought. But one may argue that this uncertainty is only "natural." A reaching out for disparate ideas, an attempt to follow paths with uncertain tendencies is characteristic of Thoreau's mind. I would attribute this naturalness of style, this unresolved irregularity of point of view in part to deliberate intention. The naturalness is parallel to the hypaethral quality of the *Week;* and when Thoreau recommends that our lives be part ordered meadow and part unordered forest in "Walking," he gives us a metaphor for his own writing. Moreover, the opposed attitudes in "The Shipwreck" (or some of them) are pitted against each other in dramatic conflict. Part of the nervous force of the chapter comes, as in much of Thoreau, from the attempt to combine and confine polarized opposites in little space. Finally, the last pages of the chapter are "more than natural," are poetic and highly artful. They constitute a beautiful if partial and transient resolution of its earlier uncertainties. The narrator has first recorded the event as it happened, then ruminated over it, and then imposed on it a unifying idea that emerges clearly at the end and functions as a remembering commentary on the issues raised by the wreck.

Like *The Maine Woods, Cape Cod* as a whole is a description of place, drawing on several visits and much reading, not a straightforward narrative of a single experience. The book contains a variety of styles and moods; it is crotchety and entertaining, as well as somber. Parts of it are slow going—Thoreau likes complete descriptions. "The Shipwreck" is, as it were, the first patch in this large quilt: it is bound to the rest but has its own distinctive character. Yet, though it can be treated as a separate unit, it sets the tone for much of the book and presents themes that are recalled and re-emphasized later. Reciprocally, the book as a whole helps us to understand "The Shipwreck." The narrative thread that ties together the various chapters is based on Thoreau's and Ellery Channing's holiday jaunt of October, 1849, beginning with their visit to the Cohasset beach. The Cape Cod landscape and weather in this season are especially undomestic and unpredictable. Man and the unstable land are at the mercy of the ocean. "The Shipwreck" and portions of the rest of the book reflect the wildness of the season, and the sense that one walks on the Cape between intervals of storm.

Thoreau seeks in this excursion just such an unfamiliar and unpredictable landscape. He goes to the Cape, he says in the first sentence of the book, "to get a better view than I had yet had of the ocean, which, we are told, covers more than two thirds of the globe, but of which a man who lives a few miles inland may never see any trace, more than of another world" (*W*, IV, 3). The excursion to the Cape is, in other words, another wandering away from towns and homes into the wild. The ocean, we saw from the early journal, is a symbol of the sublime, of an endless, abundant, terrifying nature. Thoreau's imagination seeks out the "bold," "wild," and "desolate" "grandeur" and "variety" of the sea and shore.[2] He wants, as in his mountain excursions, to get away from narrowly cultured men, to remind himself how small man is and how great nature. "I wished to see that seashore where man's works are wrecks; to put up at the true Atlantic House, where the ocean is land-lord as well as sea-lord, and comes ashore without a wharf for the landing; where the crumbling land is the only invalid, or at best is but dry land, and that is all you can say of it" (*W*, IV, 65).

But this sea, this wild nature so inspiriting to him still, is nevertheless clearly separate from him, a world entirely different. Perhaps he is influenced by his experience on Katahdin, or perhaps a landscape similarly vast and inhospitable calls up a similar response; in any case, Thoreau is facing another challenge to his early optimistic holism. Seldom does he find correspondences between man and nature in *Cape Cod*. He does not at all identify himself with particular things in the landscape, as with the white lily, the bittern, or the pond. Similarly, he finds no occasion for a cheerful erotic apostrophe to nature as in his other books—nothing like "Concord River" or the conclusion to "Ktaadn," in which he feels related to nature as to a secret source of nourishing life. If the Greeks were wrong to call the ocean "unfruitful," if, as modern science has shown, it teems with primitive animals

[2] The quoted words are from a passage at the end of *Cape Cod*, in *W*, IV, 270.

and functions as "the laboratory of continents," the walker nevertheless contemplates the laboratory from a safe distance (*W*, IV, 127, 128).

There are two stances Thoreau may take towards this separated nature. The first is to affirm it in its full distinctiveness. Though separate from man's mind, nature is yet a great *kosmos* in which all living things not only are related, but also have independent value in themselves. Thoreau's errand in *Cape Cod* is thus to discover, as in the early journal, "how good potato blows are," to observe each thing in and for itself: the sea jellies, mackeral gulls, and mosses, all with delicate organizations and yet able to live in the sea as man cannot, or the phalarope that sports with the waves, "as perfect a success in its way as the breakers in theirs" (*W*, IV, 113). In such a *kosmos* man plays a real but insignificant role. He is one more "product of the sea-slime" (*W*, IV, 186); yet this fact of his derivation constitutes his only genuine kinship with the sea.

Human disaster also contributes to the life of the *kosmos*, and from Thoreau's affirming, cosmical perspective it is not important enough to interrupt that life. When Thoreau finds beets growing wild on the Cape, he surmises that their seeds came ashore with the shipwrecked Franklin. He then moralizes, "It is an ill wind that blows nobody any good, and for the time lamentable shipwrecks may thus contribute a new vegetable to a continent's stock, and prove on the whole a lasting blessing to its inhabitants" (*W*, IV, 166). Though Thoreau first thinks of the "dreary peep of the piping plover" as "a fugacious part in the dirge which is ever played along the shore for those mariners who have been lost in the deep since first it was created," he pulls up short and adds that "the same strain which is a dirge to one household is a morning song of rejoicing to another" (*W*, IV, 71). The death of men at sea need not be felt as a catastrophe; it is a phenomenon in the life of nature, a necessary occurrence in nature's progress.

Yet even in these attempts to justify nature, shipwrecks are "lamentable." According to a second and equally pervasive point of view in *Cape Cod,* man is all important and alien nature is a grim threat. The book has no references to fancied mariners who gladly lay down their lives in the sublimity of storms. Repeatedly, human death is felt as the great fact revealed on the Cape, to which all other natural facts are subordinate. We keep hearing a muffled dirge for the dead throughout *Cape Cod,* to which the plover's peep contributes. When the thought of death comes to him, Thoreau searches for a way to make a seemly and human response to it. His recourse is often to revert to the anthropocentric, idealist Christianity of his forebears. He finds "Sit Nomen Domini Benedictum (Blessed be the Name of the Lord)"—the motto on the reverse of a French coin lying on the sand—"a pleasing sentiment to read in the sands of the seashore" (*W, IV,* 161). His moments of elegy read, in sentiment and cadence, like seventeenth-century prose, though with a Thoreauvian whimsical twist. On finding an ale bottle on the beach, he reflects:

As I poured it slowly out on to the sand, it seemed to me that man himself was like a half-emptied bottle of pale ale, which Time had drunk so far, yet stoppled tight for a while, and drifting about in the ocean of circumstances, but destined ere-long to mingle with the surrounding waves, or be spilled amid the sands of a distant shore. [*W, IV,* 117]

The ale bottle is a characteristic example of Thoreau's use of metaphor in *Cape Cod.* Instead of romantic correspondences, he seeks emblematic illustrations of the human fate, which often read like the jottings of a skeptical Father Mapple on holiday. In other words, when his romantic poetics break down, he resorts to the poetics of a Sir Thomas Browne or of one of the more lively Puritan sermon writers. As Sherman Paul points out, Thoreau intends in *Cape Cod* to remind readers of the religious earnestness of the New England past.[3] He honors the Pilgrims as pioneers in spiritual liberty, and appreciates some of their descendents on the Cape for their sober Puritan beliefs and their simple

[3] Sherman Paul, *The Shores of America,* pp. 387–388.

and hardy Puritan habits. Yet Thoreau himself, I would add, is no believer or ignorant provincial. Christian idealism is for him a "fiction" in Frank Kermode's sense, a belief that he experiments with temporarily and poetically in order to deal with the idea of death and the otherness of nature.[4]

From a man-centered viewpoint, the nature Thoreau observes on Cape Cod is inhuman, constantly threatening, the cause of death. In an extended meditation in "The Sea and the Desert," he finds, as in *Contact! Contact!,* a sublime hostility at the heart of things.

It is a wild, rank place, and there is no flattery in it. Strewn with crabs, horseshoes, and razor clams, and whatever the sea casts up,— a vast *morgue,* where famished dogs may range in packs, and crows come daily to glean the pittance which the tide leaves them. The carcasses of men and beasts together lie stately up upon its shelf, rotting and bleaching in the sun and waves, and each tide turns them in their beds, and tucks fresh sand under them. There is naked Nature,—inhumanly sincere, wasting no thought on man, nibbling at the cliffy shore where gulls wheel amid the spray. [*W,* IV, 186– 187]

This characterization of nature, however, follows directly on Thoreau's realization that man is a product of the sea-slime. Again, he is not drawing a logical conclusion, but exhibiting a many-sided truth. The ocean has created man; but at the same time nature on the seashore is inhuman. A page later the ocean itself is "a wilderness reaching round the globe, wilder than a Bengal jungle, and fuller of monsters, washing the very wharves of our cities" (*W,* IV, 188). Yet Thoreau's final reaction to this wildness is not to be appalled by it but to think of it as provid-

---

[4] Frank Kermode, *The Sense of an Ending* (New York: Oxford University Press, 1967), ch. ii. In my view, Thoreau's methods as a writer and thinker are consonant with his entertaining "fictions" rather than submitting to creeds. I would argue that nearly all his expressed beliefs— in "correspondence," for example, and even in "nature"—are more or less provisional and "fictional."

ing an opportunity for heroic adventure. "To go to sea! Why, it is to have the experience of Noah,—to realize the deluge. Every vessel is an ark" (*W*, IV, 189). In this conclusion (for the sequence of thought ends here), Thoreau has reverted to his original purpose—joyfully to confront the wild. He has put the thought of the shore as a "vast morgue" and that of the sea as a "Bengal jungle" behind him, has temporarily "forgotten" these disturbing images. Yet the pessimistic view of nature must be remembered as a feature of Thoreau's total vision. It is the predominant view in "The Shipwreck."

Nature is not felt in "The Shipwreck" as an organic whole, but only as power. Whereas the details of Thoreau's descriptions of the river and the woods in the *Week* and "Ktaadn" may be secretly bound together in the body of a *phuendos kosmos,* the texture of details in "The Shipwreck" is more like anarchic patchwork. Objects exist independently alongside each other, like natural objects in the rest of *Cape Cod,* but without the suggestion of functional connection in the *kosmos* we find even there.

A little further along the shore we saw a man's clothes on a rock; further, a woman's scarf, a gown, a straw bonnet, the brig's caboose, and one of her masts high and dry, broken into several pieces. In another rocky cove . . . . lay a part of one side of the vessel, still hanging together. It was, perhaps, forty feet long, by fourteen feet wide. I was ever more surprised at the power of the waves, exhibited on this shattered fragment, than I had been at the sight of the smaller fragments before. The largest timbers and iron braces were broken superfluously, and I saw that no material could withstand the power of the waves; that iron must go to pieces in such a case, and an iron vessel would be cracked up like an egg-shell on the rocks. [*W*, IV, 8–9]

What connects these fragmentary details is the event of the shipwreck itself, the solemn fact of the power of nature as represented by the rock and as exhibited in the scattering of human things. When that power is exercised, it leads (as the Boston handbill has it) to "Death! one hundred and forty-five lives lost at Cohasset" (*W*, IV, 5).

In Thoreau's narrative death functions like a magnet, around which diverse objects momentarily cluster. "The Shipwreck" seems entirely "natural"—in the sense that the narrator gives the impression that he is excluding nothing, reporting everything he sees—but it is also focused and unified, around human death. As his narrative proceeds, Thoreau demands, without sentimental overemphasis, our gravest attention for examples of death: for the immigrant woman who lies in a box with her sister's child in her arms, or for the drowned girl who so impressed Robert Lowell that he used Thoreau's account of her in "A Quaker Graveyard in Nantucket."[5]

I saw many marble feet and matted heads as the cloths were raised, and one livid, swollen, and mangled body of a drowned girl,—who probably had intended to go out to service in some American family, —to which some rags still adhered, with a string, half-concealed by the flesh, about its swollen neck; the coiled-up wreck of a human hulk, gashed by the rocks or fishes, so that the bone and muscle were exposed, but quite bloodless,—merely red and white,—with wide-open and staring eyes, yet lustreless, dead-lights; or like the cabin windows of a stranded vessel, filled with sand. [*W*, IV, 6–7]

This fearful picture appears in Thoreau's context as if in a factual report. We come upon it after details of the geological features of the shore, of the crowds milling about, of the mechanical activities of burial—men hammering and nailing and carting away boxes, "a sober dispatch of business that was affecting" (*W*, IV, 6). The anarchic-factual quality of the narrative is heightened by Thoreau's feeling for death itself. Death is first a moment of concentration and intensity, then one of disordering, scattering, fragmenting. At death human order dissipates for him into natural disorder, a nature no longer associated with purposeful growth,

[5] Robert Lowell, *Lord Weary's Castle* (New York: Harcourt, Brace, 1946), p. 8.

with the idea of *phusis*. The characteristic quality of his facts and metaphors in the picture of the girl is that they are without relation to each other.

The narrator's immediate response to all that he observes is to feel compassion for the sufferers and moral indignation at those spectators who, unlike those who soberly tend to the dead, are lacking in the humanity called for on such a momentous occasion: the man who stands by "chewing large quids of tobacco, as if that habit were forever confirmed with him"; the man who talks in a loud voice of the particular way the lifeboat painter broke "as if he had a bet depending on it, but had no humane interest in the matter"; the pair of men who come simply for the vulgar thrill of seeing a spectacle and cannot wait for the funeral; and the weed-collectors who search about the corpse-strewn remains of the boat for "valuable manure" (*W*, IV, 8, 9). For one of these last, the bodies of the dead are "but other weeds which the tide cast up, but which were of no use to him" (*W*, IV, 11). The narrator's critical attitude is humane, moral, man-centered. The sea, the rocks, nature—these are by implication the enemy.

But the dialectical, polarizing tendency of Thoreau's mind is at work also in "The Shipwreck." When the narrator ends his account of his visit to Cohasset and adds to it a group of isolated reflections, his direction of mind takes an unexpected turn:

> On the whole, it was not so impressive a scene as I might have expected. If I had found one body cast upon the beach in some lonely place, it would have affected me more. I sympathized rather with the winds and waves, as if to toss and mangle these poor human bodies was the order of the day. If this was the law of Nature, why waste any time in awe or pity? . . . It is the individual and private that demands our sympathy. A man can attend but one funeral in the course of his life, can behold but one corpse. [*W*, IV, 9–10]

The narrator seems to feel that his account has been one-sidedly humane. Having dwelt on man, he will say a word for nature.

(His protest on behalf of the individual and private is for my purpose secondary to his impulse to find a way back to nature.) It is as if he wished for the moment to justify nature in her most drastic manifestations. We feel the constraint of Thoreauvian exaggeration as he sympathizes with destruction, as his "sympathy with persons is swallowed up in a wider sympathy with the universe," with the tremendous, amoral natural process that throws up weeds and wrecks indiscriminately on the sands.

Thus in the midst of human tragedy Thoreau has again set up an exclusive, asocial relation to nature. But his strained sentiments are obviously not adequate to the whole truth he will convey. His next move is therefore to qualify his exaggeration. The narrator turns back from nature to consider sober men again. "Yet I saw that the inhabitants of the shore would be not a little affected by this event. They would watch there many days and nights for the sea to give up its dead, and their imaginations and sympathies would supply the place of mourners far away" (*W*, IV, 12). For Thoreau, however, this ground is untenable also. The outlook of the inhabitants of the shore is too tragic for him to endure. If he cannot affirm nature, he will effectively take man out of it, denying it any meaningful existence.

Why care for these dead bodies? They really have no friends but the worms or fishes. Their owners were coming to the New World, as Columbus and the Pilgrims did; they were within a mile of its shores; but, before they could reach it, they emigrated to a newer world than ever Columbus dreamed of. . . . I saw their empty hulks that came to land; but they themselves, meanwhile, were cast upon some shore yet further west, toward which we are all tending, and which we shall reach at last, it may be through storm and darkness, as they did. . . . The mariner who makes the safest port in heaven, perchance, seems to his friends on earth to be shipwrecked, for they deem Boston Harbor the better place; though perhaps, invisible to them, a skillful pilot comes to meet him, and the fairest and balmiest gales blow off that coast, his good ship makes the land in halcyon days, and he kisses the shore in rapture there, while his old hulk tosses in the surf here. It is hard to part with one's body, but, no doubt, it is easy enough to do without it when once it is gone. All their plans and hopes burst like a bubble! Infants by the score dashed on the rocks by the enraged Atlantic Ocean! No, no! If the St. John did not make her port here, she has been telegraphed there. The strongest wind cannot stagger a Spirit; it is a Spirit's breath. [*W*, IV, 12–13]

On its face this passage appears to be a piece of quasi-Christian rhetoric, an eloquent but almost conventional funeral sermon. (If the word-play on "old hulk" is Thoreauvian, it would not be out of place in a sermon by Father Edward Taylor of Boston, the original of Father Mapple.)[6] But why does Thoreau preach in this antique style on the immortality of the Spirit? Not, I think, out of a sudden access of piety. Rather, he is trying under the strain of the death scene to improvise a solution to a metaphysical problem. Nature as revealed at Cohasset is incompatible with man—man simply has no generous or loving relation with it. Thoreau cannot here find a way to blend the power of man *and* nature; therefore he must choose man *or* nature. But this he will not do. His stratagem is to affirm one *after* the other, that he may still affirm both. First he sympathizes with a nature devoid of spirit; then he exalts the disembodied and translated souls of the dead. Yet in jumping back and forth between these two poles, he hardly brings them together; they are split as widely apart as in *Contact! Contact!* And both extreme views are unbalanced in terms of Thoreau's usual perspective. When in his reflections the narrator turned to nature, his point of view became practically identical with that of the weed collectors. He too put the bodies of the dead on the same level with objects in nature—wind and waves, fishes and worms. When he now turns to the soul, he denies, as in *Contact! Contact!* the crucial importance that the body and the senses must have in any wanderer's life in nature. The natives who watch for the drowned are involved, soul and

[6] For an example of Taylor's preaching, see Charles Dickens, *American Notes* (1842; rpt. Harmondsworth, Eng.: Penguin, 1972), pp. 107–109.

body, with the necessity before them. The narrator, by contrast, emerges from his consideration of death by an idealist escape hatch.

> Quit, now, full of heart and comfort,
> These rude shores, they are of earth;
> Where the rosy clouds are parting,
> There the blessed isles loom forth.[7]

It is in these reflective paragraphs in "The Shipwreck" that the narrator seems particularly uncertain. (His trend of reflection is still less controlled and more varied than my excerpts would indicate.) Adopting a psychological framework, we could agree that Thoreau here is "trying to talk his way out of death," as Joel Porte puts it;[8] he may be so unnerved by the spectacle of death as to lose control over the management of his different points of view. Yet, if these reflections by themselves are confused and obsessive, they nevertheless have an appropriate place in the narrative of "The Shipwreck." As writer, Thoreau would give us an accurate transcript of his thoughts. He is bold enough to exhibit his inward indefiniteness, and then to become definite and coherent again. In an analysis of the composition of "The Shipwreck," then, we may regard the narrator's aberrations as dramatic outbursts, wayward shifts of mood. For his loss of control is temporary; the discordant conflicts in his mind are partly resolved, partly dissolved, in the working out of the chapter.

The last pages of "The Shipwreck," which tell of a second visit to Cohasset, are unique in Thoreau. He has, for once, come to the firm position that nature is separate from man and indiffer-

---

[7] Quoted by Thoreau from "verses addressed to Columbus dying," *W*, IV, 14. The verses are by Adam Gottlob Oehlenschläger; they were translated from Danish by Emerson's friend William Henry Furness. Thoreau substituted "rude shores" for "Azores" to fit his local context (W. H. Furness, *Verses, Translations from the German, and Hymns* [Boston: Houghton Mifflin, 1886], p. 58). I am indebted to Lawrence Willson for this reference.

[8] Porte, p. 184.

ent to him. This new attitude he takes with ease and assurance.
He recollects in tranquillity his earlier experience and manages
a beautifully sustained, ironic treatment of alien nature. The
ocean at Cohasset both gives to man and takes from him, but not
in either character does it correspond to man's mind or temperament. Judiciously, Thoreau balances the advantages and the
dangers of the ocean against each other (he has by now recovered
his balance, his ability to look at nature and death with detachment). He makes no attempt, as in the conclusion of "Ktaadn,"
to regard nature as innocent, and thereby to forget the terrible
aspect of nature to which he has been a witness. Rather, his
knowledge of its underlying terror is an element in his final perspective as he observes the beach.

True, the beach *seems* innocent to an uneducated observer; it
seems utterly changed from what it was at the time of the wreck.
The narrator visits it on a fiercely hot day, and the intense
weather helps to efface the storm in our minds. The scene is described as pastoral: boatmen call over the placid water like boys
in country barns. The function of the sea at this moment is to
make men and beasts comfortable. It gives relief to the traveler
from the heat; horses stand in the water or climb to the top of the
fort at Hull to feel the breeze; the narrator himself goes swimming.

The sea bathing at Cohasset Rocks was perfect. The water was
purer and more transparent than any I had ever seen. There was
not a particle of mud or slime about it. The bottom being sandy, I
could see the sea perch swimming about. The smooth and fantas-
tically worn rocks, and the perfectly clean and tress-like rockweeds
falling over you, and attached so firmly to the rocks that you could
pull yourself up by them, greatly enhanced the luxury of the bath.
. . . There were the tawny rocks, like lions couchant, defying the
ocean, whose waves incessantly dashed against and scoured them
with vast quantities of gravel. The water held in their little hollows
on the receding of the tide was so crystalline that I could not believe it salt, but wished to drink it; and higher up were basins of
fresh water left by the rain,—all which, being also of different

depths and temperature, were convenient for different kinds of baths. Also, the larger hollows in the smoothed rocks formed the most convenient of seats and dressing rooms. In these respects it was the most perfect seashore that I had seen. [*W*, IV, 16–17]

This nature is temporarily "convenient"; in other words, "man may use it if he can." The narrator's repeated emphasis on the rocks is clearly ironic—we remember Grampus and the top of Katahdin, and the weeds too remind us of the Cohasset weed-collectors. His bath is only a temporary luxury. Therefore his mind waxes luxurious and fanciful as he describes his pleasure. He indulges in illusions to ornament his hedonistic pose. It is only in fancy that he sees the water in the pools as fresh, the rocks as heraldic lions. From another, more candid perspective the sea is of the same nature as at the time when the St. John split against Grampus.

As I looked over the water, I saw the isles rapidly wasting away, the sea nibbling voraciously at the continent. . . . On the other hand, these wrecks of isles were being fancifully arranged into new shores, as at Hog Island, inside of Hull, where everything seemed to be gently lapsing into futurity. [*W*, IV, 15]

The sea is creative and destructive, gently voracious. It has made this placid scene and will eliminate it. It may be enjoyed on certain days, but a truthful observer will remember its potential wrecking power. Not all the pools it tosses up are convenient for bathing.

I saw in Cohasset, separated from the sea only by a narrow beach, a handsome but shallow lake of some four hundred acres, which, I was told, the sea had tossed over the beach in a great storm in the spring, and, after the alewives had passed into it, it had stopped up its outlet, and now the alewives were dying by thousands, and the inhabitants were apprehending a pestilence as the water evaporated. It had five rocky islets in it. [*W*, IV, 17]

This follows immediately on the narrator's appreciation of his bath. Thoreau's irony is sobering. What is "handsome" on the surface is a natural graveyard underneath. Where the alewives die is naked Nature, presented factually by the innocent-eyed narrator with the emphasis that only facts can have. He records the alewives' death and passes on without comment to the inconsequential, the fact of the "five rocky islets." The salient facts in nature are apparent only on occasion. The Thoreauvian narrator as reporter of the natural must still give evidence also of the irregularity and apparent meaninglessness of some of his impressions. The final paragraph of "The Shipwreck," however, re-emphasizes Thoreau's ironic intent.

This rocky shore is called Pleasant Cove on same maps; on the map of Cohasset, that name appears to be confined to the particular cove where I saw the wreck of the St. John. The ocean did not look, now, as if any were ever shipwrecked in it; it was not grand and sublime, but beautiful as a lake. Not a vestige of a wreck was visible, nor could I believe that the bones of many a shipwrecked man were buried in that pure sand. But to go on with our first excursion. [*W*, IV, 18]

It is typical of Thoreau that he *goes on* with his excursion; he will not be caught hamstrung in an attitude. The conclusion he manages so firmly in the last pages of "The Shipwreck" is meant only for it, not for his attempt to understand nature nor for a stage of his development nor even for *Cape Cod*. He will allow to each moment its own glory, intensity, and meaning. Nevertheless, "The Shipwreck" is an integrated and intense artistic moment in itself. It is a learning experience in which Thoreau's first impressions lead inevitably, yet naturally, to his final thoughts on nature's power and man's vulnerability.

If nature is power, is there a meaningful stance for a man to adopt toward it? The calm of the last pages of "The Shipwreck" suggests that Thoreau has temporarily found such a stance. On his second visit to Cohasset he is still attracted to nature and derives enormous sensuous enjoyment from it. But he no longer thinks an I-Thou relation with it possible. He has accepted the idea that nature is indifferent and dangerous, no longer a kindly brother. Thus he is detached and circumspect in his attitude, wary of nature and secure in himself. How has he achieved this new stance? He hints at his method of living with an alien nature, I think, in a sentence appearing among his troubled reflections on the storm: "I saw that the beauty of the shore itself was wrecked for many a lonely walker there, until he could perceive, at last, how its beauty was enhanced by wrecks like this, and it acquired thus a rarer and sublimer beauty still" (*W*, IV, 12). This is one of those momentary attempts to express fragmentary truth that Thoreau sometimes made, because he felt that the finest truths, including those apprehended in nature, were fragmentary and obscure and could be stated best in brief and suggestive sentences of insight. I interpret: The lonely wanderer achieves the detachment of the artist or artistically-minded observer. He has indeed been troubled by the evidence of tragedy on the seashore; but he is able to overcome his trouble by the Thoreauvian effort of going again and again to nature (we shall see more of this effort in *Walden*), until he finally attains a new kind of *perception,* which is for Thoreau here a truer and higher perception. He can recognize the fact of death in nature, can perceive that lamentable shipwrecks contribute to its total spectacle, drama, and meaning. From this perspective nature is not kindly or sympathetic; it is simply there for the wanderer to perceive. But when it is viewed with this educated poetic detachment, it may acquire "a rarer and sublimer" beauty than it harbored for him before his initiation into the spectacle of tragedy. Perhaps in Thoreau's own narrative of his second trip to the Cohasset shore he is describing this new beauty, as well as exposing the ironies of his new understanding. He has learned, at least for the moment, to accept nature in all its manifestations as he perceives them. He can thus see and not dismiss events like the wreck of the St. John.

This emphasis on educated poetic perception, already present in the passages on seeing in the early journal, appears again in Thoreau's late essays. In "Autumnal Tints" especially he works out at considerable length his idea of the poet as perceiver. Probably it can justly be said that Thoreau moves away in the course of his career from a conception of his relation to nature as one of mutual sympathy toward a soberer conception, according to which he perceives nature without expecting that it will offer him anything but his own perceptions in return. But he never relinquishes the idea of a generous interchange altogether; it is prominent in *Walden,* which is of course a compendium of the thoughts of many years. Moreover, his final view in "The Shipwreck," that nature is an indifferent and voracious power, is not incorporated in any distinctive way in his later work. In *Walden,* in "Chesuncook," and in the late essays he will want back one form or another of the idea that nature is a living and mysteriously beneficent whole. An attitude learned to satisfy the needs of one moment will be unlearned for other needs. Yet, in the total mosaic of Thoreau's imitation of nature, "The Shipwreck" stands out as a brilliant separate piece, the finished expression of a somber experience.

～ 7

Walden: Activity in Balance

We now turn from "Ktaadn" and "The Shipwreck," as from a dark background, to the varied light of *Walden*. Our way into *Walden* is to recognize that Thoreau expressed in it once again his sense of separateness from nature, even as he was expressing his love for it. As in much of his writing, he desires involvement with the swarming vitality of the earth that comes to life in spring and ripens through summer till it dissipates in the death of the year; but he also questions the swarming vital animal in himself, and he finds that growing beans not only invigorates him but also restricts his freedom. Yet, though he dwells at times on the brutish otherness of the natural, he manages in the course of the whole work to convey the impression that he has found joy in his life in the woods and by the pond. He conveys this without obscuring the quirks of his mind or the difficulties of his circumstances. It is an earned joy that he is expressing, one that he strives to sustain through the years he writes *Walden* against the changes in himself and the vicissitudes of nature.

True, Thoreau's moments of conscious separation from wild nature in *Walden* do not stand out so vividly as in "Ktaadn" or "The Shipwreck," nor does he aspire to heaven and abandon earth conspicuously, as he does on occasion in the *Week*. In *Walden* he deliberately leaves obscure the possibility that, as a romantic naturalist and a follower of Emerson, he may have occasion to deny his sympathy with nature; for one purpose of the book is to show that a man *can* live in nature. The paradoxes inherent in his position are to be discovered in a few careful qualifying statements, or implied in the interstices of his exaggerations. They are also evident in his revisions and expansions of the comparatively simple first (1847) version of *Walden*.[1] While studying the growth of *Walden* we can legitimately speak of a development in Thoreau's view of nature occurring coherently over a period of time. His relation to nature in the first version is comparatively simple, unconscious, and idyllic. In the seventh and final version of 1854 he has included much more of the whole conscious man. Moreover, he is by then more than ever aware of his intelligent isolation. The "I" in the 1854 *Walden* is more separated, critical, humorous, and ironical than in the *Week*, the early essays, or the first version of *Walden*, less prone to the egotistical or the natural sublime. Nowhere else does Thoreau balance his relation to nature so carefully; he is on his guard throughout against indulging any particular feeling too emphatically or exclusively. He will impress us as a sympathetic naturalist with a sense of proportion, an idealist with his feet on the ground, a writer knowingly aggressive and gentle toward nature and toward his audience.

Walden differs from Thoreau's earlier work most obviously in that its subject is not a voyage to new scenes but life in a familiar place, in "the woods." He does not explore a shore or a forest as wild areas to be appropriated by the imagination, but comes back and back to the same Walden Pond, the same nature. Thus he curbs his restless desire for imaginative freedom, confining himself in local limits. Yet this nature as he conceives it is never static. It is infinitely diverse even as it remains the same—various, fertile, mysterious, and yet one. To know it, a man must live as well as voyage in it, observing its different aspects. And to represent nature adequately, Thoreau approaches it from ever new per-

[1] This version has been reconstructed from Thoreau's manuscripts by J. Lyndon Shanley, in *The Making of Walden*, pp. 105–208.

spectives, never defining it as a whole, but offering instead a series of temporary definitions. As he makes his rounds, he conveys the sense that his appreciation deepens. *Walden* is a record of a continual, steady living with nature.

If *Walden* is a carefully pondered work in which Thoreau is at home with himself and his subject, it is still, I think, not the intensely unified work it has been called. I am happy to agree that it has enough unity and intentional structure to make us feel that it is a single whole, the art of which we can perceive and admire. But simply because *Walden* went through seven versions in nine years does not necessarily mean that it is perfectly ordered and self-consistent. On the contrary, the protracted composition of the book, far from guaranteeing its perfect unity, may indicate its diversity. If we follow Lyndon Shanley in his ascription of passages to different versions we find, for example, that while Thoreau was eager in every version to get the sum of his thoughts before the reader, he had different preoccupations at different times. Thus he was especially interested in preaching simplicity to his neighbors in 1847 (Version I), interested in representing the shimmer and beauty of the pond in 1852 (Versions IV and V), interested in amassing his disquieting description of sand formations in early spring in 1854 (Versions VI and VII).[2] The whole has the character of a carefully assembled conglomeration, not that of a single-minded expression. Thoreau matured during the writing of *Walden,* but he also maintained a respect for earlier inspirations, the manna he had eaten and digested. Thus he was somewhat reluctant to excise early passages simply because he changed his mind on a given question. He made revisions, but usually with the intention of being true to the spirit that moved him in 1845 as well as the spirit that moved him in 1854. He lets an early resolve to "fish and hunt far and wide" stand close to a later confession that he "cannot fish without falling a little in self-respect" (*Walden,* pp. 207, 213). If the earlier fishing is symbolic of his quest for wildness, it is also real and natural—Thoreau

[2] Shanley, pp. 57, 73–74, 105–137, 186–188.

caught fish that day in 1845 with John Field. Both sentiments were authentic when expressed, and both are retained in *Walden*.

I think, even, that Thoreau misleads twentieth century readers intent on unity when he uses his metaphor of the staff of the artist of Kouroo. The staff properly suggests Thoreau's careful workmanship, his vocation as artist-pilgrim, and his determination to make his book beautiful. But the fable of the staff is a set piece, like many paragraphs in *Walden*. *Walden* as a whole is unlike a staff in that it is not one object carved out of one piece of wood. Rarely elsewhere does Thoreau conceive of a work of his as a single, made object of art. (An exception is his evocation of the *Week* as a "basket" in *Walden*: "I too had woven a kind of basket of a delicate texture, but I had not made it worth any one's while to buy them"—*Walden*, p. 19. But baskets are woven of separate strands.) Even while writing and revising *Walden* he emphasizes the multiple and mosaic character of his work, his openness to varied perceptions and inspirations. His methods could easily make for disorder as well as for complexity in longer work, as he himself realized. In his journal at the pond he reflects critically on the discontinuity of the *Week*:

From all points of the compass, from the earth beneath and the heavens above, have come these inspirations and been entered duly in the order of their arrival in the journal. Thereafter, when the time arrived, they were winnowed into lectures, and again, in due time, from lectures into essays. And at last they stand, like the cubes of Pythagoras, firmly on either basis; like statues on their pedestals, but the statues rarely take hold of hands. There is only such connection and series as is attainable in the galleries. And this affects their immediate practical and popular influence. [*J*, I, 413]

Walden, by contrast, has direction, persuasiveness, and shapeliness. The essays in it are much more effectively connected—they "take hold of hands"—though they are still primarily essays, not stages in a narrative or divisions in a poem. Not only are individual chapters and sections beautifully composed, but by means of recurring metaphors Thoreau makes us sense and see delicate connections between parts of his book. Moreover, as Stanley Cavell brilliantly shows, Thoreau continually redefines his key terms—words like "labor," "amusement," and "simplicity," to mention three I touch on later—so as to create a composite philosophical discourse instilled with a power of "self-comment and self-placement."[3] But the intricate idea of the whole is not made so prominent as to overshadow individual inspirations. As Thoreau begins a major revision of *Walden* in 1852, he resolves "to set down such choice experiences that my own writings may inspire me and at last I may make wholes of parts" (*J*, III, 217). We may infer from such a resolution that the whole that is finally to emerge will be conspicuous for its choice parts. The ordinary sensitive reader, I judge, is aware of Thoreau's efforts at formal structure only occasionally; he reads *Walden* intuitively and rightly as a dense mixture of disparate materials with a sufficient but not an overinsistent unity.

Surely an effect of unity is achieved by compressing Thoreau's two and one-quarter years at the pond into one, and by allowing the "plot" of the book to conform to the cycle of the seasons. But let us look at what this structural reordering means. On the one hand, as a device for coordinating all the various ideas and phenomena contained in *Walden* it means little. The cycle of the year is a loose framework for thoughts on winter visitors and summer economies; it gives Thoreau a narrative thread, but hardly a tight plot. On the other hand, the use of Thoreau's seasonal experience helps reinforce what seems the crucial purpose of *Walden*, which is to present a self in the process of maturation and renewal. This self may be as pregnant with diverse forms as a mass of thawing clay in a Concord spring, but it is still a single self that shares in the renewal of *phusis* and *kosmos*, the single world of nature. It is, moreover, an exemplary self undergoing renewal for the benefit of the interested reader. For another pur-

[3] Stanley Cavell, *The Senses of Walden* (New York: Viking, 1972), p. 12.

pose of Thoreau's self-exhibition is to encourage the reader to undertake his own regeneration, aware that the new life he constructs may be as individual and diverse as Thoreau's own. Thus *Walden*—like the *Prelude* in this respect—is fundamentally a programmatic meditation in which formal considerations are significant but subordinate to the program and the meditative process.

In this chapter I shall be describing Thoreau's renewal not as a series of events that occur chronologically during his stay at the pond and afterwards, nor as the principal theme of that shaped artifice *Walden,* but as the chief end of his effort to relate to nature. My approach should again make for a clearer recognition of certain conflicts in Thoreau's relation to nature, conflicts he reveals in the course of his search for a balanced and thoughtful happiness. It should also emphasize that *Walden* is not only a fable of renewal but also an exhibition of an active consciousness. Thoreau writes in 1851 that he likes the idea of "a meteorological journal of the mind. You shall observe what occurs in your latitude, I in mine." "The poet must be continually watching the moods of his mind, as the astronomer watches the aspects of the heavens" (*J,* II, 403). While Thoreau is perhaps thinking of the journal itself in this bit of introspection, he describes the *Week* and *Walden* as well—both his long-pondered books are thus "meteorological."

ii

In each of Thoreau's excursions I have exhibited his willingness to set forth joyfully into nature despite physical obstacles and moral ambiguities. His enthusiastic acceptance of wild nature on the title page of *Walden* is a piece of determined exaggeration, or, as he calls it, "bragging."

I do not propose to write an ode to dejection, but to brag as lustily as chanticleer in the morning, standing on his roost, if only to wake my neighbors up.[4]

[4] This motto appears on the title page of the first edition of *Walden*

Already in his title-page boast Thoreau chooses to model himself in his tone of voice and style of self-projection on an exuberant barnyard animal. He would not at this point show, as we have seen him show in "The Poet's Delay" and "The Inward Morning," that he is sensitive to the divorce between poetic mind and nature that informs Coleridge's "Dejection." Instead, he will identify himself with wild nature, in a gesture of defiance. He will prefer the fellowship of beasts to that of common, conscious humanity. In the woods his morning companion is a Homeric mosquito whose angry buzz rejoices him alone. (No memories of stale Long Wharf flies are allowed to intrude in this setting.) His house he imagines as wholly swallowed up in nature.

No yard! but unfenced Nature reaching up to your very sills. A young forest growing up under your windows, and wild sumachs and blackberry vines breaking through into your cellar; sturdy pitch-pines rubbing and creaking against the shingles for want of room, their roots reaching quite under the house. Instead of a scuttle or a blind blown off in the gale,—a pine tree snapped off or torn up by the roots behind your house for fuel. Instead of no path to the front-yard gate in the Great Snow,—no gate,—no front-yard,—and no path to the civilized world! [*Walden,* p. 128]

If nature is aggressive, Thoreau will be also in this moment of

---

(Boston: Ticknor & Fields, 1854). Interestingly, on the title page drawn up by Thoreau for Manuscript Version VII of *Walden*—the 1854 version from which he prepared his copy for the printer—he added the following epigraph, which was later omitted from the printed book: "The clouds, wind, moon, sun and sky act in cooperation that thou mayest get thy daily bread, and not eat it with indifference; all revolve for thy sake, and are obedient to command; it must be an equitable condition, that thou shalt be obedient also.—Sadi" (quoted in *The Annotated Walden,* ed. Philip van Doren Stern [New York: Clarkson Potter, 1970], p. 141; see p. 140 for a photograph of this manuscript title page). The sentiments, Thoreau's own and Sadi's, are clearly set off in polarity against each other. The double message is that of a bragging, yet obedient, Yankee-Hindoo. Thoreau evidently decided at last to emphasize his profession of exuberance, not his profession of humility; but Version VII shows that he conceived of these two forms of feeling as opposed but necessary to each other.

involvement—a self-made Titan pitting himself against the thrusting, weedy forest.

The forest by the house is hostile to the encroachments of man, as is the forest by the logger's house in Maine. Interestingly, the above passage is already present in the first version of *Walden* and was perhaps part of what Thoreau read to Concord audiences from that version in February 1847,[5] the winter after his first trip to Maine. "No yard!" is thus of the same period as "Ktaadn." Yet in it and in *Walden* generally Thoreau pays no conscious heed to any tentative conclusions he may have reached elsewhere about nature as a place of terror. Living by the pond, he is bound to come across spectacles like the dead horse stinking in the hollow by his path; but he refuses to be overwhelmed, or even sobered, by such unpleasantness for more than an occasional sentence. His strategy is to affirm the vigorous nature around him in many varied circumstances, whether comfortable or not, and let the reader infer between the lines his silenced doubts. Thoreau will experience, even savor, nature's meanness. He is not content to present a merely humorous account of the battle between red and black ants, but will inform us exactly of the bloodiest and ugliest details, as scrutinized through a microscope. He will stare down naked Nature, parading his powers of endurance.

Nevertheless, his uncertainties as to the possibility of a relation with nature are subversively present. They come out indirectly, we shall see, in "The Bean Field," in "Higher Laws," in "Brute Neighbors," and elsewhere. They give Thoreau's effort to brazen his way joyfully through the encounter with nature an overtone of self-conscious doubt.

Thoreau, I think, insists on accepting the dead horse because he still has the visceral wish and courage to live and correspond with nature-as-growth. For him the realm of *phusis* remains one and interdependent in *Walden*. If he accepts it in one aspect, he will accept it in all. His pleasure in the aggressive forest is an ex-

[5] Walter Harding, ed., *The Variorum Walden* (New York: Twayne, 1962), p. xiv.

ample of his pleasure in growth generally; and his willingness to involve himself in the battle of ants stems from his awareness that the preying of animals on each other is a condition of growth and evolution. The idea of growth is implicit in the cycle of the seasons, emphasized in the structure of *Walden*. Believing in the health of the pattern of seasonal death and rebirth, Thoreau accepts each stage of it as necessary.

Thoreau involves himself in nature's growth at many points in *Walden*, but nowhere with such concentration and delight as in "Spring." In the year's rebirth, organic nature is felt as the single source of life; and for Thoreau all those thoughts and feelings we have seen clustered around the concepts of joy and growth come together again. Thoreau revives the image of circulation: the sand flows, and waters rise and spread over the land.

The sinking sound of melting snow is heard in all dells, and the ice dissolves apace in the ponds. The grass flames up on the hillsides like a spring fire . . . as if the earth sent forth an inward heat to greet the returning sun; not yellow but green is the color of its flame;—the symbol of perpetual youth, the grass-blade, like a long green ribbon, streams from the sod into the summer. . . . It grows as steadily as the rill oozes out of the ground. [*Walden*, pp. 310–311]

As in "A Winter Walk," the body of earth has its own inward heat to keep it alive through the winter and make it flow again in the spring. Repeatedly in "Spring" Thoreau alludes to the idea of the earth as an undying animal again in its youth. He is "cheered by the music of a thousand tinkling rills and rivulets whose veins are filled with the blood of winter" (*Walden*, p. 304). The thawing clay in the railroad cut convinces him that "Earth is still in her swaddling clothes, and stretches forth baby fingers on every side" (*Walden*, p. 308). He rejoices in "the first tender signs of the infant year." Even frost is pictured as an animal, coming "out of the ground like a dormant quadruped from its burrow." For at the heart of the "living earth" is a "great central life," a single generative force in nature, "compared with [which] all animal and vegetable life is merely parasitic" (*Walden*, p. 309).

Thoreau's organicism in "Spring" parallels Goethe's not only in the metaphysical prose poem on the leaf, in which he makes use of Goethe's hypothesis of an *Urpflanze,* but more significantly and generally in his feeling for surging creativity in nature. Behind the variegated life in the railroad cut is a Goethean god of nonmoral, daemonic creativity, "the Artist who made the world and me," who is "still at work, sporting on this bank, and with excess of energy strewing his fresh designs about" (*Walden*, p. 306). And one meaning of the railroad cut episode is the Goethean principle that the earth undergoes a continual metamorphosis in order to produce something higher.[6] "Thus, also, you pass from the lumpish grub in the earth to the airy and fluttering butterfly. The very globe continually transcends and translates itself, and becomes winged in its orbit" (*Walden,* pp. 306–307). Goethe's principles of archetypal organization and natural evolution came to Thoreau through Emerson; but Emerson's interest lay in applying them to human circumstances. Thoreau's instincts led him back to experience Goethe's original intuition for himself. He saw Goethe's principles operate where Goethe had conceived them, in growing nature.

"Spring" has the compelling complexity of Thoreau's best work not only because he makes evident the fertile sweetness of nature at the pond but also because he presents in the chapter a complete portrait of *phusis* and man's involvement with it. After he has spoken of the birth of the infant year and of the forgiveness of sins on a spring morning, he makes his most eloquent and extravagant claim for the wildness of nature and for natural violence.

We need the tonic of wildness,—to wade sometimes in marshes where the bittern and the meadow-hen lurk, and hear the booming of the snipe; to smell the whispering sedge where only some wilder and more solitary fowl builds her nest, and the mink crawls with

[6] The principle of *Steigerung.* See Chapter 4, note 3, above.

its belly close to the ground. . . . We can never have enough of Nature. We must be refreshed by the sight of inexhaustible vigor, vast and Titanic features, the sea-coast with its wrecks, the wilderness with its living and its decaying trees, the thunder-cloud, and the rain which lasts three weeks and produces freshets. We need to witness our own limits transgressed, and some life pasturing freely where we never wander. . . . I love to see that Nature is so rife with life that myriads can be afforded to be sacrificed and suffered to prey on one another; that tender organizations can be so serenely squashed out of existence like pulp,—tadpoles which herons gobble up, and tortoises and toads run over in the road; and that sometimes it has rained flesh and blood! With the liability to accident, we must see how little account is to be made of it. The impression made on a wise man is that of universal innocence. [*Walden,* pp. 317–318]

After what we know of Thoreau's penchant for plunging into *phusis,* it is not surprising to see him relishing cataclysms of weather and transformation and havoc in the ecological system. Indeed, his imagery recalls his early fantasies of engulfing: "the rain that lasts three weeks and produces freshets" and the apocalyptic rain of flesh and blood. What is surprising and even disturbing is that he should characterize the spectacle of mutual destruction in nature, which Goethe's Werther sees as "an eternally self-gorging monster," as "innocent." But Thoreau would again be true to the logic of *phusis.* Nature as an endless repetition of creation and destruction is unconscious and is therefore not properly subject to our moral categories. All plant and animal life is innocent: pine needles and excrementitious sand formations, herons and tadpoles, owls and sparrows, warring ants and peaceful partridges. If a man would be part of this growth, he must accept it as it is.

Nevertheless, I regard this climax in "Spring" as suspect, as an expression of a temporary enthusiasm. For the moment Thoreau professes to be cheered by his violent fantasy. But in *Cape Cod* he viewed the rapacity of dogs with hard cheerlessness, and generally his attitude toward natural violence is ambivalent. In the *Week,* we remember, he and his brother slaughtered pigeons and ate them, seeking to "detect the secret innocence of these incessant tragedies which Heaven allows" (*W,* I, 236). But then his hunting venture caused him to reflect on the cruelty not only of the natural man, but also of "Nature herself." She "has not provided the most graceful end for her creatures. What becomes of all these birds that people the air and forest for our solacement? . . . There is a tragedy at the end of each one of their lives. They must perish miserably; not one of them is translated" (*W,* I, 236–237). In "Higher Laws" Thoreau sees the destructiveness of the hunter as a sign of the beast within, the "reptile and sensual" in man. He would wean himself of the lust for violence. When he writes, "Nature is hard to be overcome, but she must be overcome" (*Walden,* p. 221), "nature" is the natural man in us, the man of sloth, greed, and sexual desire, who vegetates in idleness, sees himself eating fried rats and raw woodchucks, and indulges in sexual fantasies. Yet these vices of our nature are all closely related to *phusis,* to the generative and chaotic power in the external world Thoreau so much enjoys and admires in "Spring." It seems that Thoreau never resolved this quandary. He stands always in hesitation before the hog that succeeds "by other means than temperance and purity" (*Walden,* p. 219). In April 1858, he is still writing Marston Watson about it: "Is the mystery of the hog's bristle cleared up, and with it that of our life? It is the question, to the exclusion of every other interest" (*Correspondence,* pp. 511–512).

Not only the praise of wildness in "Spring," but all Thoreau's bragging of his closeness to nature is extravagant, a purposeful exaggeration of the impulse toward involvement. The frenetic tone of "No yard!" betrays the uneasiness of the attitude underlying it; Thoreau does not hold permanently to the posture of aggressiveness—sucking out the marrow of life—that he assumes in "Where I Lived and What I Lived For"; and even the mood of "Spring," lovely as it is, is too intense to be sustained. One cannot for long be so deeply in touch with the earth's circulation, nor can one ramble endlessly "into higher and higher grass" (*Walden,* p. 319).

We may expect, then, that Thoreau will also feel impelled to detach himself from nature in *Walden.* In "Higher Laws" the swing back and forth between involvement and detachment is violent and obvious. Elsewhere the conflict is indicated more subtly. I discern in a bit of stream-of-consciousness from the Hermit's meditation in "Brute Neighbors" (a strange conglomerate of Thoreau's diverse attitudes in *Walden*) a pattern of withdrawal from nature much like that in "The Thaw." The Hermit has been recalling how overcomplicated a farmer's life is; and in his enthusiasm for a simpler life he thinks of making his home still deeper in the woods. "Better not keep a house. Say, some hollow tree; and then for morning calls and dinner-parties! Only a woodpecker tapping. O, they swarm; the sun is too warm there; they are born too far into life for me" (*Walden,* p. 223). For a sentence the Hermit imagines himself happily as living like a beast in a tree, a part of nature, with only a woodpecker for a neighbor. Then his attention seems to be caught by swarming flies or insects. "They are born too far into life for me" means, I think, that the insects belong to a different world, a nature from which the Hermit feels excluded. They swarm in the sun; he keeps to his musings in the shade of his house.

In "Solitude" also, with a larger rhythm, Thoreau moves toward nature but then withdraws. "Solitude" is an essay on Thoreau's relation to nature as to a friend. It begins:

This is a delicious evening, when the whole body is one sense, and imbibes delight through every pore. I go and come with a strange liberty in Nature, a part of herself. As I walk along the stony shore of the pond in my shirt-sleeves, though it is cool as well as cloudy and windy, and I see nothing special to attract me, all the elements are unusually congenial to me. The bullfrogs trump to usher in the night, and the note of the whippoorwill is borne on the rippling wind from over the water. Sympathy with the fluttering alder and poplar leaves almost takes away my breath; yet, like the lake, my serenity is rippled but not ruffled. [*Walden*, p. 129]

For the moment Thoreau is wholly involved in nature. He is un-usually receptive, alive with all his senses, in the mood for a gen-erous interchange. As nature is "congenial," so he feels "sym-pathy" for it. Repeatedly in "Solitude" he stresses that nature gives him the companionship he needs in the woods. He experi-ences "sometimes that the most sweet and tender, the most inno-cent and encouraging society may be found in any natural object" (*Walden*, p. 131). He is sensible of "society . . . friend-liness . . . the presence of something kindred" emanating from a gentle rain (*Walden*, p. 132). Toward the end of the chapter his ardent wish for a reciprocal bond between man and nature reaches its highest pitch. He sees nature as bending to man in gestures of consolation.

The indescribable innocence and beneficence of Nature,—of sun and wind and rain, of summer and winter,—such health, such cheer, they afford forever! and such sympathy have they ever with our race, that all Nature would be affected, and the sun's bright-ness fade, and the winds would sigh humanely, and the clouds rain tears, and the woods shed their leaves and put on mourning in mid-summer, if any man should ever for a just cause grieve. Shall I not have intelligence with the earth? Am I not partly leaves and vege-table mould myself? [*Walden*, p. 138]

But this is an extravagant fantasy, the rhetorical expression of a theoretical hope. Who can tell when his moments of intelligence with the earth will arrive, or how he can use that part of himself that is nature?

All these pronouncements on Thoreau's friendship with nature are in the 1847 version of *Walden*. Thoreau seems to have later decided that the emphasis of "Solitude" was too extreme, for in a significant addition (presumably made in 1852)[7] he quietly

---

[7] See Shanley, p. 72, and *J*, IV, 291.

attempted to right the balance. First he suggests that we can be cheered in the wilderness by "our own thoughts" as well as by nature. Then he draws the consequence that our thoughts tend to separate us from nature. "With thinking we may be beside ourselves in a sane sense. . . . We are not wholly involved in Nature. I may be either the drift-wood in the stream, or Indra in the sky looking down on it" (*Walden,* pp. 134–135). This insistence on the mind's capacity for detachment is made only momentarily. It acts as a restraint on the mood, an indirect qualification of the main idea that nature and man are intimate friends. Thoreau juxtaposes his opposite view gingerly, so as not to cast doubt on the truthfulness of the main experience. It is true at times that he feels his body as one sense, that he goes and comes in nature with the freedom and ease of a natural creature. Nevertheless, the addition sets up a polarity within the chapter, complicates its mesage, and makes it truer to Thoreau's total experience.

This change Thoreau made in "Solitude" suggests that he tended to withdraw from his involvement in nature not only in particular moods like the Hermit's mood of withdrawal in the face of swarming flies in "Brute Neighbors," but also generally and increasingly in his whole life. There is other evidence that while he was writing *Walden* he reconsidered his moments of passionate commitment to *phusis,* recognizing that nature as growth did not in itself supply a framework adequate to all his experience, and perhaps suspecting that these moments were tinged with undisciplined eroticism. In *Walden,* as earlier, Thoreau would think of humans as belonging to nature in their resemblances to plants or beasts or even minerals. "What is man but a mass of thawing clay?" he asks as he looks at the railroad cut (*Walden,* p. 307). He is pleased that singing boys can sound like cows, or that he has his own "chuckle or suppressed warble" (*Walden,* p. 112), while he listens idly to the sparrow's trill. Yet, as he altered and amplified *Walden,* he portrayed himself less as a natural creature, more as a separated man. He deleted passages comparing men to plants that appear in the first version. The final text of one such comparison that Thoreau kept is a brief, crisp, Baconian metaphor to enliven a forthright assertion, while the first version is a self-intoxicated rhapsody on plant-like, natural men.

I do not value chiefly a man's uprightness and benevolence, which are, as it were, his stem and leaves. . . . I want the flower and fruit of a man; that some fragrance be wafted over from him to me, and some ripeness flavor our intercourse. [*Walden*, p. 77—final text of 1854]

So each man should take care to emit his fragrance, and perform some such office as hemlock boughs, and dried and healing herbs—I want the flower and fruit of a man—and that fragrance *as* of fresh spring life be wafted over from him to me . . .

He must serve another and a better use than any he can consciously render. We demand to discover at least some signs of life, some vegetation and putting forth of natural life in him. Some greenness, some flowering,—some ripeness.

. . . He must bring me the morning light untarnished, and the evening red undimmed—the hilarity of spring in his mirth —the summer's serenity in his joy —the autumnal ripeness in his wisdom —and the repose and abundance of winter in his silence. . . .

I would say to the anxious philanthropist—take up a little life into your pores—strike root and grow—endeavor to encourage the flow of sap in your veins—and help to clothe the human field with green.—If your branches wither strike your roots wider and deeper —send your fibres into every kingdom of nature for its contribution, and make the most of that greenness and life which the gods allot you. [1847 version][8]

Thoreau also deleted an account of a visit of natural men to his cabin, "healthy and sturdy working men, descending from sound bodies of men, and still transmitting arms and legs and bowels from remote generations to posterity."[9] It seems likely that he wished no longer to defer to such men, to whom he is so attracted

---

[8] Shanley, pp. 135, 136.
[9] *Ibid.*, p. 173.

at times in the *Week* and "Ktaadn," but to keep his distance from them. In his final characterization of Alec Therien, he has established a distance between himself and the Canadian wood-chopper that is at first absent. He has added such critical judgments as "In him the animal man chiefly was developed" (*Walden*, p. 146).[10] In the process of composition Thoreau has grown less anxious to write of himself as a part of nature, more intent on asserting his intelligent separateness.

iii

Thus, while Thoreau is intensely drawn to *phusis,* he feels at the same time that wild, growing nature, the "wild heathen Nature of the forest" as Hawthorne has it,[11] is destructive of the conscious self; he is impelled on occasion to withdraw from it because it is dangerous to the intellectual and spiritual man in him. Thoreau is antinaturalist on suitable occasions in *Walden,* not only in that he separates himself from wild and bestial men, as in *The Maine Woods,* but also in that he tries to work free from the limitations of death-generating ordinary nature, as in the *Week.* True, the tendency to fly from nature in imagination is much more strictly controlled in *Walden* than in the *Week.* There are no mountains in the neighborhood of the pond where he can float in cloudland above the dismal earth. Repeatedly he would seem to hold down the imaginative idealist in himself, tying him to "the reality that surrounds us" (*Walden,* p. 97). At the opening of "The Pond in Winter," he tells how the idealist rose up in him one winter morning, only to be stifled.

I awoke with the impression that some question had been put to me, which I had been endeavoring in vain to answer in my sleep, as what—how—when—where? But there was dawning Nature, in whom all creatures live, looking in at my broad windows with serene

[10] Perhaps this critical comment on Therien was added because he turned out to have a weakness for strong drink. See Harding, *The Variorum Walden,* p. 289.

[11] Nathaniel Hawthorne, *The Scarlet Letter* (Columbus: Ohio State University Press, 1962), p. 203.

and satisfied face, and no question on *her* lips. I awoke to an an-
swered question, to Nature and daylight. [*Walden,* p. 282]

Thoreau "gets through with nature" in *Walden* only in "Conclusion." There he expresses his aspiration toward the ideal in one
metaphor of transcendence after another. It is as if the whole
book had been preparing for these "steep transitions." The
"strong and beautiful bug" emerges into winged life from the
applewood table; the staff of the artist of Kouroo expands before his astonished eyes "into the fairest of all the creations of
Brahma" (*Walden,* p. 327); Thoreau's experience at the Pond is
remembered not for itself alone, but as a vehicle for an ascent
into "the azure ether beyond" (*Walden,* p. 325). He emphasizes
persistently in this chapter the power of thought to transcend any
natural or social condition. But the ecstatic mood of "Conclusion" comes only after the experiment is over. In the body of
Walden, this mood is kept waiting in order that the imagination
may be more closely tied to nature.

Yet the idealist who would go beyond nature makes himself
subversively felt also in the narrative at the pond. He now appears in new guises, not as a starry-eyed hero impatient to soar
beyond the confines of prose or flesh, but, for example, as a
thoughtful hermit whimsically aware of the difficulties of thought
as well as of the limiting character of nature. This is Thoreau's
persona in the meditation in "Brute Neighbors." He adopts a
similarly cagy, if more humorous and restless persona in "The
Bean Field," a remarkable chapter in which various approaches
to nature are tried out and artfully combined. At the opening,
Thoreau's attitude toward his beans is ambiguous. He exposes
his "doubleness" in bemused self-mockery; he is both involved in
nature and apart from it.

Meanwhile my beans, the length of whose rows, added together,
was seven miles already planted, were impatient to be hoed, for the
earliest had grown considerably before the latest were in the ground;
indeed they were not easily to be put off. What was the meaning of

this so steady and self-respecting, this small Herculean labor, I knew not. I came to love my rows, my beans, though so many more than I wanted. They attached me to the earth, and so I got strength like Antaeus. But why should I raise them? Only Heaven knows. [*Walden,* p. 155]

Thoreau "loves" his beans; he is attached to his earth like Antaeus, for he needs the perseverance of a Hercules. Yet while the beans grow so inexorably, his attitude toward them changes flippantly. He is ready both to admire and to ridicule his stint as a farmer. He claims not to know what to do with all this growth, nor can he find a meaning for his labor. Throughout the chapter we are made to wonder what he really thinks of beans; and toward the end he suggests that he left them entirely in contemplative moods—they became a metaphor for a higher kind of husbandry. "I said to myself, I will not plant beans and corn with so much industry for another summer, but such seeds, if the seed is not lost, as sincerity, truth, simplicity, faith, innocence, and the like" (*Walden,* pp. 163–164).[12]

"The Bean Field" cannot be explained simply as a product of the conflict between Thoreau's wish to be close to nature and his wish to leave it, though this conflict is an important stimulus here as elsewhere. What moves and excites the reader is the extraordi-

---

[12] Thoreau's "labor" in "The Bean Field" will appear in broader perspective if we think of it in terms of Hannah Arendt's meditations on nature in *The Human Condition* (1958; rpt. New York: Anchor, 1959). Labor, she posits, is the interaction of man and his body with nature, a recurrent process that sustains life. Thoreau gets strength from this involvement, this rhythmical intercourse with nature. Yet at the same time he wishes to abandon it for what Miss Arendt calls "work" and "thought." Work, by which she means among other things the fabrication of works of art, *oeuvres, Werke,* is contrasted with labor as "the unnaturalness of human existence, which is not embedded in . . . the species' ever-recurring life cycle" (p. 9). ("Thought" might include Thoreau's contemplation of sincerity, truth, and so forth.) In Miss Arendt's terms Thoreau is both *animal laborans* and *homo faber:* he participates in nature while he hoes beans, and he formally structures his experience while away from nature by writing "The Bean Field"; his practice in balancing these two kinds of living is part of his general effort to balance himself with nature.

nary mixture of attitudes and tones in the chapter—the humorous contortions, the hectic variety. Behind all this seems to be an important intention of Thoreau's in *Walden,* his wish to exhibit the shifting play of his sensibility. As he stands over his beans he shows us one style and persona after another: he is by turns humorous, reminiscent, sentimental, satirical, and solemn. At the end of the first paragraph, for example, his role shifts repeatedly. He is describing his "day's work":

My auxiliaries are the dews and rains which water this dry soil, and what fertility is in the soil itself, which for the most part is lean and effete. My enemies are worms, cool days, and most of all woodchucks. The last have nibbled for me a quarter of an acre clean. But what right had I to oust johnswort and the rest, and break up their ancient herb garden? Soon, however, the remaining beans will be too tough for them, and go forward to meet new foes. [*Walden,* p. 155]

In the first sentence Thoreau is a peaceful and well-informed Yankee farmer. In the second, he becomes, half-seriously, an enemy to woodchucks, a farmer-predator who is destructive in his natural calling and knows nature "as a robber" (*Walden,* p. 166). In the fourth he stands back and comments critically on this farmer role, once more the contemplative lover of all growing things. And at the end he drops into a matter-of-fact account of the growth of his field. A similarly complex mixture of attitudes might be found elsewhere in the chapter—the rhetorical texture is typical.

This element of play is central in *Walden,* more than in the rest of Thoreau's work. Why does Thoreau choose so to maneuver? Partly, we may be sure, to enjoy himself. As Lowell remarked, Thoreau has the instincts of a mannerist:[13] he enjoys puns and paradoxes and has a penchant for incessant intelligent qualification. But he is also playful in *Walden* for serious, delibe-

---

[13] James Russell Lowell, *Prose Works* (Boston: Houghton Mifflin, 1899), I, 371–372.

rate, related reasons. First, he would avoid the occasional solipsistic intemperateness of the *Week;* he carefully manipulates his
audience even in moments of exaggeration and speaks knowingly
and whimsically to them, not just to himself. Second, his maneuvering is part of the general attempt to reconcile the needs of
the natural man and those of the conscious man by shifting
back and forth between them. Thoreau would be like Antaeus,
and also like Apollo. Third—and this leads to a new problem—
Thoreau is practicing a strategy central to much of *Walden,* the
strategy of active uncommitment.

iv

In one of his self-portraits—this one appears early, in "Economy"—Thoreau sees himself as a Salem merchant, enormously
busy at a host of tasks necessary for his trade with the Celestial
Empire.

To oversee all the details yourself in person; to be at once pilot and
captain, and owner and underwriter; to buy and sell and keep the
accounts; to read every letter received, and write or read every
letter sent; to superintend the discharge of imports night and day;
to be upon many parts of the coast almost at the same time;—often
the richest freight will be discharged upon a Jersey shore;—to be
your own telegraph, unweariedly sweeping the horizon, speaking all
passing vessels bound coastwise. . . . It is a labor to task the faculties of a man. [*Walden,* pp. 20–21]

The merchant is a surrogate for Thoreau in numerous ways—he
is a self-reliant cultural nationalist (he carries "purely native
products . . . always in native bottoms") and an assiduous student of the requirements of his profession as poet and naturalist[14]
—but I would call attention not so much to his "business" as to
the rapid and urgent style with which he accomplishes it. The
merchant never stops moving. Nothing he does is to be lingered
over: He does not stay to be swallowed up in individual tasks,

[14] Sherman Paul, ed., *Walden and Civil Disobedience* (Boston: Riverside, 1960), p. 14, n. 1.

but moves adroitly to many different points on the shore. In other words, he is not committed to anything except his celestial trade; and he is very active. He is a prototype for what I will call Thoreau's *activity* in *Walden,* by which I mean his practice of continually changing roles, styles, and points of view to suit the occasion of the moment. It is the natural bent of Thoreau's mind to be so active, so volatile and capricious. But in *Walden,* for example in "The Bean Field," natural bent becomes technique, controlled and used for a philosophic purpose. Thoreau would show that a celestial life may be glimpsed and even possessed by a man aware, continually responsive, and always ready to abandon a tired idea for a fresh one.

An assumption behind Thoreau's activity is that no mood can be happily prolonged. He is thus unwilling to commit himself to any single attitude, vocation, or experience. "Only what is thought said or done at a certain rare coincidence is good" (*Walden,* p. 330). His view of compassion as only momentarily meaningful is of a piece with his sense of experience as valuable only temporarily. "Compassion is a very untenable ground. It must be expeditious. Its pleadings will not bear to be stereotyped" (*Walden,* p. 318). Similarly, in "The Bean Field" he prefers to view tending beans as the play of an artist, not as the labor of a farmer. "It was on the whole a rare amusement, which, continued too long, might have become a dissipation" (*Walden,* p. 162). He would say the same of his entire experience at Walden. Of his first summer there he writes, "my life itself was become my amusement and never ceased to be novel" (*Walden,* p. 112). In the advice he gives his laborer-readers on growing beans, he facetiously and earnestly suggests that they grow them only briefly. "But above all harvest as early as possible, if you would escape frosts and have a fair and saleable crop; you may save much loss by this means" (*Walden,* p. 163). Otherwise they will not have the freedom to respond as persons and friends. "Most men I do not meet at all, for they seem not to have time; they are busy about their beans" (*Walden,* p. 165).

Thoreau's method of polarity, used perhaps more consciously and more frequently in *Walden* then elsewhere, is likewise a form of his mental activity, a rhetorical device for displaying his nimbleness of mind and for avoiding commitment. The contrasting of opposites becomes an evident technique. As we know, the titles of chapters—"Reading" and "Sounds," "Solitude" and "Visitors," "Higher Laws" and "Brute Neighbors"—are set in contrasting pairs. "Sounds" follows "Reading" to show that men can learn not only from books but also from nature, from "the language which all things and events speak without metaphor, which alone is copious and standard" (*Walden,* p. 111). More subtly, Thoreau will open or close a chapter in a spirit of bemused contrariness. "Higher Laws" begin with his telling of his wish to devour a raw woodchuck, "Brute Neighbors" with the would-be-mystical meditation of a Hermit. (When the ethereally-minded Poet enters, the Hermit first mistakes him for a hound or a pig —he is the chapter's first "brute neighbor.") In some chapters the central argument or mood is established, only to be followed by qualifications. We have observed this device of construction in "Economy" and in "Solitude." Similarly, the burden of "The Pond in Winter" is that a man must have an exact knowledge of nature in order to keep his faith honest; lovely imaginings are no substitute for accuracy. Thus Thoreau criticizes the laziness and gullibility of his townsmen: "It is remarkable how long men will believe in the bottomlessness of a pond without taking the trouble to sound it" (*Walden,* p. 285). Yet at the end of this same paragraph, Thoreau turns to speak for the rights of the imagination: "This is a remarkable depth for so small an area; yet not an inch of it can be spared by the imagination. . . . I am thankful that this pond was made deep and pure for a symbol. While men believe in the infinite some ponds will be thought to be bottomless" (*Walden,* p. 287). Thoreau's juggling of polarities is by no means confined to his study of nature. For example, the play of attitudes he adopts toward railroads in "Sounds" is a conspicuous illustration of his facility in evading the march of events while keeping in touch with them.

The net effect of all his polarities is to display Thoreau's meditative and critical intelligence continually at work. By entertaining and then balancing different viewpoints, he may at first be restless and exaggerated in his sympathies, but prove himself finally judicious in his sense of proportion. His relation to nature will also be both fully represented and properly balanced.

Thoreau's doctrine of simplicity is, in one sense, a device for keeping up his activity. It is a doctrine of pleasure as well as of purity. In this sense, simplicity is a means not of denying oneself pleasure, but of insuring one's own perpetual amusement. His choice of simplicity as his personal style is an esthetic choice. He will not be encumbered with furniture: "My gay butterfly is entangled in a spider's web then" (*Walden,* p. 66). The butterfly, like the active Thoreau, is free, winged, joyful, colorful, and capricious. Thoreau's simplicity is the strategy of one irresponsible and uncommitted in a social and moral sense, responsible only to his trade with his celestial empire. Thoreau never regards an act of his as determining or final, except such necessary acts as eating through $8.74 (and this also he keeps simple). His flexibility detaches him from the ordinary run of men and gives him a sense of superiority. He runs mental circles around the responsible and propertied farmers of Concord:

In imagination I have bought all the farms in succession, for all were to be bought, and I knew their price. I walked over each farmer's premises, tasted his wild apples, discoursed on husbandry with him, took his farm at his price, . . . took every thing but a deed of it,—took his word for his deed, for I dearly love to talk . . . and withdrew when I had enjoyed it long enough, leaving him to carry it on. [*Walden,* p. 81]

Thus humorously the detached and uncommitted observer would collect the gains of his trade and, by refusing to be bound to any-

thing earthly, fashion a life and a style that is "more elastic, more
starry, more immortal" (*Walden*, p. 216).

In one sense Thoreau's activity is clearly antinatural: It de-
taches him from nature in that it frees him, at least while he
maneuvers, from the natural cycle of growth, decay, and death.
He will not be caught in such a cycle, like a mere bean-farmer,
or like those sailors whose chief business it is to transmit arms and
legs and bowels to posterity, or even like the Cape Cod natives
who watch with concern for the bodies of the drowned. (The
middle section of "The Shipwreck," we have seen, exhibits a
somewhat frantic stylistic activity as Thoreau maneuvers for position in the face of a terrible event.) Activity is in itself a means of
skirting protracted involvement of any sort, including involvement in nature. In part, it is a holding action against death and
a strategy for avoiding concern with death. This is Thoreau's
emphasis in one journal entry, where his striving for purity sounds
like a wish not to be buried alive, not to blend with the contami-
nating earth.

We must be very active if we would be clean and live our own
life, and not a languishing and scurvy one. The trees, which are stationary, are covered with parasites, especially those which have
grown slowly. The air is filled with the fine sporules of countless
mosses, algae, lichens, fungi, which settle and plant themselves on
all quiet surfaces. . . . And the sluggard is seen covered with
sphagnum. Algae take root in the corners of his eyes, and lichens
cover the bulbs of his fingers, . . . the lowest forms of vegetable
life. This is the definition of dirt. We fall a prey to others of nature's
tenants, who take possession of the unoccupied house. With the
utmost inward activity we have to wash and comb ourselves beside,
to get rid of the adhering seeds. [*J*, III, 245–246]

In *Walden*, Thoreau is always washing and combing himself, re-
vitalizing his style, shifting his approach, trying to avoid the
plague of sloth by inward activity and hectic urgency.

But only half the purpose of Thoreau's activity is to avoid the taint of death; the other half is, paradoxically, to keep in touch with nature, to be close to nature without being swallowed up in it. (Since so much of Thoreau's celestial trade is an effort to balance the advantages of involvement and detachment, this doubleness should not surprise us.) At least when his activity is under control, it allows him to maneuver continually between the poles of self and nature. He may thus come back and back to nature, see it from many perspectives, and gather together his diverse threads to make his variegated fabric. In another journal entry he resolves to write both actively and naturally. "Write often, write upon a thousand themes, rather than long at a time, not trying to turn too many feeble somersets in the air,—and so come down upon your head at last. Antaeus-like, be not long absent from the ground" (*J*, III, 107). Thoreau's total sense of nature is informed by "a thousand themes." He would not be fixedly involved in one phase of natural life, but successively involved in many.

The diversity of Thoreau's experience at Walden also leads to a diversity of approaches to nature. In a year at the pond, as distinguished from a two-week trip to Maine, he encounters nature in countless different ways. Nature appears by turns comforting and appalling, close and distant, animal and human, a source of sensuous richness and a collection of natural facts. Thus individual chapters in *Walden* are versions of particular facets of nature and man's relation to it. For example, in "Solitude" Thoreau treats nature emotionally as if it were a sympathetic friend; in "The Ponds" he both regards it affectionately and describes it factually; in "Brute Neighbors" he narrates what he knows of one part of his *kosmos,* the life of animals and insects around Walden Pond; in "The Pond in Winter" he scrutinizes nature like a practical-minded surveyor, debunking imagination while he measures what he sees in numbers. Many chapters end with meditations on nature, all distinctive, all offering distinct and even conflicting opinions. Thoreau's mind maneuvers to present diverse insights about nature, grasping each insight for a moment and passing on.

v

Thus far I have characterized the Thoreau of *Walden* as a circumspect guardian of his relation to nature. Though he tends here as earlier to lose himself in it, he checks this tendency, balancing the natural man with the intellectual in himself. Similarly, he is more cautious in his departures from nature than in his earlier work. The violent wishes to possess wild nature or to be lost in ecstatic transcendence remain; but they are ground in the mill of Thoreau's maturity. The temperateness of *Walden* is achieved not by relinquishing his passions and bents but by exercising them in combination, by balancing them against each other.

Yet to reduce *Walden* to a kaleidoscope of nature, or a compendium of attitudes toward it, is again false to the book's spirit. There is in that spirit not only nervous or cautious self-consciousness but also simple affection toward nature, and Thoreau keeps returning to this ground-tone of affection. We can think of *Walden* as providing a continual contrast between the style of activity —urgent, witty, qualifying, scintillating—and Thoreau's other basic style, that of the reverent lover of nature. Indeed, Thoreau's displays of self-consciousness and activity—his tough posturings before his neighbors, his scrupulous and various descriptions of his purpose—are written into *Walden* partly to set off his tenderness, to provide a defensive framework within which he can express tender feelings. Thus, in small, he begins "The Bean Field" with a virtuoso display of the zigzags of his mind, but relinquishes this style repeatedly in the course of the chapter to speak of his humility before nature, his recurrent sense that man with all his displays and mental trappings belongs organically to a growing *kosmos*. "The gentle rain which waters my beans and keeps me in the house to-day is not drear and melancholy, but good for me too. . . . If it should continue so long as to cause the seeds to rot in the ground and destroy the potatoes in the low lands, it would still be good for the grass on the uplands, and, being good for the grass, it would be good for me" (*Walden,* p. 131). He tries to see himself not as dominating his *kosmos,* but as realizing his proper place in it.

The pines still stand here older than I; or, if some have fallen, I have cooked my supper with their stumps, and a new growth is rising all around, preparing another aspect for new infant eyes. Almost the same johnswort springs from the same perennial root in this pasture, and even I have at length helped to clothe that fabulous landscape of my infant dreams, and one of the results of my presence and influence is seen in these bean leaves, corn blades, and potato vines. [*Walden,* p. 156]

He stands among the johnswort and the pines, a creature both natural and reflective among natural creations, a poetic intermediary between Concord and the wilderness. The chapter ends in a suggestion that the farmer's proper attitude is reverence for sun and earth and for all that they make grow, not a selfish enjoyment only of what he has made or taken for himself. "We are wont to forget that the sun looks on our cultivated fields and on the prairies and forests without distinction. . . . In his view the earth is all equally cultivated like a garden. Therefore we should receive the benefit of his light and heat with a corresponding trust and magnanimity" (*Walden,* p. 166). From its capricious-sounding beginnings the whole chapter has been working with great deftness toward this intelligent plea for reverent trust in nature.

It is in his descriptions of scenes by the pond that Thoreau's affectionate reverence for nature comes through most conspicuously: his account of bleaching the boards from James Collins's shanty, or of building a chimney in "Housewarming," or his imaginative observation of the pickerel of Walden in winter, or his evocations of spring. These are high points of the narrative, at which Thoreau has found his proper stance of detached sympathy; he observes the details around him with accuracy and with unhurried affection. He is following "the discipline of looking always at what is to be seen" (*Walden,* p. 111), but by so doing he does not eliminate himself from his descriptions—rather, feelings and imaginings emerge from facts without sharp breaks. The narrator meets nature as a Thou; he looks and is satisfied. Yet he is not swallowed or dissolved in nature; we feel his apartness. An example is Thoreau's picture of his house as it stood the first summer.

When first I took up my abode in the woods . . . my house was not finished for winter, but was merely a defence against the rain, without plastering or chimney, the walls being of rough weather-stained boards, with wide chinks, which made it cool at night. The upright white hewn studs and freshly planed door and window casings gave it a clean and airy look, especially in the morning, when its timbers were saturated with dew, so that I fancied that by noon some sweet gum would exude from them. To my imagination it retained throughout the day more or less of this auroral character, reminding me of a certain house on a mountain which I had visited a year before. This was an airy and unplastered cabin, fit to entertain a travelling god, and where a goddess might trail her garments. The winds which passed over my dwelling were such as sweep over the ridges of mountains, bearing the broken strains, or celestial parts only, of terrestrial music. The morning wind forever blows, the poem of creation is uninterrupted; but few are the ears that hear it. Olympus is but the outside of the earth every where. [*Walden,* pp. 84–85]

This passage emerges as a moment of calm in the polemical argument of "Where I Lived and What I Lived For." The house comes before us in loving detail. Thoreau tells us that he has made it, but kept it natural, and the studs still look like living trees to him. Yet it is not only a bare house, an assembling of boards, studs, doors, and chinks. After Thoreau has established in our minds a clear factual picture of something growing cleanly and simply, he surrounds his description with ideal suggestions.

Over his house he lets flow a musical and correspondent breeze that links Walden with mountains and with human myths of spirit in nature.

Another such description, more sparely factual but no less affectionate, is this of the sumach that grows near his house.

The sumach, *Rhus glabra,* grew luxuriantly about the house, pushing up through the embankment which I had made, and growing five or six feet the first season. . . . The large buds, suddenly pushing out late in the spring from dry sticks which had seemed to be dead, developed themselves as by magic into graceful green and tender boughs, an inch in diameter; and sometimes, as I sat at my window, so heedlessly did they grow and tax their weak joints, I heard a fresh and tender bough suddenly fall like a fan to the ground, when there was not a breath of air stirring, broken off by its own weight. In August, the large masses of berries, which, when in flower, had attracted many wild bees, gradually assumed their bright velvety crimson hue, and by their weight again bent down and broke the tender limbs. [*Walden,* p. 114]

The details are all evident to the reader's eyes and senses—buds, flowers, bees, the summer air, the sumach branches bending and breaking. The scene moves us specially because it displays nature in slow and beautiful circulation: sticks become tender boughs and then heavy branches that break and fall; flowers become masses of ripe red berries. The details are bound together by Thoreau's tactual and conceptual appreciation of growth, and by his sober affection for the body of nature. In both these descriptions, then, Thoreau does not regard objects he sees as isolated, but as integral parts in a living whole. Despite the variety and exactness of detail, nature is felt in them as one, one process of growth and fruition, one accumulation of facts in a *kosmos,* and one morning wind or spirit blowing through the whole.

These descriptions represent moments of stasis, still points. Briefly the observer stands opposite nature, faithfully recording what he sees. I would say here of Thoreau what Elizabeth M. Wilkinson says of Goethe in his nature poetry, that he is "actively submissive" to the scene before him. "His heart and mind submit themselves to the objects of the outer world, to know them as they are and to be transmuted by them."[15] Nevertheless, such descriptions last only for moments in *Walden*. Inevitably they lead to other styles, polemical, skeptical, humorous, or extravagant. And Thoreau has a pronounced sense that moments of reverence in nature are transient. When he tells in "Economy" of the life he has wished to lead, he describes it as one of waiting and "hearkening," standing next to nature to learn its evanescent secret.

So many autumn, ay, and winter days, spent outside the town, trying to hear what was in the wind, to hear and carry it express! . . . At other times watching from the observatory of some cliff or tree, to telegraph any new arrival; or waiting at evening on the hill-tops for the sky to fall, that I might catch something, though I never caught much, and that, manna-wise, would dissolve again in the sun. [*Walden*, pp. 17–18]

A watcher and wanderer who lives in time cannot grasp nature all at once or permanently, but must catch what little manna he can at the moment. Nature is a mystery that Thoreau is "earnest to explore," but one that he requires to be "mysterious and unexplorable" (*Walden*, p. 317). One symbol of what he would know and yet keep unknowable in nature is the disappearing loon. He never catches up with it, for he is irrevocably separated from the wildness that it represents. And this separation remains the cardinal dramatic fact of his experience. But his pains in following the loon, as in following the fox in the "Natural History," are their own reward. As Christof Tobler, Goethe's Swiss protégé, puts it in "Die Natur": "The more you win from [Nature] the better she likes it";[16] the more you attend to this mystifying goddess, the greater will be your sense of her joy and kindness.

[15] Wilkinson and Willoughby, *Goethe: Poet and Thinker,* p. 27.
[16] Goethe, *Gedenkausgabe,* XVI, 922. Tobler's prose poem, one of the most illustrious celebrations of nature in German literature, was long thought to be by Goethe. It is still included in editions of Goethe's works.

The "variety and capacity," the "vastness and mystery"[17] of nature justify the variety of approaches to it in *Walden*. Different chapters are transient approximations of "what was in the wind." Thoreau is constantly changing perspective in order to get better in position. In a passage in "Baker Farm" taken from the 1845 journal at the pond, he urges himself on to an unremitting search for new impressions as he begins this new life and work, tells himself to "fish and hunt far and wide," to "rise free from care before the dawn and seek adventures" (*Walden*, p. 207). Yet, in contrast to his other excursions, his wandering in *Walden* has a home base, a cabin to which he continually returns for self-appraisal and self-renewal. His own voyaging is imagined not as the dissipation of a restless traveler but as a circling round a center, the centered activity of a student of nature and the soul.

Circles—the cycle of the year, the movements of birds and animals, and so on—are symbolic in *Walden* of the health and ordered beauty of nature.[18] Thoreau's method of living and combining with nature, his own natural pattern of existence, can be thought of as a form of "circling." *Walden* suggests that one can know nature only by repeated visits to it and repeated returns to oneself to make sense of what one has seen. One "circles" it, then, as one walks about in it, examines it from one perspective here and another there, waits alone and wanders through the woods, lolls in the sun and works at beans, dreams and observes. In a whimsical metaphor for his "method of nature," Thoreau tells how he would not buy a farm, but would walk round it. "I think I shall not buy greedily, but go round and round it as long as I live, and be buried in it first, that it may please me the more at last" (*Walden*, p. 84). Buying a farm would spoil the perpetual

[17] "Variety and capacity" is from "Sounds," *Walden*, p. 124. It replaces "vastness and mystery," which appears in the first version of *Walden* (Shanley, p. 163).

[18] For a detailed study of circle images in *Walden*, see Anderson, *The Magic Circle of Walden*, ch. vii.

enjoyment of looking at it. He is better off in a cabin he has built himself, where his business is to be free and contemplative. In Thoreau's life as a circling poet, he strives for a continual deepening of feeling, a steady accommodation of the wayward and separated mind to nature. His manifold activity as a lover of nature is thus focused at last on one end. As we read *Walden* something similar happens to us. Our own feeling for nature deepens as we register facts, savor descriptions, share Thoreau's many perspectives, and appreciate one valuable moment after another.

vi

Reverence for nature and cautious maneuvering around it, involvement and detachment, wandering and meditation—all these attitudes and approaches are found in "The Ponds," a chapter that is the delicate center of *Walden*. When Thoreau writes in "Where I Lived and What I Lived For" of his going to the woods, or in "Conclusion" of his returning to the world, he defends his style of life and his right to his vision in active rhetoric; but in "The Ponds" he has dropped his obvious defenses. "The Ponds" lies hidden, as it were, between the bristling gates of the first and last chapters. So protected, Thoreau can write without irony of the ideal nature, the precarious combination he envisions. Walden Pond is likewise the center of nature for Thoreau, the center of the area round which he wanders. He "circles" it and keeps returning to it, continually renewing his knowledge of its detail and deepening his feeling for its mystery.[19]

[19] Thoreau's circling the mystery of the pond resembles the act of a sensitive reader, listener, or viewer who catches over and over at the spirit of a work of art by repeated initiations. Both art and nature lovers thereby enter what German critics such as Dilthey, Heidegger, and Staiger have called "the circle of interpretation," or "the hermeneutic circle." Upon entering the circle, the critic discovers repeatedly his sense of the whole from his feeling for the particular, and conversely his appreciation of particulars from his memory of the whole. See Emil Staiger, *Die Zeit als Einbildungskraft des Dichters* (Zurich: Niehans, 1939), pp. 18–20; and

"The Ponds" is also the fullest example of harmonious romantic combination in *Walden.* That is, Thoreau seeks here what he
sought earlier in the "natural Sabbath" episode in the *Week,* to
reconcile his desire to set himself above nature as a man of mind
with his desire to be wholly involved in nature. We have seen
how, in various ways, these two desires work against each other
in "Solitude," "Higher Laws," and "The Bean Field." In "The
Ponds" this polarity appears as a question of knowledge: what
should a man know, the external world that he apprehends immediately with his senses, or the glimmerings of transcendent
truth, or how may he know them both? Two ways of answering
the question are given in two familiar passages from "Where I
Lived and What I Lived For"—which I think are in a planned
polarity with each other and are meant to be opposed and compared. On the one hand, Thoreau would live in the present, investigate the facts of the world around him.

In eternity there is indeed something true and sublime. But all
these times and places and occasions are now and here. God himself culminates in the present moment, and will never be more
divine in the lapse of all the ages. And we are enabled to apprehend at all what is sublime and noble only by the perpetual instilling
and drenching of the reality which surrounds us. [*Walden,* p. 97]

On the other hand he would dream his way humbly toward
knowledge of the mystery behind the facts, trying, in imitation of
Wordsworth, to recover a child's visionary knowledge of that
mystery.

Time is but the stream I go a-fishing in. I drink at it; but while I
drink I see the sandy bottom and detect how shallow it is. Its thin
current slides away, but eternity remains. I would drink deeper; fish
in the sky, whose bottom is pebbly with stars. I cannot count one. I
know not the first letter of the alphabet. I have always been re-
gretting that I was not as wise as the day I was born. [*Walden,* p. 98]

Alexander Gelley, "Staiger, Heidegger, and the Task of Criticism," *Modern Language Quarterly,* 23 (1962), 195–216.

Both these approaches, of "drenching" oneself in "reality" (immersion in nature) and of "fishing in the sky" (searching in the ideal), are combined in "The Ponds." The natural mystery of Walden Pond has ideal elements. As Thoreau conceives it, it is both a symbol of purity and a place in nature; and neither its ideal value nor its natural reality is sacrificed in his descriptions; both are held in uncanny balance. "Walden is blue at one time and green at another, even from the same point of view. Lying between the earth and the heavens, it partakes of the color of both" (*Walden,* p. 176). These are topic sentences for "The Ponds." Walden partakes of the color and character of both earth and heaven. It has an affinity with Thoreau himself, who would combine the green of the earth and the blue of the heavens (we remember the colors of his boat from the *Week*) and who feels linked to both.

In almost every description of the pond, Thoreau takes care to suggest its double character. For example:

Sometimes, after staying in a village parlor till the family had all retired, I have returned to the woods, and, partly with a view to the next day's dinner, spent the hours of midnight fishing from a boat by moonlight, serenaded by owls and foxes, . . . surrounded sometimes by thousands of small perch and shiners, dimpling the surface with their tails in the moonlight, and communicating by a long flaxen line with mysterious nocturnal fishes which had their dwelling forty feet below, or sometimes dragging sixty feet of line about the pond as I drifted in the gentle night breeze, now and then feeling a slight vibration along it. . . . At length you slowly raise, pulling hand over hand, some horned pout squeaking and squirming to the upper air. It was very queer, especially in dark nights, when your thoughts had wandered to vast and cosmogonal themes in other spheres, to feel this faint jerk, which came to interrupt your dreams and link you to Nature again. It seemed as if I might next cast my line upward into the air, as well as downward into this element which was scarcely more dense. Thus I caught two fishes as it were with one hook. [*Walden,* pp. 174–175]

The passage is crammed with natural details, yet these are embedded in an ideal atmosphere. Nature is here in its wildness and multiplicity: the owl and the fox, the "thousands of small perch and shiners, dimpling the surface with their tails in the moonlight." In this last phrase Thoreau looks simply and joyfully at a natural event, and shows again that sensuous empathy with living creatures familiar to us from "Surely joy is the condition of life." Opposite this evident nature Thoreau portrays himself in a contemplative state of mind, dreaming, drifting, and wandering in his thought, communicating with a nocturnal mystery. In this example of combination he will join subject and object, mystical suggestion and natural detail, meditation and sensation in the rendering of one experience, will "catch two fishes with one hook."

Thoreau has taken pains to present this memory not only as a well-structured combination of the ideal and the natural, but also as a particular experience. He does not wish us to think this is an indefinite literary landscape, an imaginary garden; these things have happened when he came home from village parlors to fish for his dinner. Thus in his effort to touch reality he will again combine with nature; his poetry will be of the actual. The symbol he has chosen as a link with nature, the horned pout squeaking and squirming, is tactually so arresting that the reader also is jerked out of the dreamy atmosphere to which Thoreau has wafted him and made to recognize a natural presence. Thoreau would persuade us even of the illusion that his "fishing in the sky" here is a plausible part of his sense experience. The air is virtually as dense as the water, he suggests, and it might conceivably hold the hook that the sky-fisher casts aloft in it.

The tendency for one who aspires to romantic illumination, we have seen, is to neglect the natural and objective for the ideal and celestial; having discovered that Walden is a symbol, Thoreau might wish to dwell exclusively on its symbolic perfection. But in "The Ponds," Thoreau resists any impulse to move from "the nostalgia for the object" to the nostalgia for the beyond; he insists on feeling both, in equilibrium. A wholly idealist treatment of the pond would view it as a pure formal idea, without a bottom, a weed, a fish, or an irregularity (for the irregular is the natural). Such an idea of purity is in Thoreau's mind as he remembers Walden, but so is his memory of its sensuous reality. As he contemplates it, we may observe him offering himself the pure idealist's option, but then repeatedly refusing it, as with an informed smile, quietly insisting on the necessity of the natural in a valid description.

Some think it is bottomless. It is nowhere muddy, and a casual observer would say that there were no weeds at all in it; . . . a closer scrutiny . . . detect[s] . . . only a few small heart-leaves and potamogetons, and perhaps a water target or two; . . . and these plants are clean and bright like the element they grow in. The stones extend a rod or two into the water, and then the bottom is pure sand, except in the deepest parts, where there is usually a little sediment, probably from the decay of leaves which have been wafted on to it so many successive falls, and a bright green weed is brought up on anchors even in mid-winter. [*Walden,* pp. 178–179]

Let us read a bit between the lines: "Some think it is bottomless" (the readers of *Walden* know better); "a casual observer would say that there were no weeds at all in it" (Thoreau is no *casual* observer); "the bottom is pure sand, except in the deepest parts, where there is usually a little sediment . . . " (an important exception, for in that sediment grows the "bright green weed," the symbol of the pond's perennial naturalness). Thoreau is subtly correcting the tendency to see the pond only as an idea. This tendency is superficial; the observer who sees no weeds in the pond has not lived with it long enough or looked at it honestly. Yet Thoreau's corrections are not made in such a way as to efface or change the symbolic sketch of a perfect pond that he has planted in our minds. Idea and fact are so neatly joined that each remains valid. The pond is timeless in fancy as it is pure and bottomless; yet it exists emphatically in time, for leaves fall on it each year, decay, and make the earth in which a green weed may germinate. In turn the weed is itself the more beautiful because it has been transformed by the pure and bright water, and because it stands in relief against the pure sand.

Thoreau has placed the beauty of purity alongside the beauty of growth in the pond, but has so subtly managed the juxtaposition that no conflict is felt between them. Twice again in the chapter he manages the same juxtaposition, so that we may regard it as a controlled rhetorical maneuver, a method of presenting his conviction that purity and nature properly belong together. In the first instance he is speaking of the pond's smoothness.

If . . . you survey its surface critically, it is literally as smooth as glass, except where the skater insects, at equal intervals scattered over its whole extent, by their motions in the sun produce the finest imaginable sparkle on it, or, perchance, a duck plumes itself, or, as I have said, a swallow skims so low as to touch it. It may be that in the distance a fish describes an arc of three or four feet in the air, and there is one bright flash where it emerges, and another where it strikes the water; sometimes the whole silvery arc is revealed; or here and there, perhaps, is a thistle-down floating on its surface, which the fishes dart at and so dimple it again. It is like molten glass cooled but not congealed, and the few notes in it are pure and beautiful like the imperfections in glass. [*Walden*, pp. 186–187]

The pond is as smooth as glass, *except* for the skater insects, the ducks, the swallows, and the fish, who jump and dart in it. But Thoreau is so complacently assured in his management of narrative and tone, and he has us so confidentially under control, that he makes us see the water both as ideally calm and as sparkling with natural life.

Later in the chapter Thoreau informs us that in November there is usually "absolutely nothing to ripple the surface" (*Walden*, p. 189). One November day, however, when the pond was "remarkably smooth," he noticed "a faint glimmer" and, "paddling gently" to investigate, found himself

surrounded by myriads of small perch, about five inches long, of a
rich bronze color in the green water, sporting there and constantly
rising to the surface and dimpling it, sometimes leaving bubbles on
it. In such transparent and seemingly bottomless water, reflecting
the clouds, I seemed to be floating through the air as in a balloon,
and their swimming impressed me as a kind of flight or hovering.
. . . There were many such schools in the pond, apparently im-
proving the short season before winter would draw an icy shutter
over their broad skylight. . . . At length the wind rose, the mist
increased, and the waves began to run, and the perch leaped much
higher than before, half out of water, a hundred black points, three
inches long at once above the surface. [*Walden,* pp. 189–190]

Gently Thoreau passes from wonder at the purity of the pond to
delight at the life of the fish, yet neither is lost in the other. The
fish are emphatically natural: There are *many* schools, *hundreds*
of leaping black points, "myriads of small perch . . . of a rich
bronze color in the green water"—all the color and multiplicity
that the lover of *phusis* requires. But the fish are at the same time
images of contemplation: they are first a faint glimmer noticed
and caught by the seeker after nature; then when he closes on
them they seem to hover about him as he floats in thought. At
the end of the passage the tension between calm and motion is
for a moment dispelled, and we enjoy simply the abundance of
nature in circulation.

Thoreau has been careful in these passages to show that the
pond exists in time—he marks dates and notices signs of growth
and decay. The purity of the pond consists with its change: "It is
a mirror . . . whose gilding Nature continually repairs"; its
surface is "ever fresh" (*Walden,* p. 188). It thus enjoys a circulating, changing life without being subject to death. Thoreau
would see it mythically as a Golden Age Pond, yet not fixed in a
legend, but sensuously alive in the present. He reworks the myth:

Perhaps on that spring morning when Adam and Eve were driven
out of Eden Walden Pond was already in existence, and even then

breaking up in a gentle spring rain accompanied with mist and a southerly wind, and covered with myriads of ducks and geese, which had not heard of the fall, when still such pure lakes sufficed them. Even then it had commenced to rise and fall, and had clarified its waters and colored them of the hue they now wear, and obtained a patent of heaven to be the only Walden Pond in the world and distiller of celestial dews. [*Walden*, p. 179]

The boldness of Thoreau's imaginative speculation lies in his giving Eden a wild, American setting. Mind in the form of myth, legend, and European heritage is grafted on nature, as earlier by the Billerica hillside or on the top of Katahdin. Walden needs the myth, that it may be imaginatively enhanced, but the myth also needs Walden, that it may have contemporary relevance. The new setting, moreover, is not static or remote like a conventional image of Eden, but full of joyful change. Walden is Thoreau's example of unfallen nature, but it keeps its innocence only by perpetually renewing itself. It periodically moves, rises, and falls, and is covered with live ducks and geese every spring. The fancy is thus one of combination: myth is combined with fact and the idea of eternal innocence with nature ever in flux. We gladly accept the fiction of an American Eden because Thoreau has been effecting such combinations throughout the chapter; his romantic naturalist approach is so consistent as to have the force of persuasion.

It is the logical result of this effort of combination that Thoreau would see himself as combined or even identified with the pond. It too is "like a hermit in the woods" (*Walden*, p. 194). As he comes to the end of his meditation on Walden, he looks at it ("earth's eye," he calls it earlier) and sees himself in it. He has been thinking of God's creation of the pond:

He rounded this water with his hand, deepened and clarified it in his thought, and in his will bequeathed it to Concord. I see by its face that it is visited by the same reflection; and I can almost say, Walden, is it you?

It is no dream of mine,
To ornament a line;
I cannot come nearer to God and Heaven
Than I live to Walden even.
I am its stony shore,
And the breeze that passes o'er;
In the hollow of my hand
Are its water and its sand,
And its deepest resort
Lies high in my thought. [*Walden,* p. 193][20]

In the moment that is the poem, Thoreau denies his separation from nature. In imagination he partakes of a childlike oneness with it. The mood of the poem is one of thoughtful tenderness. The poet chooses to be simple (without ornament) in order to be at one with the pond, and this choice ushers in a flow of affection that informs his beautifully simple lines. He feels a specific affection for natural things, for the breeze and the stony shore. But he does not deny his vision of the ideal in this imagined merging, this self-naturalizing. On the contrary, the depth of the pond corresponds perfectly to the height of his thought—both poet and his symbolic brother are perfectly ideal and natural. The poem is an extreme statement of the possibility of correspondence and a momentary denial of the idea that man's consciousness divides him from nature. Yet this very extremeness of mood and thought means that he cannot keep it up; he has reached for a final combination with nature in the chapter, but one that is necessarily precarious, that will be subsumed in the restless activity of the mind. In "The Thaw" and "I am the autumnal sun" he also wrote briefly of feeling a similar oneness. Yet in the first poem he granted that his function was not to merge with nature but to stand next to it sympathetically, and before the second he explained that he felt the oneness only at

[20] *The Writings of Henry David Thoreau,* ed. J. Lyndon Shanley (copyright © 1971 by Princeton University Press); reprinted by permission of Princeton University Press.

times. In "The Ponds" also the prose that precedes the poem is more cautious and mental, less open and sweetly sensuous. Thoreau has his wits about him (at such a sober moment he still puns on "reflection"). He can "almost" say that the pond and he are one; yet in this "almost" he reveals his own aware detachment.

Nevertheless, the poem only exaggerates the sense of human harmony with nature felt throughout the section on Walden Pond. Thoreau cannot literally blend with the pond; but by circling it, by coming back and back to it in a receptive frame of mind, he may learn repeatedly to feel close to it, and may renew that original communication that must be renewed again and again if it is to be a permanent possession and a source of health. Shortly before the poem, he tells of one of these returns to nature: "It struck me again to-night, as if I had not seen it almost daily for more than twenty years,—Why, here is Walden, the same woodland lake that I discovered so many years ago; . . . it is the same liquid joy and happiness to itself and its Maker, ay, and it *may* be to me" (*Walden*, p. 193). In other words, Thoreau must make an effort of will, requiring sensitivity and humility, in order to renew his acquaintance with the pond. Like all romantics he is separate, but he *may* be intimate if he so wills.

Soon after the poem, Thoreau turns to write matter-of-fact descriptions of Flint and Goose Ponds, which are meant in their unadorned naturalness to balance the artful and moving treatment of Walden. Then he comes back briefly to his center of affection, his symbol of ideal nature. Walden and White Ponds are "Lakes of Light" (*Walden,* p. 199), illuminations on the earth's surface, links between earth and heaven. Yet this is not Thoreau's final word. The very end of the chapter twists and alters its total meaning and qualifies the very idea of combination. The ponds

are too pure to have a market value; they contain no muck. How much more beautiful than our lives, how much more transparent than our characters, are they! . . . Nature has no human inhabitant who appreciates her. The birds with their plumage and their notes are in harmony with the flowers, but what youth or maiden conspires with the wild luxuriant beauty of Nature? She flourishes most alone, far from the towns where they reside. Talk of heaven! ye disgrace earth. [*Walden,* pp. 199–200]

While Thoreau's whole narrative in "The Ponds" demonstrates how intimately he has lived with Walden, while his main view is therefore that man and nature can live in friendship, he chooses to end by stating an opposite view. Men will not, and also do not, conspire with nature. Though his last words call for an end to the disgrace of separation, he does not indicate much hope that his listeners will answer his call; for such are the difficulties of this conspiring that no human inhabitant appreciates nature; thus all men, including himself, remain more or less detached and out of touch.

Thus even "The Ponds" is polarized, even here Thoreau draws away from his delicately ordered intimacy. Ultimately, Thoreau has too many moods of mind to remain committed to any one perspective on nature, however comprehensive. The pond is only a beautiful feature of nature, not the whole of it. Thoreau, who is presenting nature in its many aspects, will not tax the reader's credulity by dwelling too long on the pure, deathless pond, removing it from its plainer and earthier surroundings. He does not bind himself to a joy, but presents his intuition of eternal nature suggestively and then moves on.

~ 8

Thoreau's Last Nature Essays

In his last years Thoreau did not falter in his ambitions. He seems to have planned elaborate books on the history of the Indian and on the natural history of Concord and its surroundings, as well as other works. The journals for this later period are voluminous and very detailed, indicating the assiduousness of his preparations. "The scale on which his studies proceeded was so large as to require longevity," as Emerson said in his Graveside Address.[1] But regardless of what Thoreau might have achieved in celebrating and revealing nature and the natural to America, he actually published or left ready for publication only a small group of writings on nature after 1855, when "The Shipwreck" and the three chapters following it in *Cape Cod* appeared: the last two parts of *The Maine Woods*, the rest of *Cape Cod*, and four essays: "Walking," "Wild Apples," "The Succession of Forest Trees," and "Autumnal Tints," all published in 1860 and 1862.[2] Whereas the later journals and travel writings are not dialectical in argument or style, the essays are; thus they are susceptible to

---

[1] Emerson, *Works*, X, 484.

[2] "Walking" was first delivered as a lecture in 1851, but it was revised before being published in the *Atlantic* in June, 1862. "Wild Apples" was delivered in Concord on February 8, 1860, and published in November, 1862, in the *Atlantic*. "The Succession of Forest Trees" was delivered in Concord in September, 1860, and published in the *New York Tribune* for October 6, 1860. "Autumnal Tints" was delivered in Worcester in 1859 and published in October, 1862, also in the *Atlantic*.

the approach adopted in this book. The most finished of his later writings, they show him still maneuvering to convey a multiple perspective on nature in order that he may express his subtly peaceful public attitude toward it.

In imitation of Thoreau in *Walden,* I have as a reader been repeatedly recognizing and "circling" his changing but constant relation with nature; I have shown that he keeps finding his desired balance, as in the fox episode, the natural Sabbath, and "The Ponds." In the last essays Thoreau consistently presents nature as a familiar ally, no longer as a problem. The essays are marked by a partial renunciation of extreme desire, and thus by a partial simplification of the public self Thoreau projects. This Thoreau is no longer erratically impatient with nature: he assumes a proper balance. On the one hand, he presents himself as a poetic observer who is clearly and distinctly human. In "Walking" the speaker still entertains the thought of merging with nature, but this merging is understood only as a means toward the end of imagining a fuller humanity. In the other essays the fantasy of wholly naturalizing the self plays no important role. On the other hand, he does not in any of the essays suggest a doubt as to whether a poetic relation with nature is possible. The top of Katahdin and the seashore laden with carcasses are happily "forgotten" by this point. The struggle against disconnection appears easier. The three essays that seem clearly to have been put together after *Walden,* "Wild Apples," "The Succession of Forest Trees," and "Autumnal Tints," are among the most serene and the least restless of Thoreau's writings. They are parts of a projected "Kalendar" of the area in which he lived, walked, and wrote, a greatly expanded "Natural History of Massachusetts," a portrait of his *kosmos* after a lifetime's study of it.[3] "Walking" is a reworking of a lecture Thoreau gave several times in the early 1850's, and as such it has both an occasional tone of bumptious bragging and an occasional reaching out for intense epiph-

[3] See Paul, *The Shores of America,* pp. 399–400.

any absent from the other essays. But it is still an essay completed in Thoreau's last years, and it too records and commends his protracted experience in a familiar nature. Thus, if earlier I have made much of episodes in Thoreau's writing in which his relation with nature is threatened, here I attempt to give a balance to my reading of him by calling attention to these affectionate essays.

The four last essays were worked over and completed during the same period, and the epistemology or method of perceiving nature implicit in all of them is much the same. Each essay is spoken by a man of unique information and experience, a walker or saunterer or wanderer in a landscape at once familiar (it is Concord) and strange (it is, in the language of "Walking," a "sainte terre," a wild and holy land). As in *Walden*, but with still more profession of authority, Thoreau presents himself in these essays as a teacher and an initiate in the art of seeing and studying nature. It can only be properly seen, tasted, "cultivated," or "improved" by the man who is in a ripe frame of mind for it. "Of course no flavors [of the local wild apples] are thrown away; they are intended for the taste that is up to them" (*W*, V, 312). As the result of his long experience the walker loves his landscape and the living spirit he perceives in it. Common to all the essays is a quiet, affectionate joy in the Concord scene mingled with an anxious concern for it; it is threatened with destruction by money-grubbing developers. At the end of "Wild Apples" Thoreau shows his prophetic outrage at the folly of men and his anguish for the disappearing land by quoting directly and without comment or twist from the Bible—something he never does at such length elsewhere. It is as if only by such a direct appeal to the book his readers most reverence can he properly warn them. The last verses he quotes show that the land disappears because men fail to perceive it. It needs true saunterers to preserve it.

Be ye ashamed, O ye husbandmen; howl, O ye vine-dressers. . . .
The vine is dried up, and the fig tree languisheth; the pome-

granate tree, the palm tree also, and the apple tree, even all the trees of the field, are withered; because joy is withered away from the sons of men. [Joel 1:11–12—*W*, V, 322]

Because New Englanders have sterilized the joy out of their hearts and forgotten how to see, they are willing to clear away the wild apple trees and sterilize the land. The withered earth corresponds to the withered joy of ignorant men.

Though the essays have much in common, each contains its own special perspective toward nature; in each Thoreau develops an approach appropriate to his particular subject. In part he manages this by altering his persona from one essay to another. One of the skills Thoreau learns as a writer is to indicate his different perspectives with a clearer consciousness of voice. In an early essay like "A Walk to Wachusett," and even in "Ktaadn," changes in the speaker's persona happen on the page without Thoreau's seeming to prepare for them. In *Walden* and the later essays, by contrast, he creates a series of roles for himself and adjusts his voice to suit his adopted role. In this sense the "activity" of *Walden* also marks the later essays. In all of them Thoreau is a saunterer who must be up to what he sees and tastes, but in each case he is projected somewhat differently: an educated savage-saunterer in "Walking," a self-pleased curmudgeon-saunterer in "Wild Apples," a poet-saunterer in "Autumnal Tints," and a naturalist-saunterer in "The Succession of Forest Trees." Moreover, each essay in itself contains a variety of voices. The main role Thoreau takes in each essay has its appropriate voice, but when he shifts his emphasis his tone and his rhetorical strategy also alter. He has developed enough astuteness and calm as an artist so that the voices do not jar against each other with interesting uncontrol as they do in "A Walk to Wachusett," "The Shipwreck," and parts of the *Week;* but in the controlled texture the variety may still be heard.

Three of the essays, "Walking," "Autumnal Tints," and "The Succession of Forest Trees," also make different philosophical points about the relation between the observer and nature. More-over, each different perspective toward nature is accompanied by a different image of it; and Thoreau adopts a different style and persona—a different mode of imagination—to give life and meaning to each image. Once we understand these differences they seem extraordinary—we wonder again if Thoreau's thought is not too diverse to be meaningful—until we remember that it is a larger aim of his philosophical-meditative method to be so diverse and inclusive. His thinking about the relation with nature is variable as well as insistent, and each of his perspectives needs momentary emphasis and exaggeration if it is to play its part adequately in his total presentation of nature. Even when, as in these essays, he is carefully summarizing his experience rather than presenting it in a narrative of intense moments, he needs the method of programmed inconsistency.

"Wild Apples" seems in my framework to require no new commentary, but the other essays are more demanding in their shifting views. I will turn to them briefly before moving to a few concluding points about Thoreau.

ii

The image of nature Thoreau presents for the most part in "Walking" is similar to that in "Surely joy is the condition of life," "Concord River," the conclusion of "Ktaadn," and "Spring":

Here is this vast, savage, howling mother of ours, Nature, lying all around, with such beauty, and such affection for her children, as the leopard; and yet we are so early weaned from her breast to society, to that culture which is exclusively an interaction of man on man,—a sort of breeding in and in, which produces at most a merely English nobility, a civilization destined to have a speedy limit. [W, V, 237]

The brave reader is invited to participate in this wildness. True, even as the invitation is heartily offered, it is in the same breath whimsically qualified. Only Thoreau would combine the universal Mother Earth with nature-as-howling-wilderness with such insouciance. This familiar compound ghost lies around us in her beauty and affection; but we may well be wary of embracing her.

Thoreau's point is one we recognize from comparable sections of the rest of his writing: a life in nature as *phusis* is brave but difficult. One has to give up not only one's physical comfort, but also one's self-assurance as a safe and separated civilized individual in order to be a walker, one daily involved with nature. Yet in *this* interaction is health and preservation; whereas in isolated civility one goes crazy by four o'clock in the afternoon, or takes refuge in a "merely English" culture as a substitute for a true one. Thus Thoreau dares us to the embrace with the leopard-mother. Inevitably we are attached from birth to her, and we would do well to seek nourishment from her. The essays opens: "I wish to speak a word for Nature, for absolute freedom and wildness, as contrasted with a freedom and culture merely civil, —to regard man as an inhabitant, or a *part and parcel of Nature,* rather than a member of society" (*W,* V, 205). The phrase I have emphasized is repeated later by Thoreau. "I would have every man so much like a wild antelope, so much a *part and parcel of nature,* that his very person should thus sweetly advertise our senses of his presence, and remind us of those parts of nature which he most haunts" (*W,* V, 225–226).

I am reminded of a famous moment from Emerson's *Nature:* "I become a transparent eyeball; I am nothing; I see all; the currents of the Universal Being circulate through me; I am part or parcel of God."[4] If the echo is deliberate, as I believe it is, it is

---

[4] Emerson, *Works,* I, 10. Thoreau also echoes Emerson's ecstatic narrative, I think, in "The Ponds," where he self-consciously makes Walden Pond into a transparent eyeball. It is not in itself surprising that he describes the pond several times as "transparent." (See *Walden,* pp. 177, 189, and especially 199: "White Pond and Walden are great crystals on the surface of the earth, Lakes of Light. . . . How much more beautiful than our lives, how much more transparent than our characters, are they!") But I would link these passages to two others in which Thoreau seems to be alluding to Emerson. A lake like Walden, Thoreau writes,

one more indication of Thoreau's choosing to mark himself off from Emerson by asserting his brotherhood with wild men and by loudly proclaiming his allegiance to and involvement with nature. For Thoreau throughout his career, as for Emerson in *Nature,* the natural world is "the present expositor of the divine mind,"[5] a constantly and compellingly evident incarnation of God. In the 1850's Emerson seemed to Thoreau to be retreating from his original appeals. He seldom showed interest in the divine detail of nature. He had become less sanguine about human freedom. He wrote essays uncongenial to Thoreau with titles like "Fate" and "Culture." He had developed in an unpredictable way, while Thoreau was still working from the premises of *Nature.* Thus "Walking" is in part a declaration of independence in which Thoreau paradoxically proves his orthodoxy: he defies the world and sticks to his original naturalist-Emersonian faith.

Even the early Emerson touched the landscape remotely, while in "Walking" the later Thoreau is still sucking the marrow from it. This is no "bare common" the speaker saunters across, but a forest irregularly laced with pathways, deserted roads, and swamps. And in imagination Thoreau pushes beyond these local limits in order to make us appreciate by exaggeration his idea of wildness.

I believe in the forest, and in the meadow, and in the night in which the corn grows. We require an infusion of hemlock spruce or arbor-vitae in our tea. . . . The Hottentots eagerly devour the marrow of the koodoo and other antelopes raw, as a matter of

---

"is the landscape's most beautiful and expressive feature. It is earth's eye; looking into which the beholder measures the depth of his own nature" (p. 186). And of Walden itself, he reports, "One [Emerson] proposes that it be called 'God's Drop'" (p. 194). Evidently, the currents of Universal Being also circulate through it. The pond not only corresponds to our human capacity for purity and transparency, but it is also pure and transparent in itself as a natural object. Thus it has its own divinity, evident in its own nature. Thoreau is discreetly reconceiving Emerson's metaphor of the self as an eye to correct Emerson's tendency toward subjective idealism.

[5] Emerson, *Works,* I, 65.

course. Some of our northern Indians eat raw the marrow of the Artic reindeer, as well as various other parts, including the summits of the antlers, as long as they are soft. And herein, perchance, they have stolen a march on the cooks of Paris. . . . Give me a wildness whose glance no civilization can endure,—as if we lived on the marrow of koodoos devoured raw. [*W*, V, 225]

Thus we are provoked into an exasperated or bemused attention: we open our civilized ears and listen. But, though Thoreau certainly wants us to attend to these extreme statements, they are used in part as a device to make us curious as to what he will say next, and thus attentive to his entire range of thought on wildness. The speaker's interaction with wild nature in "Walking" turns out to be of several sorts: he expresses desires for numerous wild landscapes, and also for wild things beyond the landscape. He might be imagined to want the marrow of raw koodoos for his breakfast, *Hamlet* and the *Iliad* for his morning reading, a walk on the Old Marlborough Road after lunch, and the sight of the sunset before retiring. All these disparate activities are made to seem encounters with wildness. It is by management of the essayist's voice that Thoreau does it: the speaker he projects is so convincing in his engaging obstreperousness that we are willing to believe him capable of saying almost anything and still landing on his feet. The disparate ideas that he entertains will turn out in the end to be truly connected. Let us think on how.

The wild nature in which Thoreau participates is both his source of power and his theatre of possibility. Because it gives him power, he impresses us continually with the vitality inherent in all wildness. Because it gives him possibility, he keeps changing the meaning of wildness. He does this cleverly and casually, while more obviously he is insisting persuasively on his constant need to return to the wild springs of life. In so far as his concept of wildness is an amalgam of possible meanings, it is built up by means of a series of associations and analogies in which different items of the series color and qualify each other. For example, the wild is associated with the West of America, then with the southwestern reaches of Concord, and finally with the western sky at sunset. Each of these "Wests" corresponds to a different spiritual fact in Thoreau's mind. He conveys his desire for them all, without eclipsing his need for nature as a whole. This casually presented series also has its direction. As the essay proceeds, the speaker's attitude becomes surreptitiously more tolerant and inclusive, and his voice becomes quieter until it attains a final exalted serenity. All the thoughtful fustian of the first pages of "Walking" leads to Thoreau's beautiful recollection of a quiet sunset and to his anticipation of "a great awakening light" shining on a redeemed meadow.

By the end of "Walking," the West is thus felt to be not only an abundantly wild and fecund landscape, but also a place of inspiration for religion and literature. Though in the main body of the essay the east stands for spiritual light and the west for fruitfulness *("Ex Oriente lux; ex Occidente* FRUX," as Thoreau braggingly rhymes it—*W,* V, 221), in the closing paragraphs the source of light has been mysteriously transferred to the west, a light that now bathes the wanderers "in a golden flood," emanating from a sun that seems "like a gentle herdsman driving us home at evening" (*W,* V, 247). Thus has wildness been gentled. The light of inspiration is native to America after all. The literate reader need not abandon his mind to savagery; he need only use the savage in himself humanely. The quiet reversal in the last pages of the essay reminds us of Thoreau's use of polarities in the composition of chapters in *Walden.* In "Walking" the reversal has been anticipated virtually from the start and intermittently throughout: the saunterer walks through swamps to his holy land; angels go to and fro in the forest. The characteristic image of nature in the essay is the leopard mother, and its obvious and central message is "in Wildness is the preservation of the World"; but the point Thoreau is making in his structure is that his interaction with wild nature finally makes the walker both fiercely exuberant and capable of inspired and sweet-tempered reflection. The wild, properly guarded, turns into the good, and nature into spirit.

iii

At the end of his brief introduction to "Autumnal Tints" Thoreau sets forth the plan of his essay: it will be a chronological record of the changing colors of a New England Fall. "I have endeavored . . . to describe all these bright tints in the order in which they present themselves. The following are some extracts from my notes" (*W*, V, 251). One could hardly wish for a flatter or a less ambitious statement of purpose. And indeed, the essay is in part just such a factual presentation of extracts and notes. But, like "A Walk to Wachusett" and "Ktaadn," "Autumnal Tints" has a second, more poetic purpose and style. If we think of it as merely descriptive, we shall at first be baffled by a curious foray into epistemology toward the end of the essay, which seems to have little direct relation to the rest. This passage, included as part of the section on "The Scarlet Oak," tells us nothing specifically about that tree. Instead, Thoreau is concerned in it with the workings of poetic observation. After urging the reader to ascend the hills in late October, he warns him that he will see nothing unless he is prepared for the landscape in his mind.

Objects are concealed from our view, not so much because they are out of the course of our visual ray as because we do not bring our minds and eyes to bear on them; for there is no power to see in the eye itself, any more than in any other jelly. . . . Nature does not cast pearls before swine. There is just as much beauty visible to us in the landscape as we are prepared to appreciate,—not a grain more. The actual objects which one man will see from a particular hilltop are just as different from those which another will see as the beholders are different. The scarlet oak must, in a sense, be in your eye when you go forth. We cannot see anything until we are possessed with the idea of it, take it into our heads,—and then we can hardly see anything else. . . . A man sees only what concerns him. . . . How much more, then, it requires different intentions of the eye and of the mind to attend to different departments of knowledge! How differently the poet and the naturalist look at objects! [*W*, V, 285–286]

Only our minds, directed through our eyes, have power to transform what is before us into beauty. Only when the saunterer is rightly disposed can he find his holy land. The passage offers a careful elucidation of this epistemological principle, which underlies all the late essays and is necessary to Thoreau's conception of a relation with nature generally. Quietly but precisely he speaks a word for the poetic observer, as he spoke a word for nature, more expansively, in "Walking." Because of this emphasis on the mind's intention, nature-as-growth-and-structure gets ignored in the passage; yet Thoreau is not asserting that this entity exists only in the mind, only that it makes its value apparent there. Even in the midst of such abstracted reflections, "Nature" casts its own pearls before us and thus has its own separate world; on our side we must be capable of seeing these gorgeous particulars and publishing their truth. Thoreau's position, then, seems to me subtly different from the one he took on occasion in the *Week,* according to which Imagination or Friendship eclipsed Nature in bright mental dawns. That position he has by now "forgotten," and he has settled for the balanced view already implicit, if uncertainly expressed, in "The Thaw," "The Poet is Nature's Brother," and "The Fisher's Son."

Yet what has happened to Thoreau's belief in nature as the source of power and energetic life? We must take it on faith; and in this sense the passage from "Autumnal Tints" is unbalanced, narrowly focused, and exaggerated, like so much of his ambitious writing. Correspondingly, the character of nature is markedly different here from the one provided her in Thoreau's trumpetings of the savage in "Walking." Nature is no she-wolf or leopard-mother, no fierce, strange, and attractive Female Presence; only in the clause in which "Nature does not cast pearls" is it personified at all; in most of the paragraph it is felt as an aggregate of "objects" in a "landscape." As a whole it is a medium or mirror in which the observer sees what concerns him. The poet sees beauty in trees; the "naturalist" sees botanical information; the New England selectman sees possibilities for his own unholy activities, or as Thoreau puts it, "a Brocken spectre of himself" (*W*, V, 287).

The emphasis in "Autumnal Tints" generally is not so much on information in itself as on the beholder-poet's power of transformation. (Whether or not Thoreau succeeds in being a "poet" in the essay is beside the point. He can at least see poetically, and that is enough to illustrate his attitude.) Thus the meditation, "the scarlet oak must be in your eye," turns out on closer reading to be a carefully conceived rationale for the poetic seeing and tinting that precedes it, and a key gloss on the essay as a whole. Much of the writing in "Autumnal Tints" is not a naturalist's record, but a poet's virtuoso display of image-making. The persona Thoreau adopts relishes the imaginative glorification of fact.

For example, the section called "The Red Maple," like the other sections of "Autumnal Tints," opens with chronology and straightforward commentary, but in the first sentence of the second paragraph the metaphors begin to multiply. Early changing and therefore prominent maples are seen as "burning bushes," aflame with a divine spirit yet not consumed by the fire. Then in a second comparison Thoreau likens a group of these trees, seen unexpectedly in a swamp, to "some gay encampment of the red men, or other foresters, of whose arrival you had not heard." Then he switches his metaphor again as he watches a single maple already red against a background of fellow maples still green: "How beautiful, when a whole tree is like one great scarlet fruit full of ripe juices, every leaf, from lowest limb to topmost spire, all aglow, especially if you look toward the sun!" Next he comes back to his earlier figure of the foresters, now rather Robin Hood's men in Lincoln Green than Red Indians. A red maple among evergreens is seen as the bearer of a "scarlet standard" for a "regiment of green-clad foresters." Finally, in a longer and more gradually paced paragraph, a maple sapling that grows unobserved "at the head of some retired valley" is transformed by means of an elaborate conceit into an example of modest probity that waits through spring and summer till "the eleventh hour of the year" to express in color its sweet and virtuous soul:

And now, in this month of September, this month of traveling, when men are hastening to the seaside, or the mountains, or the lakes, this modest maple, still without budging an inch, travels in its reputation,—runs up its scarlet flag on that hillside, . . . the tree which no scrutiny could have detected here when it was most industrious is thus, by the tint of its maturity, by its very blushes, revealed at last to the careless and distant traveler, and leads his thoughts away from the dusty road into those brave solitudes which it inhabits. It flashes out conspicuous with all the virtue and beauty of a maple,—*Acer rubrum*. We may now read its title, or *rubric*, clear. Its *virtues*, not its sins, are as scarlet. [*W*, V, 259–261]

This virtuous sapling, if not a Brocken spectre of the traveler, is a kindly reminder to him of his better nature.

In all his imaginative observations in the section on "The Red Maple," Thoreau sees what his mind is intent on seeing; his eye integrates the landscape and makes it speak back his own concerns. The very diversity of his images for the maple shows that he is not bound and confined to the actual. Instead, in a display of imaginative facility, Thoreau indulges in personification—a device he usually eschews because it obscures the actual. He turns his maples into Red Indians, green-clad foresters, and examples of solitary industry. Such a succession of metaphors might not be impressive in itself; Thoreau's mind is casually and endlessly metaphorical. But he keeps saying to the reader, Lo! Look at the tree this way and look at it this other way! Learn how powerful and various is the informed and lively seeing of the poetic eye.

The ability to see imaginatively, though it must be nourished by intercourse with nature (the emphasis of "Walking") is a human gift and opportunity (the emphasis of "Autumnal Tints").

And the alert and devoted poet alone keeps it in trust, not the selectman nor the market-man nor the driver nor the citizen—they have forgotten what they knew as children. To the poetic observer alone comes down "a purple gleam from previous years" (*W*, V, 257—surely a reminder of Wordsworth's "visionary gleam" lurks in this phrase). Indeed, because Thoreau keeps insisting on the poet's capacities and derogating the capacities of everyone else, "Autumnal Tints" seems to me marred by defensive arrogance. It is intelligent, controlled, lyrical, and modestly imaginative, but not generous. When Thoreau read it to a Worcester audience, his listeners complained that they noticed and loved fall colors as well as he. Thoreau failed to reach them because he was only trying to with part of his mind—with another part he was putting up bristling gates. On the one hand he would persuade them to use their eyes well. On the other, he would reaffirm with quiet and private defiance his own vocation as a poet-saunterer and argue for its difficulty and distinction.

iv

In "The Succession of Forest Trees," by contrast, the observations Thoreau presents are mainly those of a "naturalist." The essay was first delivered as a lecture before the Middlesex Agricultural Society—i.e., the Concord Cattle-Show—in September, 1860, and Thoreau explicitly calls the attention of his audience of local property owners and farmers to "a purely scientific subject" (*W*, V, 185). His conception of the scientific is, however, broader than most. He does more than present a conscientious proof of a sensible hypothesis.

Thoreau's subject is the operations of nature in the distribution of seeds in forests. He explains to his listeners a whole series of events that go on unobserved by them in their woodlots. Taking "a surveyor's and a naturalist's liberty" (*W*, V, 185), he has been in the habit of walking across their lots, and now he would let them know what transpires there. He informs them how stands of oaks and pines succeed each other, how the light seeds of pines are carried by winds into neighboring lands, while the heavier seeds of oaks and other hardwoods are planted by squirrels beneath full-grown pines, how in general the seeds of many different forest trees are spread by animals and birds, who plant trees unwittingly while carrying or storing acorns, nuts, and pine cones. The essay is genuinely informative, as its first audience appreciatively recognized. Thoreau presents his experience and his findings straightforwardly, soberly, correctly, in a plain style—yet with the excitement of a man who knows that he has a good case. Except for one outlandish and very strained comparison between squash seeds and hunting dogs toward the end, he virtually eschews metaphor (A seed is like a "hound" because it "points to" a three-hundred-pound squash!—*W*, V, 203.) He stays away from the mannerisms and styles of his idiosyncratic prose: there are no digressive meditations, philological puns, literary allusions, or esoteric quotations, little paradox, and only the squash-hound to remind us of extra-vagance.

It is all the more significant, then, that a scientific essay usually known and admired for its anticipation of the methods of modern forestry should also be, alongside "A Winter Walk," the least qualified and most explicit piece of pantheism Thoreau ever published. That is, he is especially careful to state that "Nature" is behind the unwitting and unremitting activity of all of us— man, beast, bird, and tree alike—and that *she* "can persuade us to do almost anything when she would encompass her ends" (*W*, V, 188). This emphasis on her quiet omnipotence is made repeatedly and at regular intervals in the course of the essay, without the qualifications and exaggerations of Thoreau's more elaborate writings. Pronouns and capital letters here are also signs of his intentions. He invariably writes "she" and "Nature" in "The Succession of Forest Trees"; in earlier work he tends to vacillate between a feminine and a neuter nature, and between upper and lower case "n's." Apparently, he wants to make clear to listeners and readers attracted to "a purely scientific subject" that an enlightened science is also reflective and religious. The information he provides should induce in them not a selfish acquisitiveness toward the earth nor a desire to anatomize it, but an intelligent and whole-souled reverence for it. Nature in "The Succession of Forest Trees" is thus imagined as a benign, mysterious, all-knowing Goddess, Parent, and Governor. The image of her as a leapard mother, or the thought of her as a theatre for the perceptions of a poet, would be out of place in this essay. Conceptually, Thoreau emphasizes not the vitality of human involvement with nature (as in "Walking") nor the human ability to conceive of beauty in the presence of natural phenomena (as in "Autumnal Tints"), but the existence and power of Nature-as-a-living-whole as she expresses herself in laws and growth, *kosmos* and *phusis*.

The first sentence of "The Succession of Forest Trees," the opening gambit as it were, already gives notice that Thoreau's account of facts is meant to serve a cause of higher truth. Thoreau writes, "Every man is entitled to come to Cattle-Show, even a transcendentalist; and for my part I am more interested in the men than in the cattle" (*W*, V, 184). The speaker will make himself at home here among his fellow animals and men; and (significantly) he will do so not as "a surveyor and naturalist" but as "a transcendentalist." This is a rare word for Thoreau, used here with personal precision and with awareness of the contemporary stigma of peculiarity attached to it. Intellectually, as a foretaste of his argument, he indicates that he approaches his subject with a particular philosophical bias. Dramatically and artistically, he is up to a familiar game, meant also in earnest: he is role-playing. Even in the straightest of his essays he indulges his crooked bent and shifts quietly but designedly from one role to another. The stance of both a transcendentalist and a naturalist are appropriate to his subject, and both are meant to be felt in the writing; indeed for Thoreau each ought to include the other.

Thoreau's transcendentalist approach to a scientific subject is close to the approach that Goethe advocated and practiced in his scientific writings. Like Goethe, Thoreau puts the subjective element back into science, but without sacrificing clarity of method or mind. In preference to using mechanical instruments he observes with his own eyes and verifies his hypothesis by experiencing the facts himself. The practical message of "The Succession of Forest Trees" is also Goethean. Man alone of all the creatures of *phusis* has a chance to understand how he affects nature—this is one reason why he is more interesting than a cow—he can pay attention to a transcendentalist. Alas, as Thoreau stresses in the final words of the essay, "men love darkness better than light" (*W,* V, 204). They prefer to remain ignorant of nature, to destroy it without realizing what they are doing, to dominate it without accepting their place in it. But a genuine Enlightenment, for Thoreau and Goethe, implies not only exactitude of mind but reverence for nature—a difficult romantic combination.

Conclusion

Joy and Life

Thoreau's numerous personae in the late essays—walker, savage, poet, naturalist, transcendentalist, and surveyor—suggest the variety implicit in his conception of nature, a conception always influenced in the moment of experience by the beholder's stance. Yet the reason nature is finally one in Thoreau's work is that it also continually gives him a common experience, felt beneath momentary deflections. This is the saunterer's perception of nature's vitality and wholeness: he hearkens while she plies the loom. And the experience makes him happy. The chief purpose of Thoreau's method of perception is the recollection and revivifying of what he calls "joy." One moral of the last essays, as of Thoreau's work generally, is "Surely joy is the condition of life." By "life" he means that growing natural life I have termed *phusis*. By "joy" he means both the pleasure of men, animals, and plants as they participate in this life, and the delight of the human observer as he reflects on what he sees. *"Think* of the young fry that leap in ponds," writes the young Thoreau. Both forms of joy, the natural and the reflective, are necessary to each other, just as a man's body and his spirit depend on each other.

Thoreau's celebration of *phusis* is perhaps less vigorous and loud in "Wild Apples," "The Succession of Forest Trees," and "Autumnal Tints" than in "Walking" and earlier writings. But the idea is central in all the late essays. In "Autumnal Tints," where we might least expect it, it is as prominent as elsewhere. We have already met the comparison of a turned red maple to "one great scarlet fruit full of ripe juices." And while otherwise the essay abounds in poetic invention of a different sort, in that autumn leaves are given poetic interest by means of a scintillating diversity of metaphors, this particular comparison of leaves to flowers and fruit persists throughout. All are clearly expressions of *phusis*.

The very forest and herbage, the pellicle of the earth, must acquire a bright color, an evidence of its ripeness,—as if the globe itself were a fruit on its stem, with ever a cheek toward the sun.

Flowers are but colored leaves, fruit but ripe ones. [*W*, V, 250]

All natural growths proceed from a single intelligent design and are variations on a single *Urphänomen*. "The Maker of this earth but patented a leaf" (*Walden*, p. 308).

Both wild apples and scarlet oak leaves are "ripe" in the last of October, and Thoreau must have thought of the two essays in which these images figure centrally as expressions of his own dying vitality when he prepared them for publication during his last months. In praising October ripeness he praises the beauty of *phusis* as it flares with brightness before receding into winter. The decay and death of leaves and grasses presages their renewal, and enforces a comforting interpretation of death in general. Though Thoreau may have given free voice to his shock and fear at the prospect of death in "The Shipwreck" and elsewhere, he returns quietly in the last essays to his early position that the death of a natural growth is a symbol of peace, not of devouring chaos. Of the purple-blossoming poke he writes,

What a perfect maturity it arrives at! It is the emblem of a successful life concluded by a death not premature, which is an ornament to Nature. What if we were to mature as perfectly, root and branch, glowing in the midst of our decay, like the poke! I confess that it excites me to behold them. . . . I love to press the berries between my fingers, and see their juice staining my hand. [*W,* V, 254–255]

Thoreau is less troubled and urgent in finding natural and reflective pleasure and peace in the late essays because he has somewhat altered the demands of his imagination. In his autumnal moods the local and ordinary are fully satisfying to him; nowhere does he speak of "getting through with nature." Instead, he relishes natural sensation slowly and makes it last. The purple stain of the poke, the savor and taste of huckleberries, are nutriment for his serenity. Even in the *Week* he found his treasure by the sands of a desolate creek, but he dreamed there more often of far Azores and of heroic combats beyond the stars. In the last nature essays he has found and assumed a settled place and stance. He is no longer tempted, except in the conscious braggadocio of his extreme statements, to defer to natural men; he knows that the saunterer is a distinct kind of visitor in nature. In his persistent preaching of the joy to be discerned in nature, he has also found his most comfortable message. For this message, implicit in much of his writing, his text might well be one known to all his contemporaries and a favorite of his own—though he gave it a distinctly unorthodox reading—the first question and response in the Shorter Catechism: "What is the chief end of man? *Ans.* Man's chief end is to glorify God, and to enjoy him forever."[6] One of Thoreau's contributions in the romantic tradition is in effect to redefine God, man, glory, joy, and forever in this text, and thereby to celebrate the gift of life.

[6] *The Confession of Faith, the Larger and Shorter Catechisms, with the Scripture Proofs at Large, Together with the Sum of Saving Knowledge* (1958; rpt. London: Wickliffe Press of the Protestant Truth Society, 1962), p. 207.

The Art of Living with Indefiniteness

Yet I would not leave Thoreau on such a wave of comfort. In this study at least his restlessness and skepticism ought to be remembered at the end. Still in the late essays we have seen him move from role to role and from prospect to prospect, thereby saving the work that finally emerges from complacency. Despite his faith in nature, some problems remain. He does not by fiat abolish the cleavage between imagination and nature, however much he plays it down; he finds the riddle of animal appetite unsolved; and he does not explain away the solemnity of death— nor would he wish to. His joyful creed, however persuasive, is a temporary stay against the possible breakdown of his romantic thinking. Thus the word "stance" is more or less right for him.

> And yet with lingering doubt I haste each morn
> To see if Ocean still my gaze will greet,
> And with each day once more to life am born,
> And tread the earth once more with tott'ring feet.
>
> [*Collected Poems*, p. 122]

"Stance" is also more or less imperfect, because Thoreau knows his nature ("I *know* the world where land and water meet"), and he meditates with constancy on his way of living with it. He combines belief and doubt in an uncanny balance, and his skeptical faithfulness is still a model of a kind of awareness.

Thus an achievement equal to Thoreau's "message" is his very refusal to have a message. "The meaning of Nature was never attempted to be defined by him."[7] An insight crucial to his art is his recognition of the natural limits of art. On the one hand, Thoreau is exceptionally aware of the value of words—their history, their current value, their scriptural and esthetic power. He took it on himself to whittle his writing into precise forms and to use these forms to speak prophetic truth. On the other hand, he is also exceptionally aware of the mutability, fluidity, and tem-

---

[7] Emerson, *Works*, X, 471.

porality of all language and all perception. Thus even as he intimates his vision of the word renewed, he refuses the temptation to convey in his work the illusion of a stable *logos*. It is as if he were conscious of a principle of Original Inadequacy in the creative human mind. An artist may strive to represent the image of perfect form he has stamped somewhere in his mind, but in practice that image is continually defaced by forgetfulness and change.

Thoreau's range of thinking and experience may be narrow, but within that range he is an incessant experimenter. One way to misunderstand and underestimate him is to fail to recognize how many divergent opinions and responses he has, how open he is to his own self-limited possibilities. This openness is manifested over and over within the very texture of his writing. Thus he evades our penchant for categorizing him in terms of his ideas, and we ought to respect that evasion to a certain extent. His writing does not come across as a set of propositions, nor usually as an artifact, but instead as the readable activity of a vigorous but unpredictable mind.

Because Thoreau not only creates closely meditated structures for his changing experience of nature but also gives himself to it, something occurs occasionally in his writing that I perhaps have not emphasized enough, that is, his willingness to be "lost."

Not till we are completely lost, or turned round,—for a man needs only to be turned round once with his eyes shut in this world to be lost,—do we appreciate the vastness and strangeness of Nature. . . . Not till we are lost, in other words, not till we have lost the world, do we begin to find ourselves, and realize where we are and the infinite extent of our relations. [*Walden,* p. 171]

When we realize "the infinite extent of our relations," we may not find it so easy to know "where we are." We "dwell in possibility," as Dickinson puts it, and suffer the shocks of an undetermined, if poetic, existence. At moments we become poor friends and neighbors to ourselves. In passages like the meditation on "doubleness" in *Walden* and the account of the visit to the summit in "Ktaadn," the experience of a vast and strange nature seems to encourage in Thoreau an uncertainty about his own individual humanity. He participates in nature's diversity by relinquishing his sense of himself. Because he is very much involved in a shifting scene, he can know himself as "the scene of thoughts and affections," not as a circumscribed human personality with a settled character. His inward indefiniteness, of which he was courageously aware, was in part a response to his chosen subject matter.

Thoreau's willingness to be open to the anarchic possibilities of perception could make him feel a nothingness in himself, as if he were "a spiritual football" or "a dandelion down that never alights." But, on the other hand, it is one of his achievements in *Walden* that he projects himself as a perceptive mind-body, an unsettled, meditative, richly inconsistent egotistical sensibility. He presents no single self-image that we can grasp and label. He narrates no straightforward cause-and-effect autobiography. He does not gratify us with a set of interrelated typical attributes. He asks us instead to go beyond these forms that we usually focus on and observe within a man thinking and feeling.

The idea of symbolic wholeness of personality is breaking down in all the great followers of Emerson. For better and for worse, Thoreau, Whitman, Hawthorne, Melville, and Dickinson—as well as Emerson himself—present us with a new conception of human identity as unsettled and protean. Thoreau has not the generalizing originality of Emerson, who brilliantly suggests this new conception of the self in "Circles" and "Experience." Nor is he aware of the woeful human loss felt by men in social circumstances when self is conceived as consciousness, as Hawthorne is aware in *The Blithedale Romance*. Nor does he realize and dramatize the conception with the strong and daring intelligence of Dickinson. Unlike these other writers, however, he has a permanent theatre and home for the protean self which he can write about in depth. He holds onto his identity by means of his imagined intercourse with nature. Though he is indebted to Emerson for the idea of nature as for so much else, he goes beyond Emerson in dramatizing over and over the loss and recovery of the self in nature. His courage to dissolve and then resolve himself may lead to honest confusion, as in "The Shipwreck," or to a beautiful reverence, as in "The Bean Field" and "Walking." Either way, it leads to a sense of open-ended discovery.

The shifting, constant nature Thoreau investigated and described is a fit subject for his kind of mind—indeed, while it is recognizable to all of us as the Massachusetts we know, it also reflects his individual mind and corresponds with it. As it requires a flexible and changing approach, so the map of his mind is full of crooked bends. As it is diverse, so the ways he comes into relation with it are diverse. If he feels separate from it, the separation itself will take different forms and will stimulate him to adopt different strategies to deal with it. The meditative weed-killer of "The Bean-Field," the cloud-scaling idealist of "Saddle-back," the disquieted observer of "The Shipwreck," and the frightened adventurer of "Ktaadn"—all are romantic personae trying to reach an accommodation with a separate nature. On the other hand, Thoreau's ability always to return to the thought of nature as a living, affectionate, and beautiful whole is a sign of his knowing how to adopt an obsession and abide by it.

Since Thoreau makes Concord and its wilder rural surroundings reflect him, his effort to understand and describe this landscape from many standpoints and even in contradictory ways is a peculiar, Thoreauvian method of being more fully, more comprehensively human. He is not content to express a fixed personality, but wants all the personal variety his perceptions will bring him. His version of nature is at once broad and subtle enough to provide a theatre for the varied tendencies of his mind. He has the courage and the intelligence to acknowledge both the natural man and the antinaturalist in himself. He cannot be the bittern or the fox, but he knows that something in him would be, and he is willing to experiment with that impulse. By refusing to deny the idea of nature, or any aspect of his sensuous experience of it, or any part of himself that would come in contact with it, he has given the romantic interpretation of nature a new experimental validity.

Index

Thoreau as Romantic Naturalist

Designed by R. E. Rosenbaum.
Composed by York Composition Co., Inc.,
in 11 point intertype Baskerville, 3 points leaded,
with display lines in monotype Baskerville.
Printed letterpress from type by York Composition Co.
on Warren's 1854 text, 60 pound basis,
with the Cornell University Press watermark.
Bound by Vail-Ballou Press
in Columbia book cloth
and stamped in All Purpose foil.